Sea Fever

Sea Fever

The true adventures that inspired our
greatest maritime authors, from Conrad to
Masefield, Melville and Hemingway

Sam Jefferson

ADLARD COLES NAUTICAL

BLOOMSBURY
LONDON · NEW DELHI · NEW YORK · SYDNEY

Adlard Coles Nautical
An imprint of Bloomsbury Publishing Plc

50 Bedford Square 1385 Broadway
London New York
WC1B 3DP NY 10018
UK USA

www.bloomsbury.com

ADLARD COLES, ADLARD COLES NAUTICAL and the Buoy logo
are trademarks of Bloomsbury Publishing Plc

First published 2015

British Library Cataloguing-in-Publication Data
A catalogue record for this book is available from the British Library.

Library of Congress Cataloguing-in-Publication
data has been applied for.

ISBN HB: 978-1-4729-0-8810
ISBN ePDF: 978-1-4729-0-8834
ISBN ePub: 9781-4-729-0-8827

2 4 6 8 10 9 7 5 3 1

Typeset in Tibere by seagulls.net
Printed and bound in Great Britain by CPI Group (UK) Ltd, Croydon, CR0 4YY

To find out more about our authors and books visit www.bloomsbury.com.
Here you will find extracts, author interviews, details of forthcoming
events and the option to sign up for our newsletters.

Contents

Acknowledgements

I would like to thank the Cruising Association for their kind co-operation in allowing me to browse through and quote extensively from their archive of Erskine Childers' logbooks. Their straightforward approach to granting me permission was a breath of fresh air. You can find out more about their work by going to: www.cruising.org.uk. Beyond that, I am indebted to my girlfriend, Ivory, and also my mother, for their help both with listening back to drafted chapters and ruthlessly hunting out grammatical errors. James Cox also deserves mention for his help with sourcing images and thank you to both Liz and Clara at Bloomsbury for invaluable work in putting the book together with great efficiency.

Ultimately, however, the biggest acknowledgement has to go to the authors who, in addition to providing me with much of my favourite literature, seem to have gone out of their way and often put themselves through extreme discomfort to provide me with billions of amusing and hair-raising incidents and anecdotes to narrate. I never realised that writers were quite so willing to suffer for their art until I started researching this book.

I would like to thank the following for allowing me to reproduce text from authors whose works are still in copyright. I am therefore indebted to: Penguin Random House for the use of quotes from Ernest Hemingway's *The Old Man and the Sea* (p95 and p115) and *The Green Hills of Africa* (p109). The Society of Authors, who administer the John Masefield estate and granted permission to quote from *Sea Fever* (p183), *New Chum* (p187, p188 and p190), *Autobiography* (p193–201 and p205), *On Growing Old* (p202–203 and p215), *Cape Horn Calm* (p206–207), *Dauber* (p210) and *Big Jim* (p212). Picador for allowing me to use quotes from Eric Newby's *The last Grain Race* (p201 and p208). The Arthur Ransome Trust for granting permission for me to use quotes from *Racundra's First Cruise* (p249, p259–260, p264–265 and p269) and *Autobiography* (p253–257).

Introduction

*If you have never been at sea in a heavy gale, you can form no idea
of the confusion of mind occasioned by wind and spray together. They
blind, deafen, and strangle you, and take away all power of action
or reflection.*

Edgar Allen Poe

Given that our oceans and seas cover about two thirds of the
planet's surface, it is hardly surprising that their influence has
always run strongly through literature. The waters of this world
have swirled through storytelling ever since the Anglo-Saxons spun
the tale of *Beowulf* and Homer narrated *The Odyssey*. To chart every
reference to sea voyages in literature would have made for a very
lengthy book indeed. But I had a different idea; I wanted to take
the opposite view and look at how the sea itself had shaped some of our
greatest writers and set them on a course that led to literary success. To
this end, I re-read my favourite books of the sea; hypnotic yarns written by
some of the greats: Melville, Marryat and Conrad, men who have written
bona fide maritime classics, and looked at their relationship with the great
waters of this world.

It didn't take long to realise that almost everyone who had written
something truly meaningful about the sea had also enjoyed a remarkably

close relationship with it. Of course it isn't exactly a revelation that the men who knew the sea intimately through working on it were best placed to write the most compelling literature about it. But although this wasn't terribly surprising, the adventures of some of these writers certainly were, in fact they were often more far fetched than the fiction their experiences helped to shape. Did you know that Joseph Conrad smuggled guns off the Catalan coast for the Carlist rebels? I did not. Nor did I realise that he later went on to command a clipper ship; the most refined and complex type of merchant sailing vessel ever built. And who would have thought that Jack London spent his youth as an oyster pirate, dodging rifle shots from the authorities while illegally dredging the mudflats of San Francisco Bay in his little yacht *Dazzler*? Meanwhile, Captain Frederick Marryat's death-defying exploits during the Napoleonic Wars simply beggar belief, while Erskine Childers' do-or-die piece of gun-running for the fledgling IRA was as breathtaking as it was bewildering. These were the revelations and the stories that needed to be told.

In all, I have rounded up 12 authors who spent long enough at sea to know it inside out aboard either ships or yachts, and who convey that knowledge through their own works of fiction. This meant omitting a good few authors of nautical classics who only wrote autobiographical works; R. H. Dana (*Two Years Before the Mast*), Joshua Slocum (*Sailing Alone Around the World*) and Eric Newby (*The Last Grain Race*) are notable absentees. I also feel rather ashamed that I didn't find space for Nicholas Monsarrat, whose *The Cruel Sea* must be up there as a nautical classic, and was shaped by his own naval experiences. Ultimately my selection could only be subjective and I am sure there will be many who can think of other worthy nominees for inclusion, but that is inevitable.

There were also a handful of other authors of works of classic nautical fiction ruled out because the author in question did not really seem to have enough true seafaring experience to qualify by my criteria. Rudyard Kipling's *Captains Courageous* was an obvious example. Kipling never served aboard any vessel and his facts for this nautical classic were gleaned second hand. Ironically, Edgar Allen Poe, quoted on the previous page, also does not appear in this book as he only made a few ocean going trips as a passenger. Then there were the marginal cases; Robert Louis Stevenson, for example, may have written a nautical classic in *Treasure Island,* but he had spent precious little time at sea when he wrote it. Yet this extraordinary man snuck into the book as I felt that his later cruises through the South Seas aboard the yacht *Casco* and trading schooner *Equator* had a profound effect on a number of his later – rather underrated – tales, such as *The Ebb Tide* and *In the South Seas.*

So who was the first writer to channel their seafaring experience into something that resembled a nautical novel? Much trawling of the archives seemed to point to one Tobias Smollett as the most plausible originator. Smollett was a somewhat curmudgeonly surgeon serving aboard the HMS *Chichester* in 1740, and it was there that he gained his seafaring knowledge. His experiences – they were almost entirely negative – made up a large proportion of his first and most popular novel, *Roderick Random.* The tale is bawdy, crass and often very silly, but in Smollett's hands the sea comes alive in a manner that no novelist had managed to convey before. Daniel Defoe had written of the sea in *Robinson Crusoe* in 1713 and given that Crusoe is marooned by it, the sea is an important element of the story, yet in his hands it is flat, uninteresting and utterly incidental – a means to an end. Crusoe sails from London and enjoys a 'good voyage' to Brazil and nothing more. Later, when a storm overwhelms his vessel, Defoe is utterly at a loss as to how to bring the scene to life and retreats into trite clichés, speaking of 'the wild sea'. Smollett, writing a few decades later, had no such problems. Witness the language he uses to describe a storm that batters his ship in the early stages of his transatlantic voyage to South America:

> *The sea was swelled into billows mountain-high, on the top of which our ship sometimes hung as if it were about to be precipitated to the abyss below! Sometimes we sank between two waves that rose on each side higher than our topmast-head, and threatened by dashing together to overwhelm us in a moment! Of all our fleet, consisting of a hundred and fifty sail, scarce twelve appeared, and these driving under their bare poles, at the mercy of the tempest. At length the mast of one of them gave*

way, and tumbled overboard with a hideous crash! Nor was the prospect
in our own ship much more agreeable; a number of officers and sailors
ran backward and forward with distraction in their looks, halloaing to
one another, and undetermined what they should attend to first. Some
clung to the yards, endeavouring to unbend the sails that were split into
a thousand pieces flapping in the wind; others tried to furl those which
were yet whole, while the masts, at every pitch, bent and quivered like
twigs, as if they would have shivered into innumerable splinters!

Finally here was an author who could fully convey the might of the ocean. Moreover, his descriptions of life below decks, and the coarse humour and camaraderie that existed among the ordinary seamen, bore the stamp of authenticity. There was more too; a frequent visitor in this and Smollett's later novels was the old sea dog; washed up on land and stumping around in a state of bewilderment. If Jack Sparrow owes a lot to Keith Richards, he owes an equal debt to the quill of an eighteenth-century novelist. Yet Smollett never truly realised that he was teetering on the edge of creating an entirely new genre, and his later books, rather like the man himself, retreated many miles from the sea.

It wasn't until the 1820s that the nautical novel was developed, and it would be two men, James Fenimore Cooper and Captain Frederick Marryat, contemporaries in the US and Royal navies respectively, who set the template. Marryat we will meet later, but Cooper got there first. These days he is best remembered for *The Last of the Mohicans,* but in his time he published several nautical novels, kicking off with *The Pilot* in 1824. Cooper had written his first novel *Precaution* because the book his wife was reading at the time was so dull she challenged him to write a better one. It was a similar premise that led to the writing of *The Pilot.* Prior to picking up his pen, Cooper had been reading *The Pirate* by Sir Walter Scott, and became so irritated at the great Scotsman's ineptitude and inaccuracy in describing the scenes set at sea that he decided to improve upon that work. He received very little encouragement in this undertaking and was frequently warned by friends and well-meaning advisors that it was a bad idea, as Cooper himself recalled:

The author had many misgivings concerning the success of the undertaking, after he had made some progress in the work; the opinions of his different friends being anything but encouraging. One would declare that the sea could not be made interesting; that it was tame, monotonous, and without any other movement than unpleasant storms, and that, for his part, the less he got of it the better. The women very generally protested that such a book would have the odor of bilge water, and that it would give them the maladie de mer. Not a single individual among all those who discussed the merits of the project, within the range of the author's knowledge, either spoke, or looked, encouragingly. It is probable that all these persons anticipated a signal failure.

They were wrong. For all these dire predictions, *The Pilot* was a success and placed the nautical novel firmly on the literary map. Cooper also went on to coin the phrase 'salty sea dog' and picked up where Smollett left off in his affectionate depiction of an honest Jack Tar.

Fenimore Cooper's career as a sailor was relatively lacking in action, but he still enjoyed more adventure in one transatlantic round trip than most of us get in a lifetime; enduring harassment from pirates and the Royal Navy, the dramatic rescue of a drowning man and many storms along the way. Yet all this was nothing compared to some of the other literary sailors, and the more I explored their lives the more I found myself bewildered by the sheer breadth of their experiences at sea. I even started to wonder if some of the seminal pieces of seafaring fiction had been written not because of any great literary merit on the author's part, but simply because the author had enjoyed such extraordinary adventures prior to writing the book. On reflection, I realised this was unfair. It is one thing to experience something remarkable and quite another to convey that experience beautifully in words. As I read more of their exploits, it was clear that all of these authors' true life adventures had been narrated by a genuine storyteller and, as such, many had been shamelessly embellished. Melville was a very good case in point, and those who have endeavoured to chart his wanderings through the South Pacific have often struggled to untangle the truth from the tall tales.

I wanted to avoid getting caught up in this untangling as much as was possible. This book is a celebration of the adventures of these remarkable writers and sailors. Whether said writer was *actually* somewhere at exactly such and such time is really neither here nor there in the grand scheme of the story. How long was Herman Melville captive in a Tahitian prison? I neither know nor care. He was there, and he was imprisoned sufficiently long to convey what captivity was like. That is all that matters to me. What harm can there be in a touch of self-mythologising as long as the substance is true?

Narrating the tales of all of these literary mariners, I was also struck by the endless quirks of fate that seemed to connect them. As an example, in 1809 James Fenimore Cooper served under Captain Lawrence aboard the USS *Wasp*. He had a fairly dull time of it and then quit the navy. Shortly afterwards, Captain Lawrence transferred to the USS *Hornet* and war broke out between Britain and America. In 1812 Captain Lawrence's latest command attacked and sank the HMS *Peacock* off Guyana. Not many miles off, the HMS *Espiegle* witnessed the attack and gave chase. Among her officers was Captain Frederick Marryat. Another strange coincidence was that the first vessel Joseph Conrad served in when he moved to Britain was *The Skimmer of the Seas,* presumably named after the James Fenimore Cooper novel. Conrad was a great admirer of Cooper.

If these are nothing more than small coincidences there are other more obvious connections between some of these writers. No less than three of the authors (Herman Melville, Robert Louis Stevenson and Jack London) traversed almost exactly the same stretch of the South Seas on their voyages. Stevenson had met with Melville prior to departing on his trip, and one can only imagine how far the tales of the old whaling man influenced the wide-eyed Scotsman before he set sail. Some years later, Jack London followed Stevenson and Melville's route aboard his own yacht *Snark* and paid homage to them both on his trip; stopping first at Nuku Hiva in order to visit Melville's paradisaical prison of Ty-Pee, and later anchoring off Samoa to visit the grave of the great Scottish author. Melville's original book *Ty-Pee* therefore indirectly helped bring about the publication of classics such as Stevenson's *The Beach of Falesa* and London's *South Sea Tales*.

There were other links too. When Joseph Conrad first 'swallowed the anchor' (sailors' parlance for retiring from the sea) and took to writing he was taken under the wing of the wonderfully named Fanny Sitwell. Some years previously Robert Louis Stevenson had been infatuated with Sitwell, and she remained a close friend and confidant until his death. Meanwhile, John Masefield and Arthur Ransome were contemporaries and friends on the London literary scene and it was Masefield – already a successful author – who urged Ransome – then fiddling around with non-fiction – to write something new and original. This pair formed an interesting contrast; writing at roughly the same time, Ransome was a pure yachtsman while Masefield had served aboard the *Gilcruix,* a mighty Cape Horn windjammer and one of the last remnants of the great fleet of merchant sail. Ransome's most salt-encrusted children's classic *Peter Duck* certainly gives more than a nod the way of Masefield, and Stevenson for that matter, in its premise, backdrop, and certain points of style.

Indeed, working my way through the literature of these authors (for the purposes of this book, I have presented them in alphabetical order), it was often striking how one had influenced another. One of the most obvious examples was between Smollett and Marryat:

Smollett: At length we arrived in a bay to the windward of Carthagena, where we came to an anchor, and lay at our ease ten days longer... if I might be allowed to give my opinion of the matter, I would ascribe this delay to the generosity of our chiefs, who scorned to take any advantage that fortune might give them even over an enemy.

Marryat: On the arrival of the squadron at the point of attack, a few more days were thrown away, – probably upon the same generous principle of allowing the enemy sufficient time for preparation.

Perhaps this is simply a damning indictment of the Royal Navy's failure to improve its practices in the 60 years that separated each respective author's active service. A slightly more subtle example of influence can be seen in

Stevenson's Long John Silver, who owes a great deal to Smollett, Marryat and Cooper in his portrayal of the ultimate bluff old sea dog. I'm sure Stevenson would not have been ashamed to admit it either.

The nautical novel could also be the forum for serious literary innovation. Marryat was one of the first authors to introduce the anti-hero, in *Frank Mildmay*, and it goes without saying that Herman Melville's *Moby Dick* remains an extremely original and ambitious piece of work. I was also struck when reading Stevenson's later South Sea works how daring they were; he was one of the few high profile authors of the late Victorian era to risk suggesting that the white colonist was certainly no more than the equal and often the lesser man to the native populace he so frequently treated with such contempt. I also found it fascinating, when reading *The Ebb Tide,* how the despotic megalomaniac Attwater, cat perched on his shoulder and rifle at his side, foreshadowed other literary villains, from Conrad's General Kurtz through to any number of James Bond's nemeses.

There are two authors on this list who seem to stand alone, almost aloof from the party. These are Erskine Childers and Ernest Hemingway. Both wrote only one true nautical novel: *The Riddle of the Sands* and *The Old Man and the Sea* respectively. While the books have little in common, I felt strongly that both broke the mould when they were written. They seem to owe very little to anyone but themselves and are both startlingly original.

Although it was often possible to trace the influence of writers from one to the next, the differences in how life at sea was evoked were marked. Masefield to me was the most quixotic; he saw the beauty of the sea with wide-eyed wonder. He could convey the sheer joy and exhilaration of flying before the wind beneath great white wings with exhilarating abandon. Yet he was also hugely talented at bringing home the misery of life aboard a ship (this contradiction in his perception of the sea is explained thoroughly later). Conrad probably knew the drudgery and routine of maritime life better than anyone bar Marryat, as he served at sea for one of the longest terms of any author included in this book. He once noted that, 'There is nothing more enticing, disenchanting, and enslaving than the life at sea.' Few knew that better than Conrad. Some of that weariness – the perception of the sea as a workplace and a cruel enslaving mistress – subtly permeates his nautical work, and it is an important point. Yet he could also convey the fine art of ship handling and the satisfaction of doing this well, better than almost anyone. These are also elements that Melville – another man who put in many hours afloat – relates vividly. His meticulous documenting of the art of whaling in *Moby Dick* illustrates his admiration for this now departed skill perfectly, while his depiction of the restlessness and boredom of being at sea in *Ty Pee* is also hugely evocative. Anyone who has worked for long stretches at sea feels some of that weariness. It is rare for a sailor, however much they love the sea, not to long for the next landfall.

It is therefore interesting to contrast these weary, working sailors, who were occasionally overwhelmed by beauty amid the mundanity of life at sea, with the leisurely yachtsmen writers who followed. Arthur Ransome is a good case in point. For him, the sea certainly didn't encapsulate enslavement; only escape, relaxation and joy. In the early days, this escape was from his demanding and often frustrating 'proper' job as a reporter on the Russian Revolution. In later years his *Swallows and Amazons* took up the theme by allowing readers, threatened by war and menaced by economic depression, to escape to a childhood utopia populated with boats. Jack London was another man to whom the sea represented little other than the tenets of freedom and escape, and this feeling permeated through all of his writing on the matter. He had once worked upon the sea as a youth, but, as a writer looking back, he approached it with nostalgia for those halcyon years and also as a yachtsman who understood the sea as a playground, not just a place of work.

Before you head out into the billows guided by this selection of nautical masters, I must stress one thing. This book is not intended to be any kind of earnest critique of the literary works of any of the authors. It is not a scholarly work, it is a celebration and appreciation of the sea by a fellow sailor. In the case of each author I wanted to convey their own special skill in evoking its moods and vagaries. I realised early on in the execution of the book that often the best way to do this was to put it across in their own words. Paraphrasing was pointless. Thus, there is a fair amount of direct quotes and I make no apology for that. I only hope that, through reading this book, you will be inspired to discover – or rediscover – some of these magical tales, and understand them all the better for knowing what the author went through in order to write them so well. Whether you are a sailor, armchair adventurer or a born and bred landlubber, I assure you that the rewards will be great.

Erskine Childers
Hidden depths

The day of 26 July, 1914 dawned fair and breezy off the coast of Howth; racing clouds, sudden bright sunshine, and the Dublin Hills glowing emerald green in the distance. Looking out to sea across the laughing, wind-whipped waters the *Asgard*, an elegant ketch, completed the scene. She was jogging along the coast under easy sail and the casual observer would have simply eyed the pretty yacht with envy, for this was a fine day for a cruise. Yet the trained eye of a sailor would have seen that something was amiss; the yacht was not making the most of the conditions; she was badly out of trim and pitching sluggishly into the seas. A close observer would also have noted the dark mood of her four crew. A tense silence had settled over them and each took their turn to scour the coastline with a furrowed brow. There was obviously serious intent behind this cruise. A cursory inspection of her cabin would have revealed all, for down below the little yacht's beautiful interior was in a terrible state; packing cases and straw were crammed everywhere, tearing into upholstery and gouging at the previously spotless woodwork. Here and there some of the contents peeked out from the packing cases. The dull metal of rifle muzzles betrayed the *Asgard*'s sinister freight. The truth was that her load line was almost submerged on account of her lethal cargo. Packed in her cabins, crammed into every locker, lazarette and hatch were hundreds of rifles destined to end up in the hands of young lads from the newly formed Irish Volunteers – forerunners of the Irish Republican Army. This voyage was not for pleasure, it had real purpose, and a highly illegal one at that.

On deck, the crew was not only tense, they were out of sorts; exhausted by a storm-tossed crossing of the Irish Sea, which had presaged interminable hours of waiting for the appointed time to deliver their deadly load. The strain of the long voyage had been almost intolerable to all; none more so than on the captain, Erskine Childers, the man responsible for this cruise into dangerous waters. Yet he remained upright and resolute as he squinted towards the breakwaters of Howth, awaiting a signal from an accomplice ashore. His wife, Molly, paced the deck in a bright red dress, the sign that they were ready. The *Asgard* was a deep yacht and had a very short tidal window during which she could enter and leave the port. Yet without an answering signal from shore, she could be sailing straight into the jaws of a trap. Minutes ticked agonisingly by. Still nothing. What awaited them inside that inviting little harbour? Friend or foe?

Noon came, and the tension was unbearable. Erskine turned to his loyal wife, now at the helm. 'I am going in', he said with quiet decision. Molly nodded in silent assent and rattled the helm down. All aboard wondered what lay in wait for them within the seemingly welcoming arms of that snug port. The yacht ghosted silently into the apparently abandoned harbour, rounded up into the breeze and furled her white wings. Childers and his wife timed the manoeuvre perfectly so that as the way fell off the big yacht and she drifted to a standstill, she was just nosing alongside the quay. Despite the extremely tense circumstances, they did it with an easy skill that only a true sailor could fully appreciate. At once, the quayside exploded into welcoming bedlam; ropes were grabbed and men swarmed aboard 'the white yacht, the harbinger of Liberty', as one observer later described her. Within minutes, the vessel was stripped of her murderous cargo. In total 900 rifles and 25,000 rounds of ammunition were taken ashore and slung over the shoulders of a hundred and more hearty lads all prepared to use them in anger in the name of freedom. Not a moment too soon either, for a crackle of signalling rockets was heard overhead. Word was out. The Royal Navy was already racing towards the port. Their patrol vessel, HMS *Porpoise,* was not far off. In an instant, the *Asgard* was once more free of the dock; the chuckle of water under her forefoot as she gathered way matched by the emotions of her elated crew on deck.

The whole improbable adventure sounds like a work of high fiction from some second-rate fantasist. Yet it is all true, and only one of the many dramas that encapsulated the quixotic life of Erskine Childers: the novelist who only wrote one novel; the quintessential patriotic Englishman who supplied arms to the Irish rebels, and, ultimately, the fanatical supporter of an Irish republic who was executed by Irish republicans.

Yet for all the complexities and contradictions within Childers' character, one thing that was unquestionable and uncomplicated was his love of the sea and exploring its undulations in a yacht. There is a reason that Childers' only novel, *The Riddle of the Sands*, is so frequently quoted by yachtsmen as their favourite book. It is because it was written by a man who truly understood and loved his subject. Every line of this short and gripping tale of amateur espionage afloat rings true to anyone who has ever felt the demented urge to set an alarm for 5am on a chill morning in order to catch the tide and sally forth down channel to pit their wits against the vagaries of wind and wave. Every ounce of his enthusiasm and love for small-boat sailing (and in particular navigating) is poured into his one masterpiece. This is the main reason it has endured.

For the uninitiated, *The Riddle of the Sands* relates the adventures of two Englishmen and their exploits in the Baltic and North Sea aboard a 30ft yacht, *Dulcibella*. Her quiet, introverted skipper, Davies, invites his erudite companion Carruthers, a bored civil servant, to go duck hunting with him. Carruthers agrees to make the trip to Flensburg despite grave misgivings about going sailing on a small yacht in October. These fears are initially well founded when he discovers that the yacht is 'a scrubby little 30 footer' and he is assigned a berth that persistently drips water on his head from a leak in the deck. Nevertheless, the simple charm of life aboard and the beauty of their surroundings gradually seduces Carruthers, and before long he rather reluctantly finds himself enjoying the trip. It is at this point that he is drawn into a web of espionage and intrigue. It transpires that Davies had previously fallen victim to the mysterious Herr Dollmann, a fellow yachtsman who used his own vessel, the *Medusa*, to lure Davies into a trap as he navigated the storm-tossed waters of the Frisian Islands on his way to the Baltic. Davies was lucky to escape with his life and, returning from the Baltic to these islands, he and Carruthers set about unearthing the 'riddle of the sands'. In the process, their amateur investigations unearth German plans to use the shallow inlets of the Frisian Islands as a springboard to invade Britain.

The book was an instant hit, and has never been out of print. Given that it was published in 1903, some 11 years before the Great War, it was extremely prescient and Winston Churchill, First Lord of the Admiralty at the time, went so far as to state that the publication of the book proved instrumental in the construction of naval defence facilities at Invergordon, Rosyth and Scapa Flow. Yet for all the book's far sightedness and even though it was among the front-runners of a new genre of espionage, neither of these factors make it the much-loved book it remains today. To understand what makes it so popular, you have to go back to the sailing and to understand that you have to look at Childers himself. Although the plot of the book is fiction laced with fact, the voyage of the *Dulcibella*, and the portrayal of most of the characters, is very real, and drawn from Childers' own adventures in those chilly waters.

Robert Erskine Childers was born in Mayfair, London, in 1870. He was from privileged stock. His uncle was for some time Chancellor of the Exchequer and his father was a highly respected academic. Despite early years of comfort and happiness, the family cocoon was shattered forever when his father contracted tuberculosis. He died at the age of 38 after only a few months battling the illness. To make matters worse, his wife Anna had kept his illness a secret and, rather than break the family up by sending her husband to a sanatorium, she had nursed him in private. When his death became known, it was Anna who found herself carted off to the sanatorium by outraged members of the family who feared she would contaminate others with the disease, and she spent seven agonising years in isolation before she died. She paid the ultimate price for her devotion to her husband and so did her children; Henry, Robert (who was always referred to by his middle name, Erskine), Constance, Sybil and Dulcibella. Although Erskine wrote to his mother he never saw her again, and, effectively orphaned, the children lived with their aunt Agnes in their mother's ancestral home of Glendalough in Wicklow, Ireland. From hereon, things became more settled for Erskine and his siblings, and they grew up enjoying the serenity and rugged, verdant beauty of this wild part of the world.

Family tragedy had shaped Erskine into a quiet, reflective character. His early life followed a path familiar to many young men from privileged backgrounds in this era: prep school, a degree from Trinity College, Cambridge and paid employment as a clerk at the House of Commons. During this period there did not seem to be anything particularly unusual about Erskine. He was noted at Cambridge for being quiet and withdrawn and continued in that vein at the House. Although he was a thorough and effective worker, this was all anybody could say about him. As a colleague observed some time later: 'He seemed a particularly quiet, almost retiring colleague who did the work allotted to him. These efficiently and without fuss, but for the rest made no great mark, and in his leisure movement, had a habit of extracting himself from all extraneous interests.' Childers himself clearly felt his employment could be rather humdrum, and in *The Riddle of the Sands* he refers to the work of a junior civil servant somewhat dismissively:

> *The plain truth was that my work was neither interesting nor important, and consisted chiefly at present in smoking cigarettes, in saying that Mr So-and-So was away and would be back about 1st October, in being absent for lunch from twelve till two, and in my spare moments making précis of – let us say – the less confidential consular reports.*

Yet, behind the tedium of work and the bland exterior, something new was beginning to emerge. Childers was leading a double life and the half of it that was spent away from his desk was every bit as action-packed, esoteric and adventurous as his office career was prosaic. Childers had taken up sailing and he took to the sport with an intensity that bordered on a fanaticism that appeared entirely out of character. It was only in later years that this intensity would fully emerge with tragic consequences.

His first dabbling with the sport was undertaken with his brother Henry, who was to be a companion on many of his later trips. In 1893 the pair opted to buy a yacht and explore the west coast of Scotland. This was towards the end of Childers' Cambridge days, and was to prove important grounding (pardon the pun) for later adventures. In recalling the moment of purchase years later, Childers reminisced:

> Our starting point was this: that we must cruise at once, visit distant places, not merely sail in one prescribed area as a matter of daily sport. It was a sound aspiration, for the essence of the cruising spirit is travel; and it is far better to familiarise the mind at once with the idea of detachment from the land than to rely too heavily on the same nightly refuge. So there followed logically the need for as stout and seaworthy a yacht as a slender purse permitted.

This vessel was *Shulah*, a 33ft yacht that the brothers purchased in Dun Laoghaire, Ireland, and determined to sail across to Scotland. In their choice, they betrayed the naiveté of novices: she was an out-and-out racing vessel; heavily canvassed, narrow and deep. A modern-day comparison would be a newcomer to cycling buying a racing bike to traverse rough mountain tracks. In this error, the pair could easily plead ignorance.

Yachting had long been a commonplace pastime but by and large it was racing that was popular, and giant racing vessels such as *Britannia* and *Shamrock*, with huge sail areas and equally huge crews, ruled the day. Yacht cruising was very much in its infancy and for most, the concept of heading out sailing in a small yacht for pleasure was a completely alien concept. True, there were a few pioneers indulging in this esoteric pursuit, but they were few and far between. Cruising yachts as a class didn't really exist when Henry and Erskine were casting around for a suitable boat and it is understandable that they settled on *Shulah*, even though they were clearly terrified of her huge mainsail.

They were soon also to discover how restrictive her extremely deep draft was. Given that the two brothers acknowledged that they were pretty green when it came to sailing, and perhaps in deference to *Shulah's* mainsail, the pair were prepared to hire a hand to show them the ropes. This step afforded mixed results, as Erskine later related rather sardonically.

> *Determined to become thoroughly grounded in the technique of yachting, we had to procure a yacht hand. One meant two, for the magnitude of our main boom and swift intuition from our speech that we were inveterate landsmen evoked from our first choice an immediate demand for a mate. The whole atmosphere of the enterprise was serious. We were barely under way and threading the crowd of yachts which lay in Kingstown harbour when we were warned to don oilskins, as there would be 'sea outside'. Clambering back to the deck clad in vivid orange, we winced at the feeling that we, like our main boom, were the objects of amused criticism. For there was no sea outside, at any rate for some miles; only a fresh offshore wind crisping the smooth waters of Dublin Bay and driving the city murk towards the cliffs of Howth. But the weather signs were held to be adverse: we found they always were – trouble might begin at any moment. So we maintained our strange armour, though it hampered our movements grievously, and by its repulsive texture and odour hastened the inevitable approach of physical distress.*

One can readily picture the friction between the working class crew and their privileged and somewhat clueless employers. Given the circumstances it is therefore perhaps understandable that it was not long before the two parties were split asunder. This happened shortly after the paid hands had managed to run the *Shulah* firmly aground in Belfast Lough. Erskine and Henry observed with great interest the efforts of their crew to build a makeshift scaffold out of spars to prop the vessel up in order to prevent her getting swamped by the incoming tide. The helpful hands resigned shortly afterwards.

Despite a newfound feeling of confidence in and understanding of the dark art of sailing, neither brother quite felt up to taking command of the vessel and instead hired a skipper. This man was evidently an alcoholic and, following another serious grounding, tried to blackmail the Childers by insinuating that they had deliberately wrecked the boat in order to claim insurance. The tipsy skipper was unceremonially discharged and a new man was hired, who thankfully seemed happy to let the brothers get on with sailing and merely kept an eye on them in the meantime.

Despite these travails, Erskine was enjoying the cruise, 'Seeing with enchanted eyes the purple hills and wine dark seas of Scotland.' They had made a start and, by the time the vessel was laid up for the winter, had a strong grasp of most of the fundamentals of navigating and boat handling. This was fortunate because when they returned to *Shulah* the following season, their latest 'skipper' lasted only a few days and from thereon the two brothers determined to make their own way. This step led to some interesting incidents, for there is little question that *Shulah* was a formidable craft for two to handle, and her huge mainsail seems to have been a permanent liability, as witnessed in this recollection by Erskine of their arrival in the anchorage of Gourock:

We came storming with magnificent nonchalance into an anchorage thickly dotted with anchor lights swaying above hulls invisible in the darkness and balefully warning us off from every discernible resting place. 'Two's enough to manage her' had been one of our smug commonplaces latterly; but six seemed scarcely enough now, with the tiller, the anchor, the lead, the sheets, the halyards, and the arrangement for a lookout all crying for attention from two harassed mariners inaudible to one another in the whistle of wind and rattle of canvas. We blundered miserably about, missing stays, gybing cataclysmically, shaving a bowsprit here and a jigger there, until more by accident than design brought up in an apparently free space, sullenly deaf to the cries of a dim figure in pyjamas on board a neighbouring craft. We turned in with a presentiment of evil, to find in the morning that we had tangled with some moorings, whose owner swept up and gave us his views on our seamanship.

Most sailors will recall fondly some similar snarl-up to this at some point in their careers, and it is worth remembering that the *Shulah* and her contemporaries did not possess a motor of any kind, so any close-quarters handling had to be done under sail. This is an infinitely more ticklish business than the handling of most boats today, whose owners are generally inclined to rely on their engines in close quarters. While this still doesn't seem to prevent comical accidents of the type described, it really should do.

It was probably incidents such as this that persuaded the brothers to sell the *Shulah* and cast around for a more suitable craft. The vessel was therefore sailed across to Ireland in order to be sold. It was on this trip that the Childers enjoyed their first solo night passage, and Erskine captures the magic of it most evocatively:

> *Who can describe the emotions of that first night, with the rapture of freedom in adventure, and the strangely paradoxical sense of added loneliness and at the same time of wider companionship? It is true that the low hiss of the foam under the lee bow takes a mysterious, almost sinister note, unlike the vivacious melody which it plays in the sparkling sunlight, and the vessel, with her slender upper rigging fretting against the stars, seems very small and isolated.*

By 1895, Childers was fully established in his job as clerk in the House of Commons and the humdrum life of London hemmed him in. The great consolation, however, was that the Commons went into recess for weeks on end during the summer. Far longer, if you can imagine it, than they do today. This afforded plenty of time for serious yacht cruising if anyone so desired. Most didn't and preferred to melt away to the various hunting, shooting and fishing activities that filled the long gaps between running the country. Those who did venture onto the water generally trod the snowy white decks of some elegant yacht anchored off the Royal Yacht Squadron in Cowes, all gleaming brass and shining varnish. Very little active sailing would have been done and most would have simply observed the numerous paid hands undertaking the actual sailing of the yacht.

In his activities, Childers was probably unique within the House of Commons. In the spring of 1895 he had purchased an 18ft yacht, open apart from a small deck at the bow, which he kept at Greenhithe on the Thames. 'She is not beautiful, but very workmanlike and I am quite satisfied with her.' Childers reflected. The vessel was named *Marguerite*, but was always rather affectionately referred to as *Mad Agnes* in reference to his aunt. This little yacht was to mould Childers into the daring and adventurous sailor he portrayed in his later novel. One of her key features was her centreboard, or lifting keel. If the boat ran aground the keel could simply be raised, enabling the boat to float off. *Mad Agnes* was also sufficiently flat-bottomed that if she got stuck between tides, she could happily dry out on the sand without tipping over at an alarming angle. This was a direct contrast to the very deep, narrow *Shulah* and it allowed Childers to explore the tortuous shallows and tidal estuaries of the east coast of England.

Childers appears to have been almost completely immune to hardship and I can do no better than quote his own description of the yacht and her accommodation arrangements:

> As for sleeping accommodation, I have a specially designed bell tent of oiled canvas, laced, (when in use) round the coaming, and bent to a halyard or runner by an eyebolt at the apex and hauled taut. The bedroom under apex is four feet six inches high. Our couches consist of two reindeer hair mattresses, which make most efficient life preserving gear.

It is not clear whether by 'life preserving' he means they floated or provided sufficient comfort to ensure the crew retained the will to live. He continues:

> Comfort was not naturally, at the highest pitch; its chief foe was bad weather, for rain complicated everything. However, management and practice did much. The tent was waterproof, and my kit could be kept perfectly dry. I spread waterproof sheets on the floor after a wet day, and I may say I never slept better on a big yacht, or even on shore. For

cooking I used two simple spirit stoves. I must admit that lack of space and the absence of a permanent roof tended to make one content with great simplicity.

Despite this patent lack of comfort, Childers had no difficulty in persuading his chums to go sailing with him. His long-suffering brother, Henry, was a faithful crewmate as always, while Cambridge pals such as Ivor Lloyd Jones and William Le Fanu seem to have filled in the gaps. Childers' logbook is full of high jinks and near scrapes: substituting their broken tiller for a mop, grappling for a match to illuminate their riding light as a steamer bore down on them on a dark night off Dover, or even tumbling into Folkestone at 4am in order to attend a fancy dress ball. The latter adventure followed a swift jaunt across the channel to Boulogne. This is no mean undertaking in an 18ft boat, particularly as this was mid-April. From hereon, Childers can be seen as one of the true pioneers of small-boat sailing and his adventures are often beyond anything that a normal, some might argue prudent, sailor would attempt. Grounding his yacht and having to kedge her off became a commonplace occurrence, while many of his trips could only have been accomplished by either a huge slice of luck, or very fine seamanship laced with plenty of daring.

Perhaps a note on the art of kedging off is necessary here. Kedging off is a procedure for dragging a grounded yacht off into deep water. It involves loading your anchor into a dinghy and rowing out while paying out the anchor chain. Once in sufficient depth, you drop the anchor and row back to your yacht. After scrambling back aboard, you then haul on the anchor chain and pray you can pull the boat back off into the deep water where your anchor is. This short description can only hint at the misery the manoeuvre often involves: the anchor is a heavy, unwieldy implement and as you row your dinghy away from the yacht, your anchor chain constantly tries to drag you back. Invariably you are soaked, and often covered with mud. In other words, it is a task to be avoided if at all possible. Yet for Childers, kedging off seemed an everyday activity; something to be relished and sought out as he explored tortuous backwaters and shoals.

An example of a typical adventure is Childers' second cruise to France, accompanied by his brother Henry. This was undertaken in late September, a period when the weather in the English Channel can be quite volatile. Indeed, some would argue that the Channel in autumn is no place for an 18ft open boat, which in bad weather could conceivably swamp and fill with water. Nevertheless *Mad Agnes* departed England with little fanfare or concern, and after a 29-hour crossing the Childers arrived off Cherbourg. This in itself was something of an epic voyage, but perhaps the most illuminating fact is that after anchoring in Cherbourg and dining out, the two brothers went their separate ways; Henry retiring to a comfortable bed at the Hotel du Louvre, while Erskine preferred the draughty pleasures of *Mad Agnes'* bell tent. He seems almost masochistic in his refusal to accept any level of comfort, though confessed that he much preferred an isolated tidal anchorage. 'I have the strongest antipathy to the dirt, odours, publicity and general discomfort of a quayside berth in a crowded basin.' This statement can be read almost word for word coming from Davies' mouth in *The Riddle of the Sands*.

From Cherbourg, the brothers cruised up the coast to Le Havre and, arriving before dawn, endured a miserable couple of hours lying off the port waiting for first light in order to find their way in. It was at this point that their adventures took on a truly hair-raising tone, as Childers relates:

> *In the first light of dawn we were approaching the land, but the mist prevented our seeing the position of the piers. Suddenly we sighted a large fishing boat just ahead, apparently running for the harbour too. We thought it safe to follow her. Suddenly the wind changed instantaneously from SE to NW, causing us to gybe all standing [no damage] and setting up a confused cross-sea in which the boat behaved admirably. Blowing a hard gale. Suddenly made out both piers at distance of 200 yards, now right to windward owing to the change of wind. When quite near we realised we could not make the entrance. The question was, would she stay [tack through the wind] in the heavy sea there was? The fishing boat failed to do so and was driven on the rocks and wrecked.*

We put her about and she stayed beautifully. We tacked out about a quarter of a mile, shipping one nasty sea, came in again, and found we gained nothing owing to the strong adverse tide. Tacked out again but nothing better.

Eventually the pair had to head to a creek some miles down the coast where the heavily battered *Mad Agnes* was allowed a well-earned rest. Childers' own spare, understated account of this terrifying incident does little to convey the utter chaos of wind screaming in the rigging and sails thrashing, as the little boat battled gamely with a howling gale and vicious cross sea that threatened to swamp and sink her at any moment. It is to the credit of both boat and crew that they survived. The Childers later discovered with some relief that the crew of the wrecked fishing boat were rescued. The vessel itself, however, was a total loss. Perhaps this incident served to cool Erskine's ardour for open-boat cruising in the autumn, for after this he took the prudent step of having his little craft shipped back to the UK aboard a cargo steamer.

Nevertheless, Erskine's adventures continued unabated. His 'thirst for the sea', as he picturesquely put it, seemed insatiable at this point and he approached it with a dedication verging on fanaticism. By now he was confident enough in his own abilities to undertake lengthy passages singlehanded; quite a contrast to those early travails aboard *Shulah* with paid hands. Childers' description of a singlehanded night passage off the Kent Coast offers a wonderful insight into the delicate balance between the thrill of being out on your own, and the almost unbearable tension of a sea passage in an open boat without anyone around to reassure you.

... off the East Swale I lost the ebb tide and off Whitstable all but a faint draught of my westerly wind. There was nothing for it but to anchor out in the open. It was a black night, with a mist just opaque enough to shroud all lights; the barometer was inclined to fall, and a swell beginning to roll in from the east was at once a presage of things to come and a source of much physical discomfort; for this was the first day of my

season in open water. Supperless, spiritless, I trimmed and hoisted my anchor light and tried to sleep.

The mast whined with every roll; with every roll there were flickings and slappings of ill tautened ropes which I had neither the energy to pacify nor the philosophy to ignore. Fevered dreams came at last, culminating in a hallucination that, like Shelley's doomed mariner 'longing with divided will, yet with no power to seek or shun', I was drifting with fatal impotence over a stormy sea. In point of fact, a brisk northeast wind had awakened my vessel into a very lively motion. In daylight this would have seemed as a very simple and welcome phenomenon; alone, in the chill depressing hour before dawn, when vitality is at its lowest and with shoals on either hand and all guides to navigation obliterated, I shivered miserably at the prospect.

Now, as always, salvation came from the cogent need to immediately do something definite and the lighting of the binnacle lamp was to find a companion, benevolent, imperturbable and at least giving one an indication of the lie of the lands and shoals. At the worst one can heave to and wait; at best, groping with lead and compass, one can make progress in a light draught boat through the restricted channels of the Kent coast.

And now dawn is breaking, grey and ghostly, a buoy is sighted and safely identified, blurred traces of the coastline appear, marks multiply and at length the sun, dispelling the last mists, dispels with them all that remains of mystery and doubt. Once more the ebb tide is under you and the mainsheet sings in its sheaves – delicious music – as you bear up for Ramsgate and the Gulf Stream. Short as a child's is the recollection of those evil night hours, keen as a child's zest for this reward, rightfully yours by conquest. And now for breakfast!

And what a breakfast it must have been after that long night! In fact, many of Erskine's crew fondly recalled that he was an excellent cook, and there is an amusing account by Erskine himself detailing the difficulty of boiling eggs and making a cup of tea while battling with steering the vessel and trimming the sails. This is truly the sort of sailing that many yachtsmen aspire to but few have the hardihood to actually carry out. Childers was different, and it is fair to say that his dedication to small-boat sailing channelled his enthusiasm and almost total lack of fear in a very worthy if slightly trivial direction. One can only look at the results when his intense personality became involved in Irish politics to see how dangerous it could become. As Childers describes Davies in *The Riddle of the Sands*: 'I saw strength to obstinacy and courage to recklessness.' Childers shared these attributes with his fictional character.

If there was one thing that Childers was not fanatical about it was his occupation. Certainly he was diligent and efficient, but that is all. He relates most vividly navigating the streets of London from his own home to Parliament; how he would gauge the direction and force of the wind and dutifully beat his way up to Westminster, mindful of any lee shores along the way. A beautiful picture of eccentricity and one that was recreated by Arthur Ransome in the opening page of his first book, *Swallows and Amazons*, when young Roger tacks up a field in the same manner. Although Childers and Ransome were contemporaries, there is no record of them meeting and it is likely that they simply shared a similar obsessive passion for the sea which led to this little coincidence.

Strangely, Childers' intense love of sailing and wild, almost reckless need for adventure, remained almost totally hidden from his colleagues, who expressed astonishment when they discovered some of the scrapes this taciturn young man had got himself into. Basil Williams, who also worked at the Commons and who became a firm friend, relates their surprise:

We were astonished when we heard that our quiet friend was wont, in the long recesses from parliamentary business allowed us in those comparatively placid times, to go away, often alone, in a little cockle shell of a boat, navigating through the storms of the Channel or the North Sea or threading his way through the complicated shoals of the German, Danish or Baltic coasts.

The reference to the German and Baltic coast is a nod to what was arguably Childers' finest (and certainly his most ambitious) voyage aboard a new vessel, *Vixen*. This trip included an exploration of the Dutch canals, a thorough investigation of the Dutch and German Frisian Islands and from thence through the Kiel Canal to Denmark before doubling back through the Frisian Islands to Terschelling, where *Vixen* was finally laid up. This being Childers, the cruise was undertaken from late September through to December and the stoical Henry was once again along for the ride. The adventure was to form the bare bones of *The Riddle of the Sands*.

Vixen was purchased in late August 1893 and it is perhaps best left to Childers to describe her. It is safe to say that it was far from love at first sight:

I have never begun a cruise under less propitious circumstances. To start with, no one could call the Vixen beautiful. We grew to love her in the end, but never to admire her. At first I did not even love her for she was a pis aller, bought in a hurry in default of a better, and a week spent in fitting her for cruising had somehow not cemented our affections. Nor could the most sympathetic of friend, tactfully avoiding the aesthetic point of view, dwell on her weatherly and workmanlike appearance. A low freeboard, a high coach house, coach roof, and a certain over sparred appearance aloft, would unnerve the most honied tongue.

Comfort below might be the flatterer's last resource, but there again the words of compliment would die on his lips. In the 'saloon' he would find but just enough headroom to allow him to sit upright; and before he could well help himself the observation would escape him that the centreplate was an inconveniently large piece of furniture.

Nothing could make the Vixen a beauty, but she proved herself to be admirably suited for the work we gave her. A couple of small bilge keels make her sit nearly upright when on the ground, a feature which we found most valuable in North Germany. As to headroom below, we very soon decided that it did not matter in the least. For heating and cooking we found a large oil stove admirable. I had the main boom and mainsail reduced and then found her handily and adequately canvassed. We were in the habit of speaking contemptuously of her seagoing qualities, but she never, as a matter of fact, justified our strictures.

The description is the same, word for word, as far the *Dulcibella* in *Riddle of the Sands* and indeed any technical or scenic description within the book is almost always taken directly from this cruise. The logbook of the voyage is still extant and bears this out beautifully. Perhaps the most delicious irony is that Childers was actually trying to get to the Mediterranean on this voyage. After fitting out his new yacht he determined to head across to France, with a rough plan to sail down to Bordeaux and from there through the Canal du Midi and onwards to the Mediterranean. This plan was scuppered by a persistent south-west wind. Childers was always loath to throw away a favourable wind, and the fateful decision was taken to head north instead and explore the canals and waterways of Holland. The rest is literary history.

The cruise was an utter epic even by modern standards. The adventurers headed inland at the Oosterscheldt and sailed as far as they could towards Rotterdam. When the waters were too restrictive to sail, they were forced to take it in turns to drag the *Vixen* from the side of the riverbank. All the while they were dogged by the youth of Holland, who seemed to take particular delight in pelting the vessel with mud, crabs and other detritus as they made their painful way back out to the North Sea at Ijmuiden. From here, the sailors determined to go wherever the wind suggested they should and as it was still blowing from the south-west, it pushed them further and further east towards the maze of channels and sands of the mysterious Frisian Islands. It was at this point that the cruise became an earnest exploration. The first taste of things to come arrived as they headed out of Lake IJsselmeer on 17 December:

The weather had broken at last for we woke to a strong bluster from the NW and the promise of more, but we were indifferent now, for we could run NE over the Zuyder Zee, behind the shelter of islands and banks. So we started double reefed before the wind. It was fine at first, but we soon had to take in [sic] third reef while heavy rain squalls fell on us in succession. It was our first experience of a kind of sailing [to] which we afterwards became quite accustomed. The channels were deep, narrow and complicated, and buoys and beacons of all shapes and colours seemed innumerable. 'We're lost' we concluded once, but we found the way in the end.

From here they ran on behind the shield of the Frisian Islands. These low, mysterious islands are little more than huge sand dunes with lonely, windblown settlements huddling behind their desolate ridges. For a couple of months in the middle of summer, the peace is shattered as tourists descend upon them, but by September the islands and their whispering sands are once more alone and magnificently desolate. Along their shores, miles of white beaches and sandbars stretch in all directions at low tide and amid them lies a maze of narrow channels and deeps. Some are buoyed and others are marked with thin sticks driven into the sand. In the UK these are called withies or booms while locals in the Frisian Islands call them pricken. Naturally, they were often vague and misleading navigational aids, as this incident from *Vixen*'s logbook illustrates:

> *Sighted a row of booms and thought we were safe as the water was deep. About ten yards from the first boom ran hard aground at six knots. Unfortunately it was about half an hour after high water. In two hours we found ourselves on a perfect Ararat [a reference to the resting place of Noah's Ark]. Seemed the highest place for miles around, with the peccant boom atop of it.*

Childers often found his charts were inaccurate and so set about discovering the true nature of the coastline. To measure depth it was necessary to make repeated casts of the lead line (a weighted line marked off with knots). This was laborious work, but something the meticulous and patient Childers enjoyed greatly. He must have felt he had stumbled upon cruising heaven, for here he could spend days on end in splendid isolation. He soon picked up on the local trader's knack of sheltering behind sandbanks to ride out a storm and frequently the *Vixen* was several days between visits to port. As their cruise progressed the weather deteriorated, but this simply served to push them inexorably on:

> *The weather was now hopelessly demoralised, and the North Sea was out of the question ... Whether this region [the Frisian Islands] is known*

to English yachtsmen I do not know; for our part, in default of better, we found it a delightful cruising ground safe in any weather and a novel and amusing mode of getting to the Elbe and so to the Baltic in a season when the North Sea would be highly dangerous to a small boat. A light [shallow] draught is indispensable, of course; ours of four feet is, I should think, the maximum for comfort, though the channels are navigated by local traders loaded down to as much as seven feet. Occasional running aground is inevitable, so that a centreboarder, which takes the ground comfortably when the plate is not in use is by far the best pattern for a boat.

By late September, the *Vixen* had made it to the island of Borkum in north-western Germany, and Childers was delighted with the contrast to Holland: 'No boys, no bother, no customs.' From this point onward, the log is a constant record of groundings, gales, fogs and the thrill of discovery. This entry from 30 September is typical:

Thick fog. Overslept and woke to bumping – dashed out in pyjamas and tried to kedge off – failed and dried. Bed again. Off about 10 and groped about for our channel in the fog.

Heating was supplied by a rather smelly paraffin stove – a Rippingille No. 3 – which is immortalised by many sardonic mentions in *The Riddle of the Sands*. The discomfort on rainy days is almost tangible as you imagine the intrepid sailors huddled down below, drying out and trying to get warm after a long day of kedging and groping through the channels of this lonely part of the world. By 1 October, Henry was clearly starting to feel the strain, for Erskine noted: 'Slight indisposition among the crew, so I landed and bought champagne and beef steak at the hotel.'

Evidently this swift action served to quell any mutinous thoughts on his brother's part. From here, *Vixen* pushed on to Cuxhaven and then through the Kiel Canal to the Baltic – a total contrast from the supremely tidal North Sea and its desolate sands. On 10th November, Henry headed back to England, his leave being up, but there was a chance he could return and

Erskine determined to keep his plans vague. He was left on his own to enjoy the beauty of the Baltic coast and sailed up to Flensburg, all narrow inlets and gentle wooded hills sloping down to the water's edge, golden brown in the late autumn sunlight. He was enchanted by the coastline, which he described as, 'the finest yachting country I had seen yet.'

All the time Childers was – unwittingly – gathering material for *The Riddle of the Sands*. One of the factors that sets the book apart from other novels is the extreme realism of the narrative. On first reading it is often hard to tell whether it is fact or fiction. This was, very simply, because most of the incidents were taken straight out of *Vixen*'s logbook and transposed into the novel. Exaggeration was rarely needed. In the characters of Davies and Carruthers, Erskine merely incorporated his own personality and that of some of his sailing friends. Basil Williams, who sailed with Erskine on many occasions, was later to observe that, 'Davies was every inch Erskine'. It is also fair to argue that Davies' own views on the threat of German invasion – so painstakingly outlined in *The Riddle of the Sands* – were much the same as Erskine's, and that these views must have been distilled on this trip. There is mention of a visit to several war memorials commemorating the German – or specifically Prussian – invasion of this area, which had previously been Danish. Interestingly both Childers' logbook and *The Riddle* are relentlessly complimentary about the Germans. As Davies observed: 'Germany's a thundering great nation, I wonder if we shall ever fight her?' This was an interesting leap to make as, prior to the 1890s, France had always been perceived as the main threat, while Germany was traditionally Britain's ally. After all, the two nations did share a royal family.

Whatever his thoughts on the burgeoning German threat, *Vixen* was now a very long way from home and it was already November. Childers was therefore seriously in need of some help, and fortunately the faithful Henry was able to make a return, bringing another paraffin stove, some rifles for duck shooting, and a prismatic compass to help them thread their way back through the Frisian Islands. By now it was very late in the season, but the adventurers pushed mercilessly on. On 29 November they received a severe dusting, as related by Erskine:

Got underway at light – determined to seek shelter at Bensersiel, a place approached by a boomed high water channel. Fearful job to get the anchor – found it bent! Groped three reefed into the Bensersiel channel and anchored outside awaiting the tide. Wind grew to an even worse gale, with heavy rain and a hurricane look to the sky. A waterspout passed us at a distance of about 400 yards. We were in the centre of a cyclone, we supposed, about 11, for the wind suddenly veered to the NE and blew a hurricane, making Bensersiel and our anchorage a lee shore. It was half flood, and we decided to start, but how to get up the anchor? Couldn't get in a link in as it was. In view of slipping it [abandoning the anchor and picking it up later] we buoyed it ready; then got up sail, three reefed and tried to sail it out of the ground. Just giving it up when it came away and we got it up. Then bore away for Bensersiel. Got into channel, but found booms almost covered by abnormally high tide and very hard to see. Henry stood forward and waved directions. Soon got into breakers and found it a devil of a situation. Fearful work with the tiller under so much sail. One or two heavy gybes at turns in the channel. When close inshore sea less bad – missed booms altogether and grounded, but blew off again. Whole population on the beach yelling. Tide so high that all clues were obscured but Henry conned her skilfully on, and we were soon tearing into the mouth of the 'harbour', about 15 feet wide at about seven knots. It was a tiny basin with not even room to round up. Tried to get sail down but it jammed: Let go anchor with a run, luffed and just brought up in time with the bowsprit over the quayside, and received the bewildered congratulations of the people, who seemed to think we had fallen from the sky.

This incident is related pretty much word for word in *The Riddle of the Sands* and one can almost feel the icy spray stinging their faces as they tear into this tiny, unlikely, port. For any yachtsmen reading this and feeling a little inferior, there is also a pleasing incident where the brothers ground their yacht near a small port and wander in to get some stores. During their absence night falls and, as they stroll back to the beach, they realise that they forgot to set their anchor light, meaning they can't locate *Vixen*. At this point they also realise, to their horror, that they forgot to drop the anchor altogether, and a frantic search reveals *Vixen* has washed some way down the beach. This incident suggests either that the brothers were getting a little complacent or, more likely, were exhausted by their adventures, and by 14 December, when *Vixen* arrived in the Dutch Island of Terschelling, the decision was taken that she should remain there until the spring, the brothers returning home by steamer.

Thus ended a truly impressive voyage, which provided Erskine with all of the raw material for his one masterpiece. Yet it would be some time before he got around to writing his tale of amateur espionage, which didn't appear until 1903. The main reason for this was that Childers was busy with other matters. In 1899 he and his friend Basil Williams had joined the City Imperial Volunteers and were sent to Africa to fight in the Boer War. Childers' adventures at war do not belong in this book, but his memoirs, *In the Ranks of the CIV*, were published on his return and, thus encouraged, Childers started work on *The Riddle of the Sands*. He was urged on by his sister Dulcibella, and it was she who persuaded him to put in the rather stilted love affair between Davies and Frau Dollmann. Childers complained at the time that the affair had been rather 'spatchcocked' into the main text. Nevertheless, the romance has its own charm and Davies' tongue-tied approach echoes an encounter during Erskine and Henry's voyage when an enthusiastic Dutch innkeeper at the port of Anjum introduced the extremely shy pair of brothers to the most attractive girls in the village. As Erskine recalled: 'They *were* pretty but it was rather an embarrassing visit as neither side knew the other's language, and we could not do much more in the social way than sit dazzled at their beauty'.

Awkward romance aside, *The Riddle* was a bestseller on publication and is still hugely popular today. Its warmth and wit, combined with intrigue and wonderful sailing sketches, have ensured its place in literary history. It wasn't the first book to foretell of the dangers of German invasion (the wonderfully titled *Battle of Dorking* by George Tompkyns Chesney, published in 1871, earns that honour), but it helped that it was so prescient and its relevance grew as the world's two great powers slowly wound up to the fateful declaration of war in 1914. Childers' novel endures largely because of its wonderful feeling of realism. It was on this wave of success that Childers met his American wife, Molly, while on a trip to Boston in 1903. The two fell deeply in love with a devotion that was to last all their lives. Vivacious, passionate and caring, she proved the ideal foil for the more introverted but equally intense Erskine. 'I'm so tremendously happy old chap', Childers wrote to Basil Williams at the time.

Marriage did not curtail Childers' sailing adventures either. *Vixen* had been sold in 1899 and there was a brief experiment with part ownership of the *Sunbeam,* but marriage also brought Childers his final command. A wedding present from his in-laws, the *Asgard,* was a beautiful ketch designed by Colin Archer, whose sturdy designs have become world renowned. It is telling that Sir Robin Knox-Johnson's famous *Suhaili*, the first vessel to circumnavigate the globe without stopping, was based on another Colin Archer design. The *Asgard* was elegant yet sturdy, comfortable, and well suited for cruising.

By now, Childers was a consummate sailor and exuded confidence, as Molly later recalled following his masterly entrance into the port of Assens during a cruise in Denmark: 'VERY tricky navigation. Erskine really has genius. It went perfectly. I was in terror and could not imagine how he knew the way. First time too. Chart no help. Absolutely without squeak.'

Molly also proved herself a fine sailor and an excellent cruising companion and, under the careful tutelage of Erskine, she soon grew in confidence. Together, the pair explored many of Erskine's old haunts and also headed deeper into the Baltic, making it all the way to Oslo. Perhaps understandably, none of these later cruises had quite the spice of his earlier adventures aboard *Mad Agnes* and *Vixen*, but still he continued to push boundaries and open up new cruising vistas. And there was one final sailing escapade to come for Childers; an adventure that was to have all the drama and suspense of *The Riddle of the Sands*. This was the Howth gun running of 1914 and, unlike *The Riddle*, the whole thing was utterly real and deadly serious. The premise behind the scheme was very simple; Erskine wanted to provide an illegal shipment of weapons to Irish Volunteers, who were agitating for an independent Ireland.

Why had Childers gone from being a loyal civil servant and noted patriot to suddenly engaging in an extremely risky undertaking, which took him into unknown and dangerous political waters? To make sense of this shift it is important to understand a bit about his allegiances. The fact was that Erskine had become more and more drawn to Irish politics and the push for home rule. Even though he appeared to be as English as a cricket field, he was more Irish than anything else and found himself being slowly drawn into the injustices his people were forced to endure. Molly supported him in his beliefs and he gradually found himself deeply embroiled with the Irish campaign. All of that fervour and 'strength to obstinacy and courage to recklessness' was no longer being channelled into footling around in yachts but into a much bigger and more serious cause. An insight into this mindset can be seen in *The Riddle of the Sands,* when Davies says the following:

> *'I can't settle down' he said: 'All I've been able to do is potter around in small boats; but it's all been wasted till this chance came. I'm afraid you wont be able to understand how I feel about it, but at last, for once in a way, I see a chance of being useful.'*

As the situation in Ireland started to reach boiling point in the summer of 1914, Erskine saw his own 'chance', and from that moment on, he was set upon the path that would eventually destroy him. The Howth gun running was a reaction to the successful Larne gun running, in which the Unionists had been armed. Now it was the turn of the Republicans and the plot involved two yachts: the *Asgard,* commanded by Childers and the *Kelpie,* commanded by an irascible young Irish sailor, Conor O'Brien, who was later to find great fame through his own cruising exploits aboard the *Saoirse.* The two vessels were to meet in Cowes on the Isle of Wight and from there make a clandestine rendezvous with a German tug off the Belgian coastline to load their shipment of weapons and bullets. From here, the two vessels would sail over to Ireland; *Kelpie* to Kilcoole and *Asgard* to Howth, a small port adjacent to Dublin. On a signal from shore, *Asgard* was to head in and unload the guns, handing them straight to the Volunteers who would be waiting at the quay. The plan was going to take some precision, due to the small window of opportunity in which a vessel of *Asgard's* depth could get in and out of

Howth. This would take skill and accuracy and there surely couldn't have been a more suitable man than Erskine Childers for the job. He was not to know it, but this dangerous undertaking was to be his final cruise.

Things started badly. The *Asgard* had been laid up in Conwy on the Welsh coast and was in a terrible state when Erskine stepped aboard. He had a tight deadline to make and the odds looked stacked against him, particularly as the *Asgard*'s mainsail was split and the vessel had not been properly commissioned that spring. Despite this delay, Childers managed to push *Asgard* hard on the long trip round from Wales to the Solent and made his rendezvous with O'Brien and the *Kelpie* only two days late, still with time to spare to get to their cargo tug off the Belgian coast. One can't help but chuckle at the thought of Childers hobnobbing with the other yachtsmen in this most genteel of settings, all the time knowing that the *Asgard* was bound on a daredevil mission that many would have looked upon with horror. The trip had all the right ingredients to satisfy Childers: a smattering of romance, more than a hint of extreme risk, a ticklish piece of tidal calculation to ensure success, and a faintly surreal aspect. Not everyone thought the same, however. An acquaintance by the name of Colonel Pipon was invited on this cruise and emphatically declined. His reasons were as follows: 'He [Childers] promised us there was no intention of using them [the rifles] as anything other than as a gesture of equality. I refused. I recognised Childers as a crackpot. Something always happens to crackpots. Something always goes wrong.'

Yet, as it turned out, after its shaky start the cruise was actually going reasonably well. *Kelpie* and *Asgard* left the Solent on 10 July 1914 and sailed on to their rather grim appointment through glorious midsummer sun and gentle breezes that barely ruffled the water. They had arranged to meet with a German tug at noon on 12 July, but the weather had other ideas. Off Beachy Head, the vessels lay totally becalmed for several hours and the crew were presented with a perfect view down the English coastline, which glinted and smouldered in the glow of a beautiful July evening. All the while, Erskine sweated over the lack of progress; they were still many miles from their rendezvous spot of the Ruylingen Lightship, situated between Dover and Gravelines. Noon the next day found them still 22 miles from their goal, with the *Asgard*'s sails hanging limp and lifeless. How Childers must have wished for an engine at this point! Yet salvation was at hand, as the gentlest of breezes sprang up and whispered in the rigging. The listless yacht came back to life and crept forward again, giving renewed hope and purpose. Yet even as the crew peered eagerly about them for the tug, they were dealt a blow. With the wind came a fog and within minutes all landmarks had been enveloped in its cloying blanket. The *Asgard* now stole forward through an eerie world of grey with only the mournful mooing of foghorns for company. All aboard strained their eyes and ears for some sign of the tug; they were now right in the vicinity of their rendezvous point.

It was Molly who made the breakthrough. Peering desperately through the mists, she made out the vague form of the tug, with a yacht moored alongside it, the *Kelpie*, which – as luck would have it – was now fully loaded and just about to cast off. Soon it was *Asgard*'s turn to load, and the fog – previously their enemy – was now a firm friend, providing a perfect cover for their illicit activities. The calm that had dogged their passage was also a huge boon as it made loading a simple operation. At this point Childers was horrified to discover that the *Kelpie* had loaded a mere 600 rifles (as opposed to her expected 750) and much less ammunition than hoped. This meant the *Asgard* was going to have to take 900 rifles, a very heavy load, yet he spared nothing to cram as much of this cargo as possible aboard his beloved yacht. Mary Spring Rice was one of the co-conspirators in this operation and recounted the dramatic events later:

> *Darkness, lamps, strange faces, the swell of the sea making the boat lurch, guns, straw, everywhere, unpacking on deck and being handed down and stowed in an endless stream – the Vaseline of the guns smeared over everything; the bunks and floors of the whole yacht aft from the fo'c'sle filled about 2'6" high with guns from side to side, men sweating and panting under the weight of ammunition boxes – a German face peering down the hatch saying, 'they will explode if you drop them'. A huge ship's oil riding light falling down through the hatch and, first onto*

my shoulder and then upside down into a heap of straw – a flare up, a
cry, a quick snatch of rescue, the lamp goes out thank god, work again,
someone drops two guns through, they fall on someone, no room to stand
save on guns, guns everywhere. On and on and on.

By 2.30am the *Asgard* was completely full and two cases of ammunition were reluctantly dumped over the side as there simply wasn't an inch more room. Stage one of the mission was complete. The *Asgard* headed for Ireland, her crew sleeping on a bed of rifles and bullets as they made their way with painful slowness up the coast, heavily laden and beating into an unexpected headwind. There were several alarming near misses along the way; firstly with the Royal Navy who were on manoeuvres off both Folkestone and Plymouth, and who succeeded in terrifying the crew of the A*sgard* during both encounters. In the first instance they fired blanks at the yacht, in the second, a destroyer came speeding directly at them and threatened to ram them. The next major scare came as *Asgard* anchored in Holyhead. Erskine needed some decent sleep and was just settling in for a snooze when a coastguard boat pulled alongside and asked to speak to the skipper. He was duly woken and coolly answered their questions regarding the last port of the yacht, tonnage, destination and such like. To the immense relief of everyone, the authorities were satisfied with Childers' half-truths and rowed away without boarding. The drama was not over yet, however, for the crossing of the Irish Sea was a brutal, tumultuous one and Erskine was not able to leave the deck for many hours as his heavily-laden vessel laboured through the storm-lashed seas. Despite this final test by the elements, *Asgard* was off Howth by 25 July and had a day to wait before her appointment. Unknown to the smugglers, there had been drama ashore, for there had been a tip-off that guns were going to be run into Howth and HMS *Porpoise* had been dispatched to patrol the area. This crisis was averted when a counter rumour was circulated that the guns were going to be run into Wicklow, and HMS *Porpoise* dutifully hurried off to hunt down the artfully placed red herring. The coast was clear and the *Asgard*'s triumphant arrival is recorded at the start of this chapter.

Fittingly, if rather tragically, this daredevil piece of seamanship was to be Childers' last ever yachting cruise. He was 44, and should have had many more years of pottering about in yachts ahead of him, but two things got in his way. First came the war with Germany, which he had presaged with such unerring foresight in *The Riddle*. Childers promptly turned British patriot again and, despite his age, served with distinction in the Royal Navy, the very force he and his friends had so dextrously dodged that fateful summer's day off Howth. Childers distinguished himself in the Cuxhaven Raid – the first time seaplanes were used to carry out an attack – and his intimate knowledge of the Frisian coastline was to prove pivotal to its success. It was one of those strange moments that followed Childers throughout his later life, where fiction and fact seemed to melt into one. Just as he had always wished for the *Riddle of the Sands* to appear to the reader as fact, now the facts of his life seemed to become more fantastical than the fiction.

Further service in the Dardanelles, and later an office job with the Admiralty, saw Childers emerge from the war relatively unscathed and awarded the Distinguished Service Cross (DSC). Yet he did not return to peace, but to his favourite subject: home rule for Ireland. He launched himself into this cause with the feverish tenacity with which he had once sought out adventure in the less fraught forum of small sailing boats. From now on, Childers was adrift on a much deeper and more dangerous ocean, and the waters were alive with sharks.

This book is primarily about seafaring literature and is therefore a far from suitable vehicle for exploring the Irish Question. Suffice to say that Childers' dogged approach saw him become one of the leading lights in the push for Home Rule. Yet he was always the outsider, the 'last Englishman', and it was a combination of this, his single-minded stubbornness and his 'reckless courage' that were to prove his undoing. Once Ireland had gained some autonomy, it promptly plunged into civil war, and by 1922 Childers was very much on the back foot. His closest ally (Michael Collins) had been shot and Childers was increasingly being portrayed as the destructive force behind the war. His conspicuous Englishness made him a convenient scapegoat and he was portrayed in the press as the evil mastermind behind the conflict in Ireland. On 10 November 1922, officers of the newly established 'free state' arrested him at his old ancestral home of Glendalough. He greeted the officers with a gun, but one of his maids intervened, throwing herself between Childers and the men. He was tried on 17 November 1922 by a court he refused to recognise and was sentenced to be executed on the rather feeble charge of possessing an automatic weapon without authority. He was executed seven days later. His final words as the firing squad lined up were: 'Take a step or two forward lads, it will be easier that way.' So Childers' life ended and with it his 'chance of being useful'.

It was a tragic, and ultimately stupid, death. Distrusted in Ireland and reviled as a traitor in England, Childers had left himself utterly isolated. At the time of his execution Winston Churchill described him as, 'That mischief making murderous renegade.' He was nothing of the sort. He was just a man earnestly trying to do his best for his mother's country. Thankfully, the passage of time has been kinder to Childers than many were in 1922 and his reputation has been restored. It is fitting that he is remembered foremost as a novelist and sailor. It is this first love of his that has endured and his ability to convey the sheer joy of 'pottering around on small boats' that has ensured his legacy is more than that of a rather quirky footnote in the history of Ireland's struggle for freedom. With that in mind, it is probably best to leave the last word to Childers himself. In an article he published in *The Times* he mused upon the madness of, 'embarking on voyages in small, half decked sailing craft, where they are drenched by day and racked by night.' Yet his conclusion sums up beautifully the very essence of why yachtsmen go to such extraordinary lengths of suffering in the name of pleasure, and provides the man himself with a fitting epitaph:

When the Sturm *and* Drang *are past, and out of the shock of the seas they glide before the weakening evening breeze into some quiet haven or cove, to drop anchor close to trees which never looked so green or cottages which never looked so snug and homely, their spirit rebounds with a leap; painful memories become sanctified, ennobled, glorious, the mystery of pain has been solved, the riddle of happiness guessed. Something has been conquered not only by power but by love; the world has grown to double its own dimensions and is seen for the first time in harmony. New values have established themselves upon the wreckage of old standards of utility and gratification.*

Joseph Conrad
Clipper ship captain turned literary titan

Of all the sailors turned writers, few enjoyed such an intimate relationship with the sea as Joseph Conrad. For him, sailing was more than just a distraction, it provided both his sole income during 20 years of wandering the globe and the framework around which his itinerant life hung. Between Conrad embarking on a career as a sailor in 1874 and when he finally turned his back on the ocean in 1893, he sailed immense distances, rounded the dreaded Cape Horn twice, meandered along thousands of miles of coast spanning the China Seas to the Mediterranean, and had worked his way up the ladder from apprentice to captain. Even this he did with a flourish, for his first command was a beautiful clipper ship, a craft that was the most perfect evolution of commercial sail. Having set the bar high as a sailor, he then proceeded to master the art of writing novels with even greater *élan*, producing a number of seminal works in addition to many beautifully crafted short stories. *Heart of Darkness, Lord Jim, Typhoon*: these are books that have long outlived their writer and endure in the memory.

Yet all of this achievement came from a most unpromising start, and things never looked darker than on a February evening in 1878 when the young sailor retired to his hotel room, a grubby little hovel in the back streets of Marseille, pressed a gun to his chest and tried to end his life. He had just lost a fortune at the card table and his life simply didn't seem worth living.

He was utterly alone, a stranger in a strange land and at this dark moment the role of perpetual outsider didn't seem one worth playing any more. He fired a bullet deep into his breast. How different the literary world would be if he had succeeded in this rather clumsy attempt at suicide. He would also have deprived himself of some of the most remarkable adventures that were later recorded, embroidered and interwoven into some of the most compelling seafaring literature ever written.

Yet, in old sailors' parlance, we are guilty of clapping on our topsails before our anchor is out of the ground, and the tale is in danger of running away with itself. This unpromising youth was 17 years old when he attempted suicide, and the act was the culmination of a tumult of catastrophes that had propelled him across Europe and landed him penniless and desperate on the streets of Marseille. Joseph Conrad was born in Poland in 1857, the only son of Apollo and Evelina Korzeniowski. Back then he was known as Jozef Teodor Konrad Nalecz Korzeniowski and was relatively wealthy, for both of his parents were from the landed gentry. Although the Korzeniowskis would certainly have classed themselves as Polish, they were technically Russian, as Poland had been plundered and divided between the Austrians, the Prussians and the Russians. Despite this, Poland had managed to maintain a strong national identity and during the nineteenth century the cry for freedom from imperialist rule rang strong and true through the region. Apollo Korzeniowski was a dreamer, a romantic and a man blessed with almost no business acumen. He managed to fritter away most of his own money and also his wife's substantial dowry on a number of ill thought-out projects. At this point he turned himself solely to the *cause célèbre* of patriotic Polish men at the time; freedom for Poland. This led to some serious errors of judgement, which resulted in the family being arrested and exiled to northern Russia in 1861. It took two years in these unforgiving climates to kill off Evelina and six years later, when Joseph was 11, Apollo followed suit. These few bald sentences encompass a world of suffering that Joseph had to endure as a child, and which perhaps explain his brooding nature in later years. He was fortunate in one respect, however; his uncle, Thaddeus Bobrowski, was a firm friend of Apollo and took it upon himself to care for his nephew. Thaddeus had none of Apollo's rashness and wilfulness and was a pragmatic and eminently sensible man. His affection for his wayward brother-in-law endured and was transferred to Joseph and at the same time he tried to instil some of his own values into his nephew. He was the perfect foil for Joseph, who was already displaying a tendency toward the kind of unthinking romanticism that had landed Apollo in such straits. In later years, Conrad would always speak of his uncle and guardian with the greatest affection and respect.

It must have come as something of a blow to Thaddeus when his young charge began to insist that he must go to sea. Given that he had never even seen the sea, and that a mariner's life was almost universally acknowledged at the time to be a dangerous and poorly paid one, this must have been viewed with some concern by Thaddeus. He saw all of Apollo's foolhardy wilfulness in the demand. Yet there seemed no stemming the youngster's desire to escape his landlocked existence, and in 1874 Thaddeus granted Joseph his wish. Using some contacts he had in Marseille Thaddeus secured him a berth as passenger aboard the *Mont Blanc*, an elderly wooden sailing vessel built in 1853. She was embarking on a round voyage to the West Indies and back and it is likely that Thaddeus hoped that the monotony and hardship of a long voyage would cure his charge of any sea fever and make him eager to return to more gainful employment.

In this assumption he was wrong, for the charm of deep-sea sailing took hold of Joseph despite the old boat taking quite a beating, as he recalled many years later:

The very first Christmas night I ever spent away from land was employed in running before a Gulf of Lyons gale, which made the old ship groan in every timber as she skipped before it over the short seas until we brought her to, battered and out of breath, under the lee of Majorca, where the smooth water was torn by fierce cat's-paws under a very stormy sky. We – or, rather, they, for I had hardly had two glimpses of salt water in my life till then – kept her standing off and on all that day, while I listened for the first time with the curiosity of my tender years to the song of the wind in a ship's rigging. The monotonous and vibrating note was destined to grow into the intimacy of the heart, pass into blood and bone, accompany the thoughts and acts of two full decades, remain to haunt like a reproach the peace of the quiet fireside, and enter into the very texture of respectable dreams dreamed safely under a roof of rafters and tiles. The wind was fair, but that day we ran no more. The thing (I will not call her a ship twice in the same half-hour) leaked. She leaked fully, generously, overflowingly, all over – like a basket.

I took an enthusiastic part in the excitement caused by that last infirmity of noble ships, without concerning myself much with the why or the wherefore. The surmise of my maturer years is that, bored by her interminable life, the venerable antiquity was simply yawning with ennui at every seam. But at the time I did not know; I knew generally very little, and least of all what I was doing in that galère. I remember that, exactly as in the comedy of Molière, my uncle asked the precise question in the very words – not of my confidential valet, however, but across great distances of land, in a letter whose mocking but indulgent turn ill concealed his almost paternal anxiety. I fancy I tried to convey to him my (utterly unfounded) impression that the West Indies awaited my coming. I had to go there. It was a sort of mystic conviction – something in the nature of a call. But it was difficult to state intelligibly the grounds of this belief to that man of rigorous logic, if of infinite charity.

Clearly Uncle Thaddeus' plan had come royally unstuck. The sea gave the youngster a real outlet for his thirst for adventure and youthful romanticism. In sending Joseph to the Caribbean, Thaddeus had certainly helped. This was a flying-fish passage as the old salts would say, all deep blue glittering water, great playful swells with feathery billowing whitecaps and steady trade winds that caressed the cheek with warmth and thrummed in the rigging. After two months of this monotonous beauty, Joseph enjoyed the thrill of raising the tropical island of Martinique, with its chattering birds, azure waters and unseen, untold adventure. Joseph was theoretically a passenger on this first trip, but would doubtless have helped with the work of the ship. Life aboard a commercial sailing ship was not an easy one. Much of the work Conrad would have been set would have been dreadfully boring, a daily drudge of cleaning and scrubbing interspersed with moments of real danger when hands were ordered up the masts to furl or set sails. It was usually the novices who were sent high into the upper yards, and death from falling was a constant threat. Yet Conrad evidently took to the work like a duck to water and the comfortable, warm-weather passage would certainly have helped ease him in to a life afloat. The only hardship would have come on the return passage, when the *Mont Blanc* would have taken a more northerly course and had to contend with slightly chillier conditions. Despite this, Conrad did not hesitate to sign on for a second trip, which again took in Martinique and also Haiti, concluding with an icy cold race up the North Atlantic to Le Havre, ending on a raw December day. It is perhaps telling that on this occasion, Joseph left the ship in Le Havre with unseemly haste, caught a train to Marseille and did not ship again for six full months. Whether he fell in love with the sea is highly debatable, but it did help satisfy Conrad's wanderlust, and he later summed up the relationship as; 'The sea has never been friendly to man. At most it has been the accomplice of human restlessness.'

Still, two lengthy voyages had at least helped to sate some of this restlessness, and he allowed himself the luxury of a six-month break. This may seem pretty decadent, but the fact was that Conrad simply didn't need to work. He received a yearly allowance from his uncle of 2,000 Francs and this was enough to afford him a life of relative comfort and idleness for extended periods ashore. His uncle may have been pressuring him to progress, but that worthy gentleman was many miles away in Poland and this gave Joseph plenty of freedom to get into scrapes. Idle evenings ashore in Marseille were whiled away in cafes and bars, enjoying the company of intellectuals and revolutionaries in this lively city. It is therefore perhaps unsurprising that this young rebel without a cause fell under the thrall of a group of Carlist agitators, sympathisers with Carlos II of Spain, who believed that he had been deprived of his throne. This had led to a number of wars, the second of which had concluded in 1876. Yet the seed of rebellion still burned within

Spain and it was the following year that Joseph and his new found comrades became involved in an operation to run guns into Catalonia for the rebels.

To this end a syndicate of four was formed, including a mysterious lady by the name of Dona Rita, who may well have been Conrad's first love – it is certainly hinted at in some of his later works. Perhaps more importantly for the purposes of this book, there was a boat involved and he certainly fell in love with this vessel. She was the *Tremolino*, a balancelle, which is an Italian derivative of the lateen-rigged dhows. Conrad later described her as follows:

> *Two short masts raking forward and two curved yards, each as long as her hull; a true child of the Latin lake, with a spread of two enormous sails resembling the pointed wings on a sea-bird's slender body, and herself, like a bird indeed, skimming rather than sailing the seas.*
>
> *Her name was the* Tremolino. *How is this to be translated? The* Quiverer? *What a name to give the pluckiest little craft that ever dipped her sides in angry foam! I had felt her, it is true, trembling for nights and days together under my feet, but it was with the high-strung tenseness of her faithful courage. In her short, but brilliant, career she has taught me nothing, but she has given me everything. I owe to her the awakened love for the sea that, with the quivering of her swift little body and the humming of the wind under the foot of her lateen sails, stole into my heart with a sort of gentle violence, and brought my imagination under its despotic sway. The* Tremolino! *To this day I cannot utter or even write that name without a strange tightening of the breast and the gasp of mingled delight and dread of one's first passionate experience.*

Joseph was to be the active member of the syndicate, meaning that he actually took the risk of being aboard while the guns were being run. The captain was a Corsican by the name of Dominic Cervoni, a flamboyant moustachioed man who appeared to fear very little:

> *He was perfect. On board the* Tremolino, *wrapped up in a black caban, the picturesque cloak of Mediterranean seamen, with those massive*

moustaches and his remorseless eyes set off by the shadow of the deep
hood, he looked piratical and monkish and darkly initiated into the most
awful mysteries of the sea.

Several successful runs lined the syndicate up perfectly for the catastrophe that followed. For this fateful voyage, Conrad had borrowed about 3,000 Francs from his uncle, and all of this was stored in gold pieces in his money belt, which fatefully, he hid in a locker. The crew featured Cervoni's own nephew Cesar, and it was this shifty individual who betrayed the conspirators, forewarning the authorities of their plans. Running along the coast of Spain, a Spanish coastguard vessel was spotted and the crew pushed the *Tremolino* hard in order to evade it until they could make good their escape under cover of darkness. The little *Tremolino* flew like a bird before the rising gale and all were hopeful of escape until her great mainsail was unexpectedly torn from its yard by a heavy gust of wind. Close inspection revealed that this had been weakened by tampering. With the *Tremolino* disabled, Cervoni opted to run the vessel close inshore and destroy her by ramming her on to the rocks. Once ashore they would then easily be able to escape the coastguard. It was at this point that Joseph went to retrieve his Uncle's 3,000 Francs from the locker, only to discover that they had been stolen. There was no time for recriminations and the *Tremolino* was duly shattered on the unyielding rocks of the Spanish coastline. The crew took to the dinghy, but not before Cesar had been knocked into the water. To everyone's surprise, the unpopular crewmember sank like a stone and did not resurface. The rest of the crew survived and were able to escape, but it was soon abundantly clear that Cesar had stolen the money belt and it had been his own duplicity and the weight of the gold that had drowned him.

Conrad was left to return to Marseille with all the makings of a truly marvellous novel. Many of the elements of the tale were used in one of his last books, *The Arrow of Gold*. Of course, this was scant consolation to a shipwrecked 20 year old, who now found himself very heavily in debt to his uncle. Ashamed of his misadventures, he returned to Marseille and dug himself deeper into trouble by borrowing a further 800 Francs and gambling it away in an attempt to recoup the loss. After a night at the card table, he returned to his hotel room at rock bottom; utterly alone, penniless, and hopeless. He couldn't bring himself to admit his errors to his uncle, as they all too closely resembled those of his father before him. His attempt on his own life was driven by despair. There is some speculation that the wound to his chest was actually inflicted during a duel over the mysterious Dona Rita, but if this is so, we will never know, for Conrad took the exact details to his grave. All we can fully establish is that Uncle Thaddeus was duly informed of his nephew's troubles and headed to Marseille to sort them out. In a later correspondence with a close friend, he wrote that Joseph had been injured in a suicide attempt and that they had opted to cover up the embarrassing truth by fabricating the story of a duel.

Conrad was to fully repent his Carlist adventures, and in a later recollection, he couched them in much less colourful words:

> All this gun-running was a very dull if dangerous business. As to intrigues, if there were any, I didn't know anything of them. But in truth, the Carlist invasion was a very straightforward adventure conducted with inconceivable stupidity and a foredoomed failure from the first. There was indeed nothing great there worthy of anybody's passionate devotion.

It was time for a change and the decision was taken that Joseph should pursue a career in the British Merchant Navy. This was partly because the French were very strict about the number of voyages non-French nationals could make aboard their ships. The British were less fussy and besides, Thaddeus had other pragmatic reasons for pushing this switch. In his lengthy letters with his wayward nephew, he patiently explains how important it is for Joseph to gain a new nationality, for as a Russian citizen, he was eligible for National Service. With life in the French Merchant Navy out of the question, Britain seemed like a good bet, although one which young Joseph doubtless approached with some trepidation, particularly given that he didn't speak much English. Nevertheless, in 1878 he turned his back on Marseille, and Thaddeus duly shelled out 400 Francs for a passage aboard a humble cargo steamer, the *Mavis*, which took him to London via Constantinople and the Black Sea. Once he had arrived in London, Joseph promptly wired his uncle asking for some more money and at this point, his long-suffering relative finally lost his patience, writing back as follows:

> *Ponder for a moment what you have perpetrated this last year and ask yourself whether you could have met with such patience and forbearance even from a father as you have with me, and whether some limit should not have been reached?*
>
> *You were idle for nearly a whole year, fell into debt, purposely shot yourself – at the worst time of year, tired out and with the most terrible rate of exchange – I hasten to you, spend 2,000 roubles – to cover your needs I increase your allowance. Was all this not enough for you? I agreed to your sailing in an English ship, but not to staying in England, travelling to London and wasting my money there! I can give you only one piece of advice – not a new one – 'arrange your budget within the limits of what I give you' for I shall give you no more! Make no debts for I will not pay them, DO SOMETHING and don't remain idle. Don't pretend to be the rich young gentleman and wait for someone to pull your chestnuts out of the fire – for that will not happen. If you cannot get a ship then be a clerk for a time. But do something, earn something. If you learn what poverty is, that will teach you the value of money. I have no money for drones and have no intention of working so that someone else can enjoy himself at my expense.*

You can almost feel Thaddeus tearing a hole in his writing paper as his pen scratches out his utter frustration with this feckless youngster. The letter touches quite heavily on work, a necessary evil, which Joseph was long to have an awkward relationship with, as he later distilled in his short story *Heart of Darkness*. 'I don't like work – no man does – but I like what is in the work – the chance to find yourself. Your own reality – for yourself not for others – what no other man can ever know. They can only see the mere show, and never can tell what it really means.'

For the first time Joseph had to fully face up to this. He truly needed to find himself for he must have felt truly abandoned; out on his own with no direction home. The desolation and loneliness of his situation must have been utterly crushing. Yet, just when things didn't look like they could get any worse, he headed to Suffolk. He had secured a berth as a seaman aboard the *Skimmer of the Sea*, a small barquentine plying coals between Newcastle and Lowestoft.

Sadly Conrad never put down in words the emotions he felt when he arrived in this humble town and signed on aboard the modest little ship. There is little doubt he would have felt like his fortunes had taken a tumble. In Marseille, he had friends, spoke the language and had clearly enjoyed the climate and cosmopolitan buzz of a thriving port. Lowestoft was far from cosmopolitan and, to make matters worse, Conrad found that the people of Suffolk spoke no known language or at least spoke in such an impenetrable dialect that he had no chance of understanding. In French ships he had been treated as an apprentice (this basically means a trainee officer, separate from the ordinary seamen). The *Skimmer of the Sea* would have observed no such niceties. She was as rough and ready as they came, a prime example of the British coasting trade, a business for tough men who navigated, not with sextant and chronometer, but by feel and memory – the sound of a dog barking onshore could ward them off in fog. They understood the coast intimately and could read wind shifts and changes in the weather almost by intuition. Yet, for a youngster aboard, the overriding theme was backbreaking work. An example of the kind of tough labour in which Conrad would have been employed was the process of loading and unloading. Steam winches were rarely used in vessels of this size, so the *Skimmer*'s cargo of coal would have been winched in and out by hand. Day after day of this 'dollying' as it was known was necessary. The old sailors called this kind of work 'Armstrong's Patent' and many suffered badly ruptured muscles from years of overdoing it.

Joseph worked aboard the old barquentine for a little under three months. During this time she made six passages between Newcastle and Lowestoft and no doubt provided an excellent learning experience for him. Even if he was already a reasonable sailor, all the nautical terms he had learned in France were now redundant and he would have had to start over. Yet he was clearly making progress and felt confident enough to sign off the *Skimmer* and head back to London in order to secure a more glamorous berth.

The year was 1878 and the docks of the city were still crowded with beautiful sailing ships. Some of the legendary clipper ships still survived and were thriving in the Australian wool run. This trade was the last stand of clipper ships before they were supplanted by the humdrum steamship. Every year a fleet of 20 or so of the fastest sailing ships in the world sailed out from London to the ports of Sydney and Melbourne and awaited the season's wool clip. Once loaded, they raced around Cape Horn to London in order to catch the March wool sales. Racing was intense and dominated by the legendary former tea clippers *Cutty Sark* and *Thermopylae*. An example of the kind of work done by these boats can be witnessed in 1889 when *Cutty Sark* caught up and overhauled the supposedly invincible mail steamer *Britannia* as she raced into the Bass Strait on her way to Sydney. Here was doomed romance and beauty aplenty!

Whether tales of the clippers seduced Conrad is not clear, although he certainly wrote in reverent tones about them in later years. Certainly he was always slightly scornful of steamships and their 'plodding' progress across the sea, as he described it. It is also clear that he sought out interesting and unusual vessels, which appealed to his romantic nature, and it was perhaps this that led him to a berth in a clipper ship.

Stumbling into a shipping agent's office, Joseph asked in broken English for a berth and, after an initial rebuttal, the agent relented and informed the young sailor that there was an apprentice's position available aboard the *Duke of Sutherland*, an Aberdeen-based vessel built of wood in 1865. Although she was described as a clipper, it appears that her powers were very much on the wane by the time Conrad stepped aboard. A couple of slow runs in the wool trade could damage the reputation of a ship, which would then generally find itself relegated to less glamorous – and less profitable – trades. As it was, the passage that Joseph took in 1879 was to be the *Duke of Sutherland*'s last as a wool clipper. She took 108 days to get out to Sydney, a rather stark contrast when compared with the 76 days set by the clipper

Pericles – the fastest passage of the year to Sydney and a full month quicker than the *Duke of Sutherland*'s voyage.

Although the old vessel was clearly struggling, Joseph was finding his feet and the young mariner was remembered many years later by one of his shipmates, Henry Horning:

> *Conrad occupied one of the top bunks and I the lower. He was a Pole of dark complexion and black hair. In his watches below he spent all of his time reading and writing English; he spoke with a foreign accent. I can well remember his favourite habit of sitting in his bunk with his legs dangling over the side and either a book or writing material in his lap. How he came to occupy a bunk in the half-deck instead of one in the topgallant forecastle is quite beyond me.*

This is an interesting insight not only into Joseph as a rather bookish seaman, but also into the snobbery of young Horning. The reference to Conrad occupying the half deck rather than the topgallant forecastle is telling. The half deck was where all of the privileged young gentlemen apprentices trained to become officers. The topgallant forecastle was where the poorer sailors were lodged. Generally professional sailors had fewer aspirations to become an officer and the insinuation is that Conrad, as a foreigner, had no place with the young gentlemen. This is ironic, as the Pole probably had an allowance to match even the most spoilt apprentice, yet he was clearly seen as an outsider, an anomaly. This theme would crop up throughout his life, and run through his later novels. What Horning also reveals is that Joseph was finally knuckling down. Thaddeus's endless nagging seemed to be paying off and, shortly after signing off from the *Duke of Sutherland* at the end of a long return voyage around Cape Horn to London, Joseph put himself in for his Board of Trade examination in order to obtain his second mate's certificate.

This exam was an ordeal at the best of times, as the Board of Trade attempted to put into words the very fluid and complicated practice of sailing a square-rigged ship in all sorts of challenging circumstances. To qualify, you needed four years of sailing experience 'before the mast'. Conrad had just enough time under his belt but the examiner clearly eyed this unusual candidate with scepticism. In fairness, his record of discharge from a motley selection of ships looked none too promising and he proceeded to give the aspiring officer the grilling of his life. Conrad later recalled the examination with eloquence:

It lasted for hours, for hours. Had I been a strange microbe with potentialities of deadly mischief to the Merchant Service I could not have been submitted to a more microscopic examination. Greatly reassured by his apparent benevolence, I had been at first very alert in my answers. But at length the feeling of my brain getting addled crept upon me. And still the passionless process went on, with a sense of untold ages having been spent already on mere preliminaries. Then I got frightened. I was not frightened of being plucked; that eventuality did not even present itself to my mind. It was something much more serious and weird. 'This ancient person,' I said to myself, terrified, 'is so near his grave that he must have lost all notion of time. He is considering this examination in terms of eternity. It is all very well for him. His race is run. But I may find myself coming out of this room into the world of men a stranger, friendless, forgotten by my very landlady, even were I able after this endless experience to remember the way to my hired home.' This statement is not so much of a verbal exaggeration as may be supposed. Some very queer thoughts passed through my head while I was considering my answers; thoughts which had nothing to do with seamanship, nor yet with anything reasonable known to this earth. I verily believe that at times I was light-headed in a sort of languid way. At last there fell a silence, and that, too, seemed to last for ages, while, bending over his desk, the examiner wrote out my pass-slip slowly with a noiseless pen. He extended the scrap of paper to me without a word, inclined his white head gravely to my parting bow. When I got out of the room I felt limply flat, like a squeezed lemon, and the doorkeeper in his glass cage, where I stopped to get my hat and tip him a shilling, said: 'Well! I thought you were never coming out.' 'How long have I been

in there?' I asked, faintly. He pulled out his watch. 'He kept you, sir,
just under three hours. I don't think this ever happened with any of the
gentlemen before.'

Second Officer Korzeniowski now had his qualification; what he lacked was
a ship, and this was not as easy to procure as might be expected. Fortune
was on his side, however, and he was able to gain a berth through the time-
honoured practice of the pierhead jump. It so happened that as Joseph was
prowling the London Docks in search of a job he got wind that the second
mate of the wool clipper *Loch Etive* had been seriously injured and would be
unable to sail. The ship was scheduled to depart and Conrad hurried along
the wharves to the Loch Etive to meet with her skipper, Captain Stuart. The
meeting was later used in one of his fictional works, *Chance*, as follows:

> *I suppose he had heard I was freshly passed and without experience as*
> *an officer, because he turned about and looked at me as if I had been*
> *exposed for sale. 'He's young' he muttered. 'Looks smart though.. You're*
> *smart and willing (this to me sudden and loud) and all that aren't you?'*
> *I had just managed to open and shut my mouth, no more, being*
> *taken unawares. But it was enough for him. He made as if I had*
> *deafened him, with protestations of my smartness and willingness.*

Captain Stuart promoted his third mate to second and made Conrad his
new third. This position is often given to senior apprentices trying to make
up the time to sit their second mate's examination. Both first and second
mates are in charge of the two separate watches of men and the third mate
simply fills in. If the position wasn't terribly prestigious, Conrad had
certainly struck gold with regard to the ship. The *Loch Etive* was one of a
number of extremely fast clippers owned by Aitken and Lilburn's Loch
Line, which specialised in the Australian trade. To serve in the Loch Line
was the rough sailing equivalent of the Cunard Line or P&O services today.
The *Loch Etive* was not quite as fast as some of their earlier clipper ships,
but she benefitted from being commanded by one of the finest captains

in the world at the time. Captain Stuart was a dour old Scotsman who had previously skippered the *Tweed*, a quirky vessel out of which he had coaxed some extraordinarily fast passages. He had made the *Tweed*'s name and she had made his. Conrad soon ascertained that his captain was in mourning for his old ship, and seemed to console himself by wringing the last ounce of speed out of his new one, as Conrad noted later:

> *It was hopeless for Captain Stuart to try to make his new iron clipper equal the feats which made the old* Tweed. *There was something pathetic in it, as in the endeavour of an artist in his old age to equal the masterpieces of his youth – for The* Tweed's *famous passages were Captain Stuart's masterpieces. It was pathetic, and perhaps just the least bit dangerous. At any rate, I am glad that I have seen some memorable carrying on to make a passage. And I have carried on myself upon the tall spars of that Clyde shipbuilder's masterpiece as I have never carried on in a ship before or since.*

It was during this voyage from London to Sydney and back that Conrad also got his first taste of real responsibility aboard ship, for the second mate was taken ill and Conrad was briefly put in charge of a watch of men. The experience sounds truly terrifying, for Captain Stuart clearly did not make life easy for his young officers, as this encounter between the two illustrates beautifully:

> *He was, I must say, a most uncomfortable commander to get your orders from at night. If I had the watch from eight till midnight, he would leave the deck about nine with the words, 'Don't take any sail off her.' Then, on the point of disappearing down the companion-way, he would add curtly: 'Don't carry anything away.'*

It was in this tough school that Conrad learned the art of being an officer and there can't have been many more exacting arenas than the wool trade in which to learn: after a run down the Atlantic, the hard work really started off the Cape of Good Hope. From here the clippers 'ran their easting down', blown before the wild winds of the Roaring Forties, which howl unrestricted around this empty part of the globe. Dipping far south in search of fresh westerlies, the rigging of a ship would be adorned with icicles, the deck a maelstrom of confused water and icy spume flying inboard with the force of buckshot, cutting to the skin and freezing to the bone. The seas were often immense and daunting and the vessels driven almost under by their commanders. It was here that the rigging of the ship, always thrumming, would start to emit a deep roaring moan and the whole vessel would tremble like a leaf. This description by Conrad of a gale in the southern ocean gives some insight into the suffering and terror and beauty:

> *For a true expression of dishevelled wildness there is nothing like a gale in the bright moonlight of a high latitude. The ship, brought-to and bowing to enormous flashing seas, glistened wet from deck to trucks; her one set sail stood out a coal-black shape upon the gloomy blueness of the air. I was a youngster then, and suffering from weariness, cold, and imperfect oilskins which let water in at every seam.*

Arrival in Sydney must have been a blessed relief and there was a brief pause as ship and crew girded their loins for the run back home around Cape Horn; once more, the vessel would enter the screaming wasteland of the Roaring Forties with only the lonely albatross and the howling westerly wind for company. It was here that Conrad was involved in the dramatic rescue of a small Danish brig, which was right on the verge of sinking when the *Loch Etive* reached her and launched her boats with unseemly haste, as Conrad recalls:

> *We made a race of it, and I would never have believed that a common boat's crew of a merchantman could keep up so much determined fierceness in the regular swing of their stroke. What our captain had clearly perceived before we left had become plain to all of us since. The issue of our enterprise hung on a hair above that abyss of waters which*

will not give up its dead till the Day of Judgment. It was a race of two ship's boats matched against Death for a prize of nine men's lives, and Death had a long start. We saw the crew of the brig from afar working at the pumps – still pumping on that wreck, which already had settled so far down that the gentle, low swell, over which our boats rose and fell easily without a check to their speed, welling up almost level with her head-rails, plucked at the ends of broken gear swinging desolately under her naked bowsprit.

Her bulwarks were gone fore and aft, and one saw her bare deck low-lying like a raft and swept clean of boats, spars, houses – of everything except the ringbolts and the heads of the pumps. I had one dismal glimpse of it as I braced myself up to receive upon my breast the last man to leave her, the captain, who literally let himself fall into my arms. It had been a weirdly silent rescue – a rescue without a hail, without a single uttered word, without a gesture or a sign, without a conscious exchange of glances. Up to the very last moment those on board stuck to their pumps, which spouted two clear streams of water upon their bare feet. Their brown skin showed through the rents of their shirts; and the two small bunches of half-naked, tattered men went on bowing from the waist to each other in their back-breaking labour, up and down, absorbed, with no time for a glance over the shoulder at the help that was coming to them.

It was a dramatic rescue and the culmination of a truly adventurous and educational trip. Conrad signed off in London and went in search of a new vessel. The choice of his next berth clearly illustrates that his thirst for adventure was far from quenched. She was the *Palestine*, an ancient ship under the command of the equally ancient and wonderfully named Captain Beard. Despite his advanced years, this was Captain Beard's first command and from the first this little man enchanted Conrad. He offered him the berth of second mate for the *Palestine*'s voyage round to North Shields to load coal. From there, she would make the long haul around the globe to Bangkok. This shabby little vessel was a million miles away from the smart *Loch Etive*, but her dilapidated air and epic voyage appealed to the romantic in Conrad and he eagerly signed on.

The passage did indeed prove to be a challenge and is narrated in Conrad's short story, 'Youth'. The bare facts of it are as follows: the *Palestine* (renamed '*Judea*' in 'Youth') headed from London around to North Shields and ran straight into a series of equinoctial gales. It took her a month to reach her destination, by which time she had lost the berth booked for her and had to wait some weeks to load. While in dock, she was hit by an out-of-control steamer and further delayed while repairs were carried out. Setting out to Bangkok in November, she struggled down channel against a succession of gales and after a month of being battered by the elements she was seriously leaking. Fortunately, progress had been so slow that Falmouth was a two-week sail away, so while the hands pumped for their lives, the *Palestine* limped back to port. Despite the hardship, Conrad was clearly enjoying the trip, as he recalled in 'Youth':

> As soon as we had crawled on deck I used to take a round turn with a rope about the men, the pumps, and the mainmast, and we turned, we turned incessantly, with the water to our waists, to our necks, over our heads. It was all one. We had forgotten how it felt to be dry.
>
> And there was somewhere in me the thought: By Jove! this is the deuce of an adventure – something you read about; and it is my first voyage as second mate – and I am only twenty – and here I am lasting it out as well as any of these men, and keeping my chaps up to the mark. I was pleased. I would not have given up the experience for worlds. I had moments of exultation.

On finally reaching Falmouth, carpenter and crew effected repairs, the ship sailed again and promptly started leaking anew. Once more she returned to Falmouth, where most of her cargo was unloaded and the shipwrights got to work on her. She was then reloaded but leaked worse than ever. By now the vessel was becoming something of a joke, as Conrad related:

They towed us back to the inner harbour, and we became a fixture, a feature, an institution of the place. People pointed us out to visitors as 'That 'ere bark that's going to Bankok – has been here six months – put back three times.' On holidays the small boys pulling about in boats would hail, 'Judea, ahoy!' and if a head showed above the rail shouted, 'Where you bound to? – Bankok?' and jeered.

In all, the vessel was six months in Falmouth but when they finally made good their escape there were no further dramas until they neared their destination. At this point ill-fortune descended again, when a wisp of smoke was detected rising from the main hatch; the *Palestine* was on fire. This was probably due to her cargo of coal getting damp through all the leaks and being loaded and unloaded for repairs.

Spontaneous combustion of a cargo was an ever-present danger back in those days of leaky wooden ships and the crew now set to work pumping water back in to the boat they had spent so long emptying, while the vessel proceeded on her course. She was tantalisingly close to her destination, but after several days of containing the blaze, the barque finally blew her decks off, sending many of the crew flying overboard. Fortunately the weather was calm and a steamer that was close at hand offered to tow them, as Java was within striking distance. The tow only succeeded in fanning the flames however, and the line was cut. The steamer offered to take the crew to safety, but Captain Beard declined, preferring to stick with his ship until the bitter end. The crew took to the ship's boats and awaited the death of their doomed vessel. It came thus:

Between the darkness of earth and heaven she was burning fiercely upon a disc of purple sea shot by the blood-red play of gleams; upon a disc of water glittering and sinister. A high, clear flame, an immense and lonely flame, ascended from the ocean, and from its summit the black smoke poured continuously at the sky. She burned furiously, mournful and imposing like a funeral pyre kindled in the night, surrounded by the sea, watched over by the stars. A magnificent death had come like a grace,

like a gift, like a reward to that old ship at the end of her laborious days.
The surrender of her weary ghost to the keeping of stars and sea was
stirring like the sight of a glorious triumph.

And that was the end of the *Palestine* debacle. It took Conrad and his crew
three hours or so to row to Java and he was able to observe for the first time
the East and all the mysteries it held. It was a significant moment, for these
waters were to provide the inspiration for many of his tales.

Yet he did not tarry for long here and returned to Britain in a more
prosaic manner as passenger on a steamer. His next vessel was the
Riversdale, a ship which sailed to Madras via Africa. At this point Conrad
signed off due to a dispute with the skipper. It appears that the captain was
a heavy drinker and was suffering from delirium tremens when he arrived
in Madras. He ordered Conrad to fetch a doctor, which he did, informing
him that the captain was suffering from an alcohol-related illness. This
unfortunately got back to his captain, who promptly dismissed his second
mate. This could have left Conrad in a bit of a fix; many sailors ended up
stuck 'on the beach' in eastern ports and Conrad obviously did not have a
reference from the *Riversdale*. Fortunately, he headed to Bombay and easily
secured a berth aboard the beautiful full-rigged ship, the *Narcissus*. Any
stain on his character regarding the *Riversdale* had been cleared once that
vessel had left Madras, for her skipper immediately wrecked her despite
the weather being perfectly calm and clement. An official inquiry found
that the ship was many miles off course, and gave a good insight into her
drunken captain by stating: 'Either he did not know where he was going,
in which case there was culpable recklessness; or, he did not know where
he was, in which case there was equally culpable negligence or ignorance.'
The skipper's certificate of competence was suspended for twelve months.
Conrad was clearly best off out of the *Riversdale* and returned to London
aboard the *Narcissus*, the elegant ship that was to provide the setting for
his later book, *The Nigger of the Narcissus*. On returning to London, he
had gained enough sea time to sit his examination for First Mate and was
once more tormented by the Board of Trade examiner who set him the most

impossible theoretical situations from which he had to rescue a wayward square-rigger. He later recalled:

> *The imaginary ship seemed to labour under a most comprehensive curse. It's no use enlarging on the never ending misfortunes; suffice it to say that, long before the end I would have welcomed with gratitude the opportunity to exchange into the* Flying Dutchman.

Despite these travails, he successfully attained his first mate's certificate and shipped aboard another big square-rigger, the *Tilkhurst*, which made a round trip to Singapore and back without incident. On being discharged, Conrad sat his master's certificate and also applied to become a British citizen. He was successful on both counts and at the age of 24 had achieved a great deal. For his uncle Thaddeus it was a very proud moment; a triumph of his own sensible, pragmatic nature over the natural instinct of the Korzeniowskis to go off the rails. He wrote effusively to his nephew praising him for his achievements. It was a far cry from the angry missive he had sent on Conrad's first arrival in London.

Although Conrad was now technically a captain, it was common to spend several years as first mate before stepping up to command, and this is exactly what he did, signing on aboard the *Highland Forest*, another big windjammer. He joined the vessel in Amsterdam during an epic cold snap. The weather was so cold that the cargo was frozen upriver and, as a result, the crew were all discharged. To add to the loneliness, the captain was also absent and would not join the vessel until just prior to departure. Conrad later recalled the chilly desolation of this frustrating time beautifully:

> *Notwithstanding the little iron stove, the ink froze on the swing-table in my cabin, and I found it more convenient to go ashore stumbling over the arctic waste-land and shivering in glazed tramcars in order to write my evening letter to my owners in a gorgeous café in the centre of the town. It was an immense place, lofty and gilt, upholstered in red plush, full of electric lights and so thoroughly warmed that even the marble tables felt*

tepid to the touch. The waiter who brought me my cup of coffee bore, by comparison with my utter isolation, the dear aspect of an intimate friend. There, alone in a noisy crowd, I would write slowly a letter addressed to Glasgow, of which the gist would be: There is no cargo, and no prospect of any coming till late spring apparently. And all the time I sat there the necessity of getting back to the ship bore heavily on my already half-congealed spirits – the shivering in glazed tramcars, the stumbling over the snow-sprinkled waste ground, the vision of ships frozen in a row, appearing vaguely like corpses of black vessels in a white world, so silent, so lifeless, so soulless they seemed to be.

Eventually the cargo did arrive and, in the absence of the captain, Conrad was responsible for loading the ship. This was not as easy as one might think, for sailing ships were tricky vessels and no two were the same. Load some down by the stern and they would be sluggish in light weather but fly before a storm. Down by the bow might lead to the opposite being true, but not always. Load a vessel with the cargo too high up and she might become unstable or 'crank', load her too low and she would be too 'stiff' and not roll naturally. It was vital to load a ship to suit her personal requirements. Conrad did not know the *Highland Forest*, and had to do the best he could. Sadly, it was not good enough, as he discovered on Captain McWhirr's arrival:

Without further preliminaries than a friendly nod, McWhirr addressed me: 'You have got her pretty well in her fore and aft trim. Now, what about your weights?' I told him I had managed to keep the weight sufficiently well up, as I thought, one-third of the whole being in the upper part 'above the beams,' as the technical expression has it. He whistled 'Phew!' scrutinizing me from head to foot. A sort of smiling vexation was visible on his ruddy face. 'Well, we shall have a lively time of it this passage, I bet,' he said.

Neither before nor since have I felt a ship roll so abruptly, so violently, so heavily. Once she began, you felt that she would never stop, and this hopeless sensation, characterizing the motion of ships whose centre of gravity is brought down too low in loading, made everyone on board weary of keeping on his feet. The captain used to remark frequently: 'Ah, yes; I dare say one-third weight above beams would have been quite enough for most ships. But then, you see, there's no two of them alike on the seas, and she's an uncommonly ticklish jade to load'.

It is perhaps understandable that after many months of this interminable rolling and jerking the *Highland Forest* lost one of her lighter spars from aloft, and it is poetic justice that the offending spar should strike the man responsible on the back. Conrad was seriously injured by the blow and was laid up for many months in a hospital in Singapore. When he finally got back on his feet he made another unusual move; signing up as first mate aboard a small coasting steamer, the *Vidar*, which plied her trade along the numerous colonial outposts of the China Seas. This was quite a leap from treading the deck of a big square-rigger, and would demand an entirely different skill set, for the little steamer threaded her way through some of the most treacherous waters in the East. Conrad came to understand them intimately and described them perfectly:

'The China seas north and south are narrow seas. They are seas full of every-day, eloquent facts, such as islands, sand-banks, reefs, swift and changeable currents – tangled facts that nevertheless speak to a seaman in clear and definite language.'

Once again, he was on a steep learning curve but was proving to be an adaptable sailor. He was five months aboard the *Vidar*, exploring the steamy, sweltering coast and observing closely some of the strange, broken down characters who occupied these outposts of colonialism; drinkers, despots over tiny kingdoms, madmen, they were all here, including one Dutch trader called Olmeijer, who was to become the central character in his first novel, *Almayer's Folly*. After five months of happily tramping this interesting coast he signed off rather abruptly:

Suddenly I left all this. I left it in that, to us, inconsequential manner in which a bird flies away from a comfortable branch. It was as though all unknowing I had heard a whisper or seen something. Well – perhaps! One day I was perfectly right and the next everything was gone – glamour, flavour, interest, contentment – everything. It was one of these moments, you know. The green sickness of late youth descended on me and carried me off. Carried me off that ship, I mean.

You would swear that he was doing little more than research for future novels, yet Conrad claims it never even occurred to him to take up writing at this point in his life. Besides which, one of his most momentous adventures was just around the corner, for a strange twist of fate was about to land the young officer his first command: the *Otago*.

The circumstances of his gaining this command were, on the face of it, extremely fortunate. While awaiting a passage home from the East, he lodged at a sailors' home in Singapore. While he was loafing there he was invited to take command of a small barque, which was stuck in nearby Bangkok following the death of her previous skipper. Conrad eagerly accepted the offer of command, headed to Bangkok and this is where the trouble started. He narrates the early days of his command in *The Shadow-Line* a short story in which he confesses to a degree of trepidation: 'A strange sense of exultation began to creep into me. If I had worked for that command ten years or more there would have been nothing of the kind. I was a little frightened.'

Little wonder either; at 29 Conrad was unusually young to gain command of a ship, and his rather erratic and itinerant lifestyle meant that he had served far fewer hours as an officer than many of a similar age with the same qualifications. Nevertheless, the first sight of the trim little *Otago* as he arrived in Bangkok by steamer seems to have dismissed his fears and doubts:

I leaned over the rail of the bridge looking over the side. I dared not raise my eyes. Yet it had to be done – and, indeed, I could not have helped myself. I believe I trembled. But directly my eyes had rested on my ship all my fear vanished. It went off swiftly, like a bad dream. Only that a dream leaves no shame behind it, and that I felt a momentary shame at my unworthy suspicions. Yes, there she was. Her hull, her rigging filled my eye with a great content. That feeling of life-emptiness which had made me so restless for the last few months lost its bitter plausibility, its evil influence, dissolved in a flow of joyous emotion. At first glance I saw that she was a high-class vessel, a harmonious creature in the lines of her fine body, in the proportioned tallness of her spars. Whatever her age and her history, she had preserved the stamp of her origin. She was one of those craft that, in virtue of their design and complete finish, will never look old. Amongst her companions moored to the bank, and all bigger than herself, she looked like a creature of high breed – an Arab steed in a string of cart-horses.

She was indeed a sweet little vessel; built of iron in Glasgow in 1869. She was 147ft long, which was a handy size for a first command, and evidently pleasing to the eye. That, however, was about as far as Conrad's good fortune went, for the ship was languishing in Bangkok in unusual circumstances. It appears that after the death of her previous captain, a Mr Snadden, the mate, Mr Born, had taken her to Bangkok rather than the more cosmopolitan Singapore. His reason for this was that he realised he had a far greater chance of gaining command of the vessel if she was stuck in some backwater rather than busy Singapore. This led to immediate friction between Conrad and Born. What is more, the mate seemed utterly spooked by the death of Captain Snadden, who is described in *The Shadow-Line*:

He used to keep the ship loafing at sea for inscrutable reasons. Would come on deck at night sometimes, take some sail off her, God only knows why or wherefore, then go below, shut himself up in his cabin, and play on the violin for hours – till daybreak perhaps. In fact, he spent most of his time day or night playing the violin. That was when the fit took him. Very loud, too.

According to Born, his former skipper had thrown the offending instrument overboard on the night he died. Whether this tale is merely a bit of poetic licence from Conrad we will never know. What there is no doubt about is that Snadden had left a pretty tangle behind him for the new skipper to unthread. The ship's accounts were in a terrible mess, and her crew was ailing with disease after too long spent in the unhealthy air of Bangkok. Yet work must go on, and after loading a cargo of teak logs – rather picturesquely aided by local elephants, the *Otago* was ready for sea with orders to head to Sydney. The first part of this trip was tortuous, with fickle breezes fanning vessels through a maze of reefs towards the Sunda Strait, which divides Java and Sumatra and is the gateway to the Indian Ocean and freedom. Things did not go well from the start; *Otago* was towed out of Bangkok and ghosted along before a few catspaws (a gentle puff of breeze that soon dies away again) and shortly afterwards the wind died completely. Then she lay for days motionless and sweltering in the heat. To make matters worse, it was soon evident that many of the crew were seriously ill with cholera, dysentery and fever. As the vessel drifted, the men grew increasingly sick. The relationship between Conrad and his first mate was also distilling into one of mutual dislike. This was not helped by the fact that Mr Born was ailing with fever, and his terror that the ship was under the curse of the departed Captain Snadden seemed reinforced by the deathly calm. Conrad describes their relationship:

> *To begin with, he was more than five years older than myself at a time of life when five years really do count, I being twenty-nine and he thirty-four; then, on our first leaving port (I don't see why I should make a secret of the fact that it was Bangkok), a bit of manoeuvring of mine amongst the islands of the Gulf of Siam had given him an unforgettable scare. Ever since then he had nursed in secret a bitter idea of my utter recklessness.*

The scare he refers to occurred when Conrad opted to stand in toward some islands off Bangkok in order to get the benefit of the evening land breeze. No breeze materialised and the *Otago* was left drifting helpless and too close to land for comfort. By now it was clear the crew was too sick to continue, and Conrad discovered that Captain Snadden had sold off the ship's supply of Quinine and substituted it with an unknown white powder. This was the final straw and a course was set for Singapore. It took her 21 days to stagger there and she finally arrived flying a flag of distress. Conrad's first voyage as captain was over and it had clearly been a thoroughly testing experience. In Singapore a new crew was shipped and from hereon things generally went without a hitch, the *Otago* arriving in Sydney in May of 1888.

Interestingly, the services of the fractious mate, Born, were retained and Conrad grew to value his strengths. This picturesque description gives a good insight into the manner in which business was conducted aboard the *Otago:*

He was worth all his salt. On examining now, after many years, the residue of the feeling which was the outcome of the contact of our personalities, I discover, without much surprise, a certain flavour of dislike. Upon the whole, I think he was one of the most uncomfortable shipmates possible for a young commander. If it is permissible to criticise the absent, I should say he had a little too much of the sense of insecurity which is so invaluable in a seaman. He had an extremely disturbing air of being everlastingly ready (even when seated at table at my right hand before a plate of salt beef) to grapple with some impending calamity. I must hasten to add that he had also the other qualification necessary to make a trustworthy seaman – that of an absolute confidence in himself. What was really wrong with him was that he had these qualities in an unrestful degree. His eternally watchful demeanour, his jerky, nervous talk, even his, as it were, determined silences, seemed to imply – and, I believe, they did imply – that to his mind the ship was never safe in my hands. Such was the man who looked after the anchors of a less than five-hundred-ton barque, my first command, now gone from the face of the earth, but sure of a tenderly remembered existence as long as I live. No anchor could have gone down foul under Mr. Born's piercing eye. It was good for one to be sure of that when, in an open roadstead, one heard in the cabin the wind pipe up; but still, there were moments when I detested Mr. Born exceedingly. From the way he used to glare sometimes, I fancy that more than once he paid me back with interest. It so happened that we both loved the little barque

very much. And it was just the defect of Mr. Born's inestimable qualities
that he would never persuade himself to believe that the ship was safe in
my hands. But upon the whole, and unless the grip of a man's hand at
parting means nothing whatever, I conclude that we did like each other at
the end of two years and three months well enough.

Despite this rather strained relationship, both captain and mate were able to settle into the *Otago* after the dramatic start and evidently enjoyed the experience. The clipper was next despatched to Mauritius. This exotic little outpost of the French empire was a beautiful stopover and Conrad welcomed the chance to mix with the local society and practise his French. He even had time to fall in love with one Eugenie Renouf and seems to have proposed to her a couple of days before the *Otago* was scheduled to sail. To his horror he discovered she was already betrothed and he departed Mauritius somewhat melodramatically proclaiming that he would never again set foot on the island. This proclamation was to return to haunt him a year later, when, following passages to Madagascar and Melbourne, the *Otago*'s owners secured another charter to Mauritius. Conrad begged them to explore new avenues of trade in the East, but the charter was secured and that was that. As a result, Conrad resigned his command in 1889. Within a couple of months he was back in London, having returned by passenger steamer. He was understandably ready for a break and, only a few days after settling in to lodgings in London, he determined to start writing a book, which was eventually shaped into his first novel, *Almayer's Folly*.

He may have started the ball rolling on his literary career, but this was 1889 and *Almayer's Folly* wasn't published until 1895. For now his future was still very closely tied up with ships and the sea. Conrad had already reached the peak of his seafaring career and was casting around for the next great adventure. He settled upon Africa and the roots of his decision are clear from his short novel, *Heart of Darkness*:

I had then, as you remember, just returned to London after a lot of Indian
Ocean, Pacific, China Seas – a regular dose of the East – six years or so,

and I was loafing about, hindering you fellows in your work and invading your homes, just as though I had got a heavenly mission to civilize you. It was very fine for a time, but after a bit I did get tired of resting. Then I began to look for a ship – I should think the hardest work on earth. But the ships wouldn't even look at me. And I got tired of that game too.

Now when I was a little chap I had a passion for maps. I would look for hours at South America, or Africa, or Australia, and lose myself in all the glories of exploration. At that time there were many blank spaces on the earth, and when I saw one that looked particularly inviting on a map (but they all look that) I would put my finger on it and say, 'When I grow up I will go there.' The North Pole was one of these places, I remember. Well, I haven't been there yet, and shall not try now. The glamour's off. Other places were scattered about the Equator, and in every sort of latitude all over the two hemispheres. I have been in some of them, and ... well, we won't talk about that. But there was one yet – the biggest, the most blank, so to speak – that I had a hankering after.

True, by this time it was not a blank space any more. It had got filled since my boyhood with rivers and lakes and names. It had ceased to be a blank space of delightful mystery – a white patch for a boy to dream gloriously over. It had become a place of darkness. But there was in it one river especially, a mighty big river, that you could see on the map, resembling an immense snake uncoiled, with its head in the sea, its body at rest curving afar over a vast country, and its tail lost in the depths of the land. And as I looked at the map of it in a shop-window, it fascinated me as a snake would a bird – a silly little bird. Then I remembered there was a big concern, a Company for trade on that river. Dash it all! I thought to myself, they can't trade without using some kind of craft on that lot of fresh water – steamboats! Why shouldn't I try to get charge of one? I went on along Fleet Street, but could not shake off the idea. The snake had charmed me.

It was with such a careless rationale that Conrad approached the *Societe Anonyme pour le commerce du Haut Congo* about the possibility of working for them as skipper. They accepted and Conrad signed a contract committing himself to work on a steamer plying the trading outposts of the upper Congo. The Congo River is divided into three navigable sections that are divided by a series of rapids and waterfalls. To reach his command, Conrad would be obliged to undertake a long overland trek to Kinshasa where he would join the steamer. Much of this disastrous trip is narrated in *Heart of Darkness* which, according to Conrad, strays 'a little, only a very little' from the actual facts. King Leopold II of Belgium, keen to attain a colony for his country, had established the Congo Free State in 1884. What happened next was the transformation of the Congo into a place of unspeakable cruelty. An example of the horrors inflicted is that rubber plantation workers who did not reach their quota of rubber had their hands amputated as punishment. Some of the worst crimes ever committed were taking place here and it was into this maelstrom of intolerable degradation and disease that Conrad ventured in. Like the rest of the world, he would have been utterly unaware of the state of things beforehand, and what he saw on his travels was seared indelibly onto his conscious.

The first rumblings of misgiving came on the trip down the coast of Africa to the Congo. He wrote with concern to a friend about receiving the disquieting news that 'sixty per cent of the company's employees return to Europe before they have completed even six months service. Fever and dysentery!' He saw other things that filled him with foreboding, as described in *Heart of Darkness*:

> *Once, I remember, we came upon a man-of-war anchored off the coast. There wasn't even a shed there, and she was shelling the bush. It appears the French had one of their wars going on thereabouts. Her ensign dropped limp like a rag; the muzzles of the long eight-inch guns stuck out all over the low hull; the greasy, slimy swell swung her up lazily and let her down, swaying her thin masts. In the empty immensity of earth, sky, and water, there she was, incomprehensible, firing into a continent.*

Conrad made his way up the Congo River to Matadi and then had to make the overland trip to Kinshasa. This was a painful trek and Conrad did well to arrive there with his health intact. He was disgusted with most of the white people he met on the way, who for the most part were unsavoury desperadoes looking to make a quick fortune exploiting the local populace. Conrad noted in his diary that he would 'try to avoid making acquaintances as much as possible'. During his trek upriver, Conrad relates seeing an endless succession of dead and mutilated bodies along the trail. In Kinshasa, his spirits took a further tumble, as he discovered that his command, the *Florida* was badly damaged and would not be back in commission for several months. In the meantime he was assigned to provide back-up to the skipper of the steamer *Roi de Belges*, which was soon to be despatched upriver to the Stanley Falls. One of the purposes of this trip was to pick up one of the company's agents, Klein, who was seriously ill. During the course of this trip also, Conrad was forced to take command of the *Roi de Belges*, as her skipper was taken ill. This would have been a new challenge to Conrad, for handling a river steamer in restricted waters, often extremely fast flowing, is very different from being in charge of a ship in the open sea. It required an almost completely new skill set and the fact that the trip was accident-free is much to Conrad's credit. Despite the rapid and untroubled trip, Klein died before the steamer returned to Kinshasa, and with his burial the bare bones of *Heart of Darkness* were laid out. If other authors, most notably Robert Louis Stevenson, had hinted that perhaps the imperialism of the 'civilised' world was not always beneficial, Conrad's book was set to blow the lid completely off that myth. *Heart of Darkness* was to document the true rapaciousness, greed and horror of imperialism gone wrong with the unflinching eye of a man who had headed into Africa full of optimism and returned from the interior repulsed.

On returning to Kinshasa, Conrad saw quite clearly that there was no hope of a permanent command, and fell out with some of the company directors. To make matters worse, he had finally succumbed to the malaria and typhoid that were decimating the populace and he had little choice but to return home or die. He relates the trip down the Congo thus:

I got round the turn between Kinshasa and Leopoldville more or less alive, although I was too sick to care whether I did or did not. I arrived

at the delectable capital of Boma, where before the departure of the
steamer which was to take me home I had the time to wish myself dead
over and over again with perfect sincerity.

The following passage in *Heart of Darkness* puts things even more bluntly:

I have wrestled with death. It is the most unexciting contest you can
imagine. It takes place in an impalpable greyness, with nothing
underfoot, with nothing around, without spectators, without clamour,
without glory, without the great desire of victory, without the great fear
of defeat, in a sickly atmosphere of tepid scepticism, without much belief
in your own right, and still less in that of your adversary.

When he finally made it back to London, it was clear that the experience
had nearly destroyed him, and it was to be a return to his old friend and
adversary, the sea, that restored him. It took him eight months to convalesce
from his various ailments, but when he did he found that fortune had not
completely turned her back on him after all. Captain Cope of the famous
passenger clipper *Torrens* offered him the position of first mate. Initially
Conrad expressed reservations about his health, but Cope admonished
him by saying it was 'no good moping around ashore'. It proved to be just
the tonic he required. The *Torrens* was a very beautiful ship, which took
passengers on the round trip from London to Adelaide. Unlike the wool
clippers that Conrad had earlier served aboard, she was able to sail back to
England by the slightly easier Cape of Good Hope route. This was to make
life more comfortable for her passengers but also made things much more
pleasant for the crew. The *Torrens* had established an excellent reputation for
herself and, loaded down with passengers rather than cargo, she was a very
comfortable and civilised ship. Basil Lubbock, unquestionably the foremost
historian of clipper ships described her thus:

She was without doubt one of the most successful ships ever built, besides
being one of the fastest, and for many years she was the favourite

passenger ship to Adelaide. A beautifully modelled ship and a splendid sea boat, she was very heavily sparred. In easting weather she would drive along as dry as a bone, making 300 miles a day without wetting her decks. But it was in light winds that she showed up best, her ghosting powers being quite extraordinary. The flap of her sails sent her along two or three knots, and in light airs she was accustomed to pass other clippers as if they were at anchor.

Conrad served as mate for the duration of two round the world voyages aboard this thoroughbred and she seemed to go a long way to replenishing his diminished stocks of energy and wellbeing. There is a fascinating insight into the mate of the *Torrens* given by the writer John Galsworthy, who travelled aboard as a passenger in 1893:

He was superintending the stowage of cargo when I first met him. Very dark he looked in the burning sunlight. Tanned with a peaked brown beard, almost black hair and dark brown eyes over which the lids were deeply folded. He was thin, not tall his arms very long, his shoulders broad. He spoke to me with a strong foreign accent. He seemed to me strange on an English ship.

The chief mate bears the main burden of sailing a ship. All the first night he was fighting a fire in the hold. None of us seventeen passengers knew of it until long after. It was he who had most truck with that tail of a hurricane off Cape Leeuwin and later with another storm. He was a good seaman, watchful of the weather, quick in handling the ship – considerate with the apprentices – we had one unhappy Belgian among them, who took unhandily to the sea and dreaded going aloft and Conrad compassionately spared him all he could. With the crew he was popular; they were individuals to him, not a mere gang. He was respectful if faintly ironic with his whiskered stout old English Captain, for Conrad had commanded ships and his subordinate position was only due to the fact that he was still convalescent from the Congo experience which nearly killed him. Many evenings were spent on the poop, even then a great teller of a tale. He had already nearly twenty years of tales to tell. Tales of ships and storms of Polish revolution, of his youthful Carlist gun running adventure of the Malay seas and the Congo; and of men and men.

This is a fine portrait of the final evolution of Conrad the sailor; affable yet a consummate professional and clearly at the top of his game. In 1891 he signed on for his last voyage aboard the *Torrens* and, although he had no idea at the time, it would be his final voyage as a professional seaman. He was only 36, yet had packed more adventure into those years afloat than most manage in a lifetime. He married a young lady named Jessie George three years later and the dream of the sea seemed to slowly fade as his writing career picked up. Still, his retirement from the sea was always somewhat half-hearted and his pining for it often screams out in his writing. His love of the sea was far from blind however: 'There is nothing more enticing, disenchanting, and enslaving than the life at sea,' he once observed. This is a man speaking of his work, but what a seductive workplace it was for him and what adventures it meted out to him along the way! For all that the sea was his career, he clearly longed for it in his later years and sums up the sense of loss he felt beautifully in *Chance*, the book which, in 1913, fully launched him as a literary titan. He describes Marlow thus:

Marlow had retired from the sea in a sort of half hearted fashion some years. From year to year he dwelt on land as a bird rests on the branch of a tree, so tense with the power of brusque flight into its true element that it is incomprehensible why it should sit still minute after minute. The sea is the sailor's true element and Marlow, lingering on shore, was to me an object of incredulous commiseration like a bird which, secretly should have lost its faith in the virtue of high flying.

A sad epitaph to his seagoing life, yet his loss was our gain, for by turning to his pen he felt he became one of the last chroniclers of commercial sail's pinnacle of elegance. His writings helped to record and bring alive a way of life that existed for centuries and was snuffed out in a matter of decades. His eloquence has helped at least keep the memory of these brave seafaring days alive, and make future generations aware of the great beauty we have lost in the pursuit of efficiency and utility. As he summed it up himself:

> *History repeats itself, but the special call of an art which has passed away is never reproduced. It is as utterly gone out of the world as the song of a destroyed wild bird. A modern ship does not so much make use of the sea as exploit a highway with a thudding rhythm in her progress and the regular beat of her propeller, heard afar in the night with an august and plodding sound as of the march of an inevitable future. But in a gale, the silent machinery of a sailing-ship would catch not only the power, but the wild and exulting voice of the world's soul.*

James Fenimore Cooper
The first of the nautical novelists

The seafaring novel is now such a well-established genre that it seems entirely natural that an author should create an entire story with ships, sailors and the sea as the focal point. The same could certainly not be said back in 1823 when James Fenimore Cooper sat down to write what is now recognised as the first true nautical novel. Some previous authors – most notably Tobias Smollett – may have devoted sections of a novel to the sea, but it was Cooper who saw the real potential of dedicating an entire book to the subject. The result was *The Pilot,* a book which proved to be an immediate success, both in Cooper's homeland, America, and abroad.

You could call Cooper a visionary for making the leap of imagination required to dream up a novel of the sea. Certainly *The Pilot*'s concept was outlandish and the author noted at the time that he was met with opinions from friends and advisors that were 'anything but encouraging', but he pressed on. So what made him persist? The answer is less to do with vision and more to do with stubbornness and a desire to show the world's most successful novelist how it was done.

It all came about when Cooper – now best remembered for his classic *The Last of the Mohicans* – was already rapidly establishing himself as a pioneer of the fledgling American literary scene, found himself in conversation with a friend over the merits of Sir Walter Scott's bestselling novel, *The Pirate*. These days, Scott's novels have recently fallen out of favour, but in the nineteenth century, his works were considered almost beyond reproach. While his friend was impressed with the accuracy with which Scott represented the sea, Cooper was not. The upshot was to have a profound effect on nautical literature, as Cooper noted:

> *The result of this conversation was a sudden determination to produce a work which, if it had no other merit, might present truer pictures of the ocean and ships than any that are to be found in* The Pirate. *To this unpremeditated decision, purely an impulse, is not only* The Pilot *due, but a tolerably numerous school of nautical romances that have succeeded it.*

So it was nothing more than a quirk of fate and a bit of bloodymindedness that brought about the birth of a new genre. Yet if the starting point was a strange one, the results were impressive. Right from the start, the author showed that he was able to portray the sea in a manner beyond the ability of a landsman such as Scott. In his hands the sea came alive. Witness this early passage from the book:

> *The short day of that high northern latitude was already drawing to a close, and the sun was throwing his parting rays obliquely across the waters, touching the gloomy waves here and there with streaks of pale light. The stormy winds of the ocean were apparently lulled to rest; and, though the incessant rolling of the surge on the shore heightened the gloomy character of the hour and the view, the light ripple that ruffled the sleeping billows was produced by a gentle air, that blew directly from the land. Notwithstanding this favorable circumstance, there was something threatening in the aspect of the ocean, which was speaking in hollow but deep murmurs, like a volcano on the eve of an eruption.*

It was clear that here was a man with a great deal of love, empathy and understanding of the sea, and there was good reason. Not only had Cooper served as an able seaman aboard a merchant ship, he had also been a midshipman in the US Navy. Furthermore at the time he was writing *The Pilot,* he was also the owner of a small whaling ship, the *Union,* a contemporary vessel of Herman Melville's *Acushnet.* Here was a man who had an intimate knowledge of ships and the sea and was able to translate that understanding, both technical and emotional, onto the written page. He did just that with great success and went on to write a number of classics of the sea including *The Red Rover, Afloat and Ashore, The Skimmer of the Sea* and *The Sea Lions.* In the process, he was also responsible for coining the term 'salty sea dog' now firmly embedded in the English language and conjuring up the kind of hearty old tar that Cooper so enjoyed portraying in his books.

Yet, if his seafaring credentials were impeccable by the time he sat down to write *The Pilot* in 1823, the signs certainly hadn't looked very promising during his early childhood. He was born in 1789 in Burlington, New Jersey. He was not there long, for his father had been fortunate enough to inherit great swathes of land in the wake of the American War of Independence. Cooper Sr set about colonising some of his land, and determined to establish his very own settlement on the shores of Lake Otsego in New York State. This was Cooperstown, which is now best known to sports fans as the location of the National Baseball Hall of Fame. Cooper's father built a sizeable mansion where the extended family was able to enjoy the rewards of their colonising work. They may have been pioneers, but they were very successful ones, and comfort and privilege were never far away as their children grew up. None of this steered young James towards the sea to any great extent. Certainly he grew to love and appreciate the great outdoors, and in particular Lake Otsego, but it is doubtful he even saw the great open expanse of the Atlantic until he was in his teens.

Perhaps the turning point came when he blew up his schoolmate's door. Cooper was attending Yale at the time and must have seriously fallen out with one of his classmates. The upshot was grave, for Cooper opted to surreptitiously shove a cloth funnel through the keyhole of his rival's door and pour home-made gunpowder into it. Once full, he twisted the funnel tight and set it alight. The results were immediate and alarming, not only terrifying his classmate, but also causing considerable damage to the door. Combine this with other hellraising incidents, most notably locking a donkey into the recitation room of the school, and you will perhaps not be too surprised to learn that young Cooper was expelled. Our future author was gaining a reputation as a troublemaker and, back then, the natural course for such tearaways was to run away to sea. After several months spent languishing at home considering his options, this is exactly what Cooper decided to do. He was 16 and had no clear idea of what he wanted from life. There is no question that he was an adventurous soul and if there was one thing life at sea almost guaranteed, it was untold adventure as well as a chance to travel, visit foreign shores and observe different cultures. It was not long before young Cooper was scouring the wharves of Philadelphia in search of a vessel. Weeks of fruitless enquiries ensued and it wasn't until he switched his search to New York that his luck changed, for he managed to secure a berth aboard the *Sterling*, a smart ship-rigged boat, which had been built the previous year in Maine. It is possible that it was a family connection that enabled him to secure the berth. If this is so, then clearly any parental objections to his going to sea had evaporated. Certainly, there is no mention in any of Cooper's recollections of conflict between his family and himself, so it seems likely that they rapidly reconciled themselves to his career move.

The ship was loading flour in New York and was bound for England. From here, her captain, a Mr Johnston, would have to scout around for the next cargo and see what he could get. Cooper signed on as an ordinary seaman. Aside from the ship's boy, this was the lowest rank aboard, one rung below the able seamen, who were more experienced sailors and received slightly better pay. As such, life would have been tough aboard. Cooper would have messed with the rest of the ordinary and able seamen in the fo'c'sle, exposed to all the crudities and heartbreaking privations that were a sailor's lot in 1806. No doubt this would have come as a shock to the genteel Yale boy, but he seems to have taken it all in his stride. The ship appears to have been friendly and well run, being family-owned by Captain Johnston, his father and his brother. Over the next few decades the American merchant marine was to gain a reputation for extremely tough and unsympathetic officers, but in 1806 this was not the case at all and Cooper, along with the other 16 members of the crew, could look forward to a relatively comfortable passage.

I have read biographies of James Fenimore Cooper that have managed to cover his seagoing exploits in roughly two paragraphs. This is surprising because, while it is true that his seagoing life was not chock full of adventure, there is certainly enough incident on his passages in the *Stirling* to fill a decent-sized book. We are fortunate when looking into the details of the voyage that they were actually written about in full by one Ned Myers, a shipmate and friend of Cooper's aboard the *Stirling*. This account was part of an autobiography published, with the help of Cooper, many years later in 1843. As such it gives a very good idea of the mixture of excitement and misery a sailor could look forward to when undertaking a passage in the early 1800s. It is also a remarkable insight into the maiden voyage of one of America's most celebrated early authors. Although the book is based on Myers' reminisces there is no question the pair pooled their memories to create the chapter on the *Stirling*.

Things did not start out altogether well for either Cooper or Myers, for shortly after departing, they were sent aloft, with comical results, as Myers explained:

That afternoon we lifted our anchor, and dropped down abreast of Governor's Island, where we brought up. Next day all hands were called to get under way, and, as soon as the anchor was short, the mate told Cooper and myself to go up and loose the fore-top-sail. I went on one yard-arm and Cooper went on the other. In a few minutes the second mate came up, hallooing to us to 'avast,' and laughing. Cooper was hard at work at the 'robins,' and would soon have had his half of the sail down in the top, had he been let alone; while I was taking the gaskets from the yard, with the intention of bringing them carefully down on deck, where it struck me they would be quite safe. Luckily for us, the men were too busy heaving, and too stupid, to be very critical, and we escaped much ridicule. In a week we both knew better.

This act of attempting to untie the sails from the yards shows just how green the novice sailors were. The incident also illustrates the tolerant nature of the officers, and both boys appear to have enjoyed the trip across. Certainly there is precious little grousing in Myers' journal and the entire Atlantic crossing is summed up in a couple of sentences:

> *Our passage was long and stormy. The ship was on a bow-line [beating in to the wind] most of the time, and we were something like forty days from land to land. Nothing extraordinary occurred, however, and we finally made the Bill of Portland. The weather came on thick, but we found a pilot, and ran into St. Helen's Roads and anchored. The captain got into his boat, and taking four men pulled ashore, to look for his orders at Cowes.*

The ship had sailed in the notoriously stormy month of October and it is little surprise that they received a bit of a dusting down. In terms of passage length, forty days was fairly normal for that time, although it was certainly nothing to write home about and other vessels more favoured by the wind could do it in half that time even back then. Nevertheless, it was a passage without any death or suffering en route and, in 1806, that was a real bonus. Cooper also found himself for the first time within sight of a foreign shore and the *Stirling*'s arrival off the English coast must have sent a thrill down the spine of a youngster hungry for exploits on foreign shores. If he was excited, he was soon to witness drama here that would instil within him a profound lack of trust in the English: a theme that ran through many of his novels.

As the *Stirling* lay off Cowes awaiting orders, Cooper gazed across at the verdant slopes and low cliffs of the Isle of Wight. He knew he was looking at the land of his forefathers. Yet by 1806, the average American's attitude towards the English was complex. America had declared independence in 1776 and only truly won it in the 1780s. This new nation was looked upon with great condescension by the English as troublesome upstarts who had exploited French hostility to the British in order to wriggle free from the yoke of imperialism. It was at sea that the arrogant attitude of the English was most apparent, and Cooper was soon to witness it first hand. The problem came about because Britain was still at war with France and there was a desperate need for able-bodied seamen to man the Royal Navy, which scoured their territorial waters looking to seize fit and able sailors from unsuspecting merchant vessels. They could only legally do this 'press ganging' if the sailor was British, and this was where the blur between American and British citizenship caused real problems. A man could have lived in America all his life and be in his heart American, but it was easy for the Royal Navy to prove that, at least technically, he was still British and force him to sign up for king and country. During the savage Napoleonic War, this was often as good as a death sentence and it is exactly what happened to the crew of the *Stirling*. The incident is described by Ned Myers:

That afternoon it cleared off, and we found a pilot lying a little outside of us. About sunset a man-of-war's cutter came alongside, and Mr. Irish was ordered to muster the crew. The English lieutenant, who was tolerably bowsed up, took his seat behind the cabin table, while the men came down, and stood in the companion-way passage, to be overhauled. Most of the foreigners had gone in the boat, but two of the Americans that remained were uncommonly fine-looking men, and were both prime seamen. One, whose name was Thomas Cook, was a six-footer, and had the air of a thorough sea-dog. He filled the lieutenant's eye mightily, and Cook was very coolly told to gather his dunnage, as he was wanted. Cook pointed to his protection, but the lieutenant answered – 'Oh! these things are nothing – anybody can have one for two dollars, in New York. You are an Englishman, and the King has need of your services.' Cook now took out of his pocket a certificate, that was signed by Sir John Beresford, stating that Thomas Cook had been discharged from His Maj. Ship Cambrian, after a pretty long service in her, because he had satisfactorily proved that he was a native-born American. The lieutenant could not very well dishonour this document, and he reluctantly let Cook go, keeping his protection, however. He next selected Isaac Gaines, a native New Yorker, a man whose father and friends were known to the captain. But Gaines had no discharge like that of Cook's, and the poor fellow was obliged to rowse up his chest and get into the cutter. This he did with tears in his eyes, and to the regret of all on board, he being one of the best men in the ship.

Cooper, due to his wealthy background, would almost certainly have had documentation of citizenship, enabling him to escape this fate. Things got worse when Captain Johnston headed up to London in order to discharge his cargo of flour. Threading their way up the Thames to one of the greatest cities on earth at the time, Cooper was deeply impressed by the huge fleet of merchant vessels anchored in the river and particularly the great 'forests of masts' he saw. But it was while they were here that another embittering incident took place. Thomas Cook, the man who had previously escaped the navy while the *Stirling* had been off the Isle of Wight, took the time to visit the Admiralty during the ship's stay in London. He headed there in the company of Cooper in order to settle some money he was owed for his services in the *Cambrian*. He was told to return in a few days and leave his certificate of discharge – the document that had previously saved him from impressment – with the Admiralty in the meantime. Almost inevitably, in the intervening days he was captured by the press gang and never seen again. It is clear that such incidents infuriated Cooper. Nevertheless, he was able to enjoy taking in some of the sights of the great city while the *Stirling* loaded shingle preparatory to the next leg of her voyage, which would take her around to Aguilas in Murcia, Spain.

On a chill January day, the *Stirling* took leave of the turgid lower reaches of the muddy old Thames and headed for warmer climes. As the crew hunched against the icy blasts of wind that ruffled the darkened waters of the English Channel, all must have felt a wave of apprehension. Ahead lay the Scilly Isles and beyond Ushant and the dreaded Bay of Biscay, feared by sailors from time immemorial. The route to Aguilas would take the *Stirling* straight across this notorious bight of water in the very depths of winter. Exposed to the fearful south-westerly gales that lash the French coastline through this gloomy season, a ship could rapidly be battered into submission by wind and wave, become embayed in Biscay and driven ashore on the great fangs of rock which hem its shoreline. However, although the passage was indeed stormy, it was not to be the weather that caused the *Stirling* the trouble on this leg, but rather other shipping. Clear of Biscay and running into warmer climes off the Portuguese coast, the *Stirling* was followed by a mysterious stranger. I will leave it to Cooper and Myers to tell the story:

While running down the coast of Portugal, with the land in sight, we made an armed felucca astern, and to windward. This vessel gave chase; and, the captain disliking her appearance, we carried hard, in order to avoid her. The weather was thick, and it blew fresh, occasionally, in squalls. Whenever it lulled, the felucca gained on us, we having, a very little, the advantage in the puffs. At length the felucca began to fire; and, finding that his shot were coming pretty near, Captain Johnston, knowing that he was in ballast, thought it wisest to heave-to. Ten minutes after our main-top-sail was aback, the felucca ranged up close under our lee; hailed, and ordered us to send a boat, with our papers, on board her. A more rascally-looking craft never gave such an order to an unarmed merchantman. As our ship rose on a sea, and he fell into the trough, we could look directly down upon his decks, and thus form some notion of what we were to expect, when he got possession of us. His people were in red caps and shirts, and appeared to be composed of the rakings of such places as Gibraltar, Cadiz and Lisbon. He had ten long guns; and pikes, pistols and muskets, were plenty with him. On the end of each latine-yard was a chap on the look-out, who occasionally turned his eyes towards us, as if to anticipate the gleanings. That we should be plundered, every one expected; and it was quite likely we might be ill-treated. As soon as we hove-to, Captain Johnston gave me the best spy-glass, with orders to hand it to Cooper, to hide. The latter buried it in the shingle ballast. We, in the cabin, concealed a bag of guineas so effectually, that, after all was over, we could not find it ourselves.

Captain Johnston proceeded to swing out the jolly boat in order to row across to the pirate ship, for that is undoubtedly what she was – and ascertain the *Stirling* and her crew's destiny. Fate had other ideas, however:

There lay the felucca, waiting for the boat; and the men were reluctantly going into the latter, when the commander of the felucca waved his hand to us, his craft fell off and filled, wing-and-wing, skimming away towards the coast, like a duck. We stood gaping and staring at her, not knowing what to make of this manoeuvre, when 'bang!' went a heavy gun, a little on our weather quarter. The shot passed our wake, for we had filled our topsail, and it went skipping from sea to sea, after the felucca. Turning our eyes in the direction of the report, we saw a frigate running down upon the felucca, carrying studding-sails on both sides, with the water foaming up to her hawse-holes. As she passed our stern, she showed an English ensign, but took no other notice of us, continuing on after the felucca, and occasionally measuring her distance with a shot. Both vessels soon disappeared in the mist, though we heard guns for some time. As for ourselves, we jogged along on our course, wishing good luck to the Englishman. The felucca showed no ensign, the whole day. Our guineas were found, some weeks later, in a bread-locker, after we had fairly eaten our way down to them.

It was a narrow shave and there was more to come, for shortly afterwards the *Stirling*, so recently saved by the Royal Navy, almost fell victim to it, coming very close to being run down by a vessel from the British Fleet, which lay off Cape Trafalgar on the Spanish coast. Cooper was to play an important role in saving the ship:

The captain ordered our helm hard up, and yelled for Cooper to bring up the cabin lantern. The youngster made one leap down the ladder, just scraping the steps with his heels, and was in the mizzen rigging with the light, in half a minute. That saved us. So near was the stranger, that we plainly heard the officer of the deck call out to his own quarter-master to "port, hard a-port--_hard_ a-port, and be d----d to you!" Hard a-port it was, and a two-decker came brushing along on our weather beam-- so near, that, when she lifted on the seas, it seemed as if the muzzles of her guns would smash our rails.

After this, the trip was incident-free and the *Stirling* battled through the narrow bottleneck of the straits of Gibraltar into the azure waters of the Mediterranean and skirted the Spanish coast around to the great port of Cartagena. After a brief period of quarantine, she was able to proceed to Aguilas and load a cargo of Barilla, a plant that produces sodium carbonate, used in washing powder. Some weeks later she tripped her anchor and headed back to England, being almost hurled out of the Mediterranean by a strong Levanter, one of the great winds that roar across this stretch of water, particularly in spring. After a fortnight she was once again off the English coast, swinging to her anchor in Carrick Roads, Falmouth. It was while she lay in quarantine here that there was a repeat of the humiliating plundering of the *Stirling*'s crew by British naval officers. The loss of a Falmouth-born man known simply as 'Bill' was particularly scarring, as Cooper and Myers related:

> *The press-gang was soon on board us, and its officer asked to have the crew mustered. This humiliating order was obeyed, and all hands of us were called aft. The officer seemed easily satisfied, until he came to Bill. 'What countryman are _you_?' he asked. 'An American – a Philadelphian,' answered Bill. 'You are an Englishman.' 'No, sir; I was born–' 'Over here, across the bay,' interrupted the officer, with a cool smile, 'where your dear wife is at this moment. Your name is _____ _____, and you are well known in Falmouth. Get your clothes, and be ready to go in the boat.'*
>
> *This settled the matter. Captain Johnston paid Bill his wages, his chest was lowered into the boat, and the poor fellow took an affectionate leave of his shipmates. He told those around him that his fate was sealed. He was too old to outlive a war that appeared to have no end, and they would never trust him on shore. 'My foot will never touch the land again,' he said to Cooper, as he squeezed his young friend's hand, 'and I am to live and die, with a ship for my prison.'*

Such high-handed incidents sickened Cooper, and his views on the British were no doubt hardening rapidly as the voyage progressed. From Falmouth, the *Stirling* proceeded once again to London. It was here that an incident occurred that cemented the friendship between Cooper and Myers, which was to bear fruit many years later. Myers had been fooling around and had jumped across the bulwarks in order to board a vessel that was moored alongside the *Stirling*. The youngster somehow lost his footing and fell between the two boats. He seemed certain to drown, for he could not swim a stroke, but Cooper intervened:

... hearing my outcry, he sprang down between the ships, and rescued me from drowning. I thought I was gone; and my condition made an impression on me that never will be lost. Had not Cooper accidentally appeared, just as he did, Ned Myers's yarn would have ended with this paragraph.

After this piece of casual heroics, Cooper, the much chastened Myers and the rest of *Stirling*'s crew had to wait several months in London River before finally returning to America. Aside from a brief meeting in 1809, it was to be many years later, in 1842, that Cooper and Myers crossed paths again. By that time Cooper was one of America's most successful novelists and Myers had endured a lifetime of hardship and adventure at sea. He read Cooper's book, *The Pilot*, and wrote to his former shipmate. Cooper was delighted to hear from him and invited his former shipmate into his home, where he remained some weeks. The upshot was *Ned Myers,* which affords a great insight into the US Mercantile marine and navy during these formative years.

The last leg of this voyage turned out to be a lengthy one and, during an interminable few weeks spent tacking to and fro in an endeavour to get out of the English Channel, the *Stirling* was once again boarded by the Royal Navy who tried to seize a Swedish sailor. It was at this point that the infuriated Cooper 'got into a little fight' with the English officers, and it is perhaps fortunate that the captain intervened. The Swedish sailor was so adamant that he would not serve in the Royal Navy that the English eventually left him alone. The rest of the passage was lengthy and Captain Johnston had to head as far south as Corvo in the Azores before he picked up a fair breeze that finally bowled them home. The *Stirling* had been away over a year and Cooper had garnered an affection for the sea that lasted until the day he died. He had also witnessed enough English bullying and brutality to make his next move clear; he wanted to join the US Navy.

There is little doubt that this decision was, at least in part, the result of the chastening encounters with the Royal Navy during his adventures aboard the *Stirling*. English arrogance when dealing with America was never more evident than in the manner in which they simply strode aboard American ships and plundered them of men. This was to be one of the key factors that led to outright war between the two countries in 1812. Cooper was clearly outraged by what he had witnessed and his ardour was to be further stoked when he returned to America. When he arrived in New York, the city was abuzz with the latest British outrage; the *Leopard–Chesapeake* affair, a diplomatic disaster for the British. In short, troubles had started when a number of sailors had deserted the HMS *Melampus* off the US coast. An order was given to search any US vessel for these men. Rumour had it that they had joined the US frigate *Chesapeake*, just departed for a cruise of the Mediterranean. As ill-fortune would have it, the *Chesapeake* ran in to the HMS *Leopard*. The American frigate was still in a state of extreme disorganisation, having just made her departure. By contrast, the *Leopard* appeared ominously ready for action, her gunports already open and decks cleared for action. The *Chesapeake*'s commander received an officer who had been sent from the *Leopard* by stating that he was under no obligation to surrender any deserters.

The British officer returned to the *Leopard* and within minutes the British ship opened fire upon the *Chesapeake*, pouring broadside after broadside into the unprepared American ship. On board the *Chesapeake*, officers and men raced around in a panic, and in the general confusion, no one was even able to find a match or spark to ignite a cannon. Right at the end of a fierce 15-minute pounding, a single cannon discharged its shot into the *Leopard*'s side but it was more of a poignant symbol of impotence than a meaningful retaliation, and shortly afterwards, the *Chesapeake* surrendered and the *Melampus* deserters were returned. The *Chesapeake* limped back to port with a tally of three men dead and 18 seriously wounded. The frigate was also a wreck. The result was public outrage. These days it is hard to imagine America as a bullied underdog but in the early 1800s, she was, and Cooper wanted to do his bit, signing on as a midshipman in the US Navy in 1808.

There is little doubt that he had visions of seeing active duty in order to right some of the wrongs that the English had inflicted on his country. Certainly, it felt as if America was just waiting for the spark that would cause the country to explode into war. Yet, just as had been the case aboard the *Chesapeake*, the country was unprepared and the spark was lacking. War would not come until 1812 and, in the meantime, Cooper discovered that life in the navy in peacetime could be an extremely tedious business. His service was something of an anti-climax. He never seemed to gain a position of any permanence and, although the thunderclouds of war with Britain darkened the skies and rumbled, peace remained in place. Cooper initially served on the USS *Vesuvius*, which was in such a terrible state of repair that she rarely went anywhere. Following this, he was transferred to Oswego on Lake Ontario to help supervise the building of the USS *Oneida*, a brig that was intended for use in the expected war with Britain.

This was probably the most interesting assignment Cooper had in the navy. Oswego was a tiny backwood on the shores of the great lake and the arrival of a huge band of carpenters, blacksmiths and naval officers must have made quite an impression. It must also have been fascinating for the aspiring young sailor to witness a vessel being built from scratch. Indeed, much of what he observed found its way into one of his later books, *The Crater*. In the meantime, the many months spent in this peaceful, remote back of beyond provided rich material for two of his early novels, *The Pioneers* and *The Pathfinder*. This material was further augmented by an epic pleasure trip – in one of the *Oneida*'s boats – up the Niagara River to the mighty falls. Cooper took in the dramatic scenery and wove these spectacular and lonely backdrops into his later writing. By spring 1809, the smart little vessel they were building was almost ready, but delays in finding personnel meant that she would not actually sail until 1810. It is therefore understandable that Cooper became restless, longing for active service. In September 1809 he requested leave from the navy and attempted to secure a berth on a merchant vessel. He failed and, again, the British were at least partly to blame for this. At the time that Cooper went looking for a berth, American trade was utterly stagnant following the Embargo Act of 1807, implemented by President Thomas Jefferson. This legislation, preventing trade with either Britain or France, was the result of incursions such as the impressment that Cooper had witnessed aboard the *Stirling*. America did not feel strong enough to stand up to either Britain or France and therefore went for sanctions in order to punish both. The result was mild punishment for America's enemies and wholesale punishment for American traders, as the sanctions were returned with interest. Merchant shipping was paralysed, and it says much for the depression of trade in America at this time that an active and experienced seaman could not find a berth. Cooper returned to the navy and things seemed to be looking up, for he secured a berth on the USS *Wasp*, later described by Cooper as 'a beautiful and fast cruiser'. Her captain was James Lawrence, a most active and daring commander, who would later perish while commanding the aforementioned USS *Chesapeake* in her epic defeat by the HMS *Shannon*. He was later immortalised for his words, 'don't give up the ship' as he was taken down to the sick bay of the *Chesapeake* having received a mortal wound.

Both ship and commander were top notch but Cooper was rapidly realising that the navy in peacetime can be a tedious workplace and, aside from a few coastal trips, the *Wasp* was by and large idle. The young midshipman's main role was rounding up reluctant recruits, which must have rankled somewhat.

Cooper therefore cut a frustrated figure, brimming over with thwarted ambition: a man waiting for some meaningful action to occur. Yet all the waiting was to be in vain, for as he twiddled his thumbs and looked forward to the inevitable outbreak of war, something far more momentous occurred; he fell in love with a girl by the name of Susan DeLancey. 'I loved her like a man,' he later recalled 'and told her of it like a sailor.' If this was so, Susan also signalled the end of his life as a sailor. The couple were married on New Year's Day 1811, Cooper having already resigned his commission aboard the *Wasp*. His days afloat were over and Cooper now looked to the land for a living. It therefore must have been galling for the fervent young patriot to have to observe from a distance the dreadful bloody nose that the US Navy gave the cocksure and overconfident British during the ensuing war of 1812–15. Certainly Cooper was later to document much of the action with barely disguised glee. Whether it was a promise to his wife, or simple pragmatism that prevented Cooper from returning to the sea and the heat of battle, we will never know.

Henceforth, Cooper became a landowner, gentleman and businessman, but life was not as simple as it had seemed in the carefree days of his youth in Cooperstown, and he was often under heavy financial pressure. This didn't stop him from investing in the whaling vessel *Union*, which made several voyages in pursuit of sperm whales, and certainly seems to have helped to keep him afloat financially. His visits aboard this vessel at the end of her trips were always a source of pleasure to the retired sailor, and his knowledge of the business must have been invaluable. It wasn't until 1820 that Cooper wrote his first novel, *Precaution*. The circumstances were spontaneous and off the cuff. He was reading a rather dreary novel and happened to remark to his wife that he could do better himself. Susan responded by challenging him to do just that, and the rest is history.

Cooper slowly established himself as one of the great pioneers of American literature. In doing so, he truly was a pioneer, as prior to this it was largely accepted that novels were written in Europe and it was not financially viable to be a full-time author in America. Cooper proved it *was* possible and paved the way for Melville, Hawthorne and many more besides, remaining a staunch patriot and retaining that early disdain for the English. It is telling that his first nautical novel – *the* first nautical novel – *The Pilot,* was based on the story of John Paul Jones, regarded as the founder of the American Navy and a man who, during the War of Independence, became the scourge of the Royal Navy after leading a number of dashing attacks on English and Scottish ports, which badly damaged British morale.

In later years Cooper became the leading biographer of the US Navy and his cataloguing of the early history of the force remain important historical sources. Yet it was his nautical fiction that was the most striking illustration of his relationship with ships and the sea. He was clearly very much in love with life afloat and this hankering for salt air and open horizons seeps through all that work. Joseph Conrad was later to observe:

[Cooper] loved the sea and looked at it with consummate understanding. In his sea tales the sea inter-penetrates with life ... His descriptions have the magistral ampleness of a gesture indicating the sweep of a vast horizon. They embrace the colours of sunset, the peace of starlight, the aspects of calm and storm, the great loneliness of the waters, the stillness of silent coasts, and the alert readiness which marks men who live face to face with the promise and the menace of the sea.

Ernest Hemingway

A strange fish

You did not kill the fish only to keep alive and sell food, he thought. You killed him for pride and because you are a fisherman. You loved him when he was alive and you loved him after.

Hemingway's The Old Man and the Sea

By the time of his death, Ernest Hemingway had become a hideously bloated parody of himself. The year was 1961 and Hemingway was the most famous author in the world. He was 62 years old; his faculties were shot to hell and he was utterly dissipated. Years of boozing had frayed his nerves to the point where he was utterly paranoid. He had become deluded, obsessed with the idea that the FBI was tapping his phone. In the meantime, his legendary writing powers were so diminished that his last attempt to write a meaningful paragraph had reduced him to tears. Evidently deciding it was time to sign off, he took his own life by putting a shotgun to his head.

Since then, Hemingway's larger-than-life persona has been stretched and distorted still further, until the myth surrounding this hard living, hard drinking, self-hating ball of machismo and ego is hard to make any sense of at all. He clearly had a mean streak a mile wide and made plenty of enemies – even among his friends. Since his death, there have been so many hatchet jobs on his personality that it becomes hard for any Hemingway scholar not to end up hating him. Yet for all the bluster and swagger, and his wanton treachery towards his friends, there comes a point when only the hardest hearted could not feel a bit sorry for the man. For me, this point is around 1951, the moment when the façade of all those years of boasting and braggadocio starts to crumble and you see him for what he really is: a confused, pathetic and rather desperate middle-aged man capable, now and again, of creating literary magic. This was also around the time he sat down to write to *The Old Man and the Sea*, his final masterpiece and a work of real sensitivity and beauty. The book distilled all that Hemingway loved about the sea and deep-sea fishing into one story, stripped bare of everything but a profound understanding of nature, the sea and the magic of man's relationship with both its unfathomable depths and the creatures therein. It is unquestionably one of the great pieces of maritime literature.

Given the reflective beauty of the book, it is interesting to understand the circumstances in which it was written and what made the man who wrote it. Hemingway's story has been told so many times that I don't really want to go into too much detail about his youth, so I will be brief. He was born many miles from the sea in Illinois in 1899. The second of six children, his father was a doctor and a stern disciplinarian who often handed out brutal beatings to his kids. Hemingway rapidly grew to hate his rather eccentric mother, perhaps because she insisted in cladding him in girl's clothes in his early years. Young Hemingway showed an aptitude for writing, and after leaving school was a cub reporter on the *Kansas City Star*. He had a longing to travel, and World War One gave him a great excuse. He tried to enlist, but failed on account of bad eyesight and instead signed up for the Red Cross in 1918, serving on the Italian front. He was only 18 and witnessed first hand the horror of one of the most brutal conflicts the world has seen. He was injured badly and also commended for his bravery. Returning home, he married Elizabeth Hadley Richardson and the couple soon headed to Paris after Hemingway, now a reporter for the *Toronto Star*, was made European correspondent. It was in decadent Paris that Hemingway was to become a leading light of what became known as 'the lost generation': a group of bohemians, artists, writers and intellectuals. Surrounded by writers and poets such as Ezra Pound, James

Joyce, F. Scott Fitzgerald and Gertrude Stein, Hemingway began to find his own voice as a writer. His clipped narrative and lean, hard, athletic prose was new and exciting. He published his first full-length novel, *The Sun Also Rises,* in 1925 and was immediately propelled to the forefront of his profession. It's a book that is pure Hemingway: sex, death, drunkenness, bullfighting, fishing and machismo are all there in spades. Lionised in the press for his talents, Hemingway worked hard to live up to his reputation and it didn't seem to have a great effect on his personality. Perhaps success came too easily to the young author. Certainly there seems to have been a horrible price to pay down the line.

By the time he had published *A Farewell to Arms* in 1929, Hemingway's fame was assured and he was showered with plaudits, already marked out as one of the great authors of his time. Something else happened in 1929. Back in Illinois, his father shot himself. Hemingway may never have liked his father, but his suicide understandably left profound scars. It is perhaps no coincidence that around this time he suffered something of a crisis of confidence as a writer. Throughout the 1930s he struggled with where to go and how to evolve. He did all this with the eyes of the world on him – some willing him to fail. His huge ego and the raw machismo that he paraded around won him many enemies and when he tried to evolve and adapt, the critics savaged him. Hemingway was furious.

He rallied in 1940 with *For Whom the Bell Tolls,* but following that, writer's block and self-doubt seemed to bite hard. He produced only one book in the next decade, *Across the River and into the Trees,* and it was panned. He retreated to his home in Cuba, and into himself, his booze and his great love, deep-sea fishing. By the time 1951 rolled around and he sat down to write *The Old Man and the Sea* the general perception was that he was a spent force. He was now over 50. His heavy drinking, always seen as an essential part of his macho persona, was now simply embarrassing. He generally got through a quart (roughly a litre) of whiskey a day in later years. His love life was also a huge embarrassment: while his fourth wife, Mary, stalked the corridors of the couple's well appointed Cuban home, another woman vied for the author's attention. This was Adriana Ivancich, a beautiful Italian who, at 21 years of age, could very easily have been Hemingway's daughter. In fact, this sad old man referred to her as just that, 'daughter', but lusted after her in a most unfatherly manner. He had already declared his love for her earlier that year during a visit to Europe. Since then, he had been imploring her to visit him in Cuba and she had obliged, arriving there with her mother. Hemingway had been eyeing her covetously ever since and, although their relationship was never consummated, he sat down to write his seminal piece of literature in an atmosphere that must have been charged with sexual tension, frustration and fury. These circumstances were clearly favourable to the author, for the result was a book overflowing with purity, simplicity and beauty. Very few writers have managed to articulate the almost symbiotic feeling that comes from being intimate with the sea. The book is all about love, respect and being part of something great and unfathomable, and he put his whole being into it. He himself recognised this, as he wrote to his publisher: 'This is the prose I have been working for all my life that should read easily and simply and seem short and yet have all the dimensions of the visible world and the world of a man's spirit. It is as good prose as I can write now.'

To understand how a man with such a reputation for being a colossal boor could have come up with prose of such delicate sensitivity, one has to understand more about Hemingway and his relationship with the sea. We have already touched upon his complicated romantic life, but in all honesty on the morning he decided to end it all, there was probably only one true love left for him and that was his little fishing launch, *Pilar*. She had stuck with him through three marriages and innumerable crises. She had also provided him with some of his happiest and most contented times when he and *Pilar* had whiled away the days off the Cuban coastline, fishing the Gulf Stream for hours at a time in search of marlin, tuna and mako sharks. It was these hours out in the 'stream' that provided Hemingway with the knowledge and understanding to write his final masterpiece.

Growing up in Illinois, Hemingway had always loved the great outdoors and particularly fishing, which he undertook on the many rivers that surrounded his home in the town of Oak Park. The family had a number of rowing boats and later a powerboat to engage in this pursuit. Yet it was not until the 1920s, when Hemingway was based in Europe, that he was fully introduced to the joys of big-game fishing. Big-game fishing is a sport that has been around since the beginning of the twentieth century and involves heading offshore and 'trolling' lines with bait or lures at slow speed in the hope of attracting big fish such as tuna, marlin and shark. Hooking these fish can be difficult, as they often simply nibble at the bait. While the fish is toying with its food, the fisherman has to 'slack' the line in order to allow his prey to fully swallow the hook. Once this has happened, the fisherman can 'strike', pulling the line tight and dragging the hook deep into the innards of the fish. From hereon it is a battle between man and fish, the fisherman constantly slacking and reeling in until his prey is exhausted and can finally be landed on deck. The struggle can go on for hours at a time and is hugely physical. With his brawny physique, love of manly pursuits and relish for a good set-to, it was only going to be a matter of time before Hemingway got involved. His first forays came when he was working as foreign correspondent for the *Toronto Star* and he wrote about it in one of his lifestyle features in that paper. The year was 1922 and Hemingway was not even on the radar as a novelist, but his promise shines through in his narrative:

> *A big tuna is slate blue, and when he shoots up into the air from close beside the boat it is like a blinding flash of quicksilver. He may weigh 300 pounds and he jumps with the eagerness and ferocity of a mammoth rainbow trout. Sometimes five and six tuna will be in the air at once in Vigo Bay, shouldering out of the water like porpoises as they herd the sardines and then leaping in a towering jump that is as clean and beautiful as the leap of a well hooked rainbow.*

This was written after an early fishing trip from the port of Vigo in northern Spain, and shows that Hemingway was already entranced by the great beauty and power of the fish. Yet it wasn't until he returned from Europe in 1928 that he was able to take up the sport in earnest. The now-famous author had moved back to his home country and settled in Key West, at the very tip of Florida. It was a ramshackle backwood in those days and Hemingway revelled in the pleasant climate and azure seas, '... the best place I've ever been anytime, anywhere, flowers, tamarind trees, guava trees, coconut palms. Got tight last night on absinthe and did knife tricks'.

He couldn't have chosen a finer spot to take up fishing, for the 75-mile-wide channel between Key West and Cuba marks the beginning of the Gulf Stream, a warm, swift flowing current. Funnelled up from the Caribbean by the trade wind, this river of warm water can rush through the Straits of Florida at anything up to five knots. This great current then races on up the US coast all the way to Newfoundland before splitting in two, one half flowing down to the African coast and the other racing across to Northern Europe. The meeting places of great bodies of water have always contained multitudes of fish and the Gulf Stream is no exception. Its waters have provided a rich food source since man first began to fish. Hemingway had located himself at one of the great pulsing jugulars of fishing and as the years slipped by this great swirling vein of water was to become his lifeblood. He described it in an article he wrote for the gentleman's magazine *Esquire*:

> *In the first place, the Gulf Stream and the other great ocean currents are the last wild country there is left. Once you are out of sight of land and of other boats you are more alone than you can ever be hunting and the sea is the same as it has been since before men ever went on it in boats. In a season fishing you will see it oily flat as the becalmed galleons saw it while they drifted to the westward; white capped with a fresh breeze as they saw it running with the trades; and in high rolling blue hills the tops blowing off them like snow.*

Truly this was a wonderful playground, but it would not be until 1932, some four years after he first arrived in Florida, that Hemingway would discover the full potential of his position. Prior to this, he had simply messed around, dipping a toe into the mighty stream now and again. But in 1932 he took the plunge. Joe Russell, proprietor of *Sloppy Joe's*, one of Hemingway's favourite bars in Key West, also owned a small fishing launch, the *Anita,* and the pair decided that they would take this vessel on a two-week fishing trip with a few friends. During the prohibition years, Russell had used the *Anita* to smuggle vast quantities of illegal alcohol from Cuba into Key West, so he was intimate with the Straits of Florida. He headed the *Anita* out into the stream and across to the coast of Cuba where they could fish for some of the monsters of the deep, particularly Marlin. Hemingway was rapidly hooked (pun intended). Two weeks turned into two months and still the writer was entranced. Days fishing in the stream were followed by wild nights out in the magical old city of Havana, where there was music in the cafes at night and revolution in the air. The daiquiris and mojitos flowed, the streets throbbed to the rhythm of the rumba and Hemingway revelled in it all. He wrote of this time with great enthusiasm:

We fished along that coast for 65 days... It is wonderful. The Gulf Stream runs almost black and comes right in to the shore. The marlin swordfish go by, swimming up the stream like cars on a highway. You go in to shore on a boat and look down to see the wrinkles in the white sand through the clear water. It looks as though you would strike bottom. They have beaches miles and miles long, hard white sand and no houses for twenty miles. We go out in the morning and troll the stream go in to swim and get back somewhere at night. Sometimes sleep on the boat, sometimes on the town.

'The town' was one thing, but it is clear that daytime fishing remained the main draw for Hemingway and he pursued the sport with enormous diligence. Quite simply, he wanted to be the best fisherman on the planet, and he studied the art with all the intensity of a man possessed. Although at first he was fairly indiscriminate with what sort of fish he hooked, he soon realised the greatest prize out there was marlin and his love affair with hooking and killing this fish lasted the rest of his life. Marlin is a breed of swordfish, coveted by sport fishermen the world over due to its size, elusiveness, strength and speed. Blue and black Marlin are the most sought-after of the breed, and a female marlin can exceed 450kg (1,000lbs) in weight and can swim at speeds of up to 80km (50mph). To take on such a creature with a rod and line is not something to be sniffed at, and Hemingway loved the physicality of the fight and the satisfaction of showing off your catch at the end of the day. He articulated the excitement of hooking such a beast with great eloquence:

> He [the fisherman] can see the slicing wake of the fin, if he cuts toward
> the bait, or the rising and lowering sickle of his tail if he is traveling, or
> if he comes from behind he can see the bulk of him underwater, great
> blue pectorals widespread like the wings of some huge underwater bird,
> and the stripes around him like purple bands around a brown barrel.
> To feel that fish in his rod, to feel that power and that great rush, to be a
> connected part of it and then to dominate it and to master it and to bring
> that fish to gaff, alone and with no one else touching rod, reel or leader,
> is something worth waiting many days for.

Yet there was more than this to his fascination with the sport; in the past he had followed bullfighting and taken up fly fishing with a similar degree of obsession, but the enthusiasm had waned. Out in the stream, things were different. Hemingway articulated his deep fascination with the Gulf Stream thus:

> Because the Gulf Stream is unexploited country, only the fringe of it ever
> being fished, and then only at a dozen places in thousands of miles of
> current, no one knows what fish live in it, or how great size they reach or
> what age, or even what kinds of fish and animals live in it at different
> depths. When you are drifting, out of sight of land, fishing four lines,
> sixty, eighty, 100 and 150 fathoms down in water that is 700 fathoms
> deep, you never know what may take the small tuna that you use for bait.
> It may be a marlin that will jump high and clear off to your right and
> then go off in a series of leaps, throwing a splash like a speedboat in a
> sea as you shout for the boat to turn with him watching the line melting
> off the reel before the boat can get around. Or it might be a broadbill
> that will show wagging his great broadsword. Or it may be some fish
> that you will never see at all that will head straight out to the north west
> like a submerged submarine and never show and at the end of five hours

the angler has a straightened out hook. There is always a feeling of excitement when a fish takes hold when you are drifting deep.

It was during this early period, fishing aboard the *Anita*, that Hemingway was first introduced to an old Cuban fisherman by the name of Carlos Gutierrez. Hemingway was like a sponge during this period, attaching himself to anyone who knew more than him about deep-sea fishing and soaking up all the information he could gather until the subject of his attention was wrung dry. Gutierrez, who had fished the stream since 1884, had much knowledge to pass on, and one story that fascinated Hemingway was to lie dormant within the recesses of his brain until 1951, when it simply spilled out onto the page, forming *The Old Man and the Sea*. He mentioned Gutierrez's tale briefly:

An old man out in a skiff out of Cabanas hooked a great marlin that, on the heavy sash cord hand line, pulled the skiff far out to sea. Two days later the old man was picked up by fishermen sixty miles to the eastward, the head and forward part of the marlin lashed alongside. What was left of the fish, less than half, weighed eight hundred pounds. The old man stayed with him a day, a night, a day and another night while the fish swam deep and pulled the boat. When he had come up the old man had pulled the boat up on him and harpooned him. Lashed alongside the sharks had hit him and the old man had fought them alone out in the Gulf Stream in a skiff, clubbing them, stabbing at them, lunging at them with an oar until he was exhausted and the sharks had eaten all that they could hold. He was crying in the boat when the fishermen picked him up, half crazy from his loss, and the sharks were still circling the boat.

This was to be the first stirring of *The Old Man and the Sea*. After another season aboard the *Anita*, Hemingway took the plunge and bought his own boat. The year was 1933 and he had just returned from a season of big-game hunting in Africa when he placed the order for *Pilar*, a Wheeler Playmate cabin cruiser some 38ft in length. This was a fairly modest vessel straight off the production line, but she was a sleek little motorboat, pleasing to the eye and capable of running at 16 knots or so if required. Hemingway had her especially customised for fishing and painted black. She was comfortable enough to sleep six with a further two in the cockpit if the weather permitted. Hemingway was immensely pleased with his purchase and hired two crew whom he kitted out with matching uniforms with the name of his command, *Pilar*, monogrammed onto their sailor suits. If that sounds a little overblown for a cabin cruiser, the more acute reader may have noted that in 1933 America was in the grip of the great depression. Millions were unemployed; the country stared into the abyss. Hemingway went fishing on a shiny new boat with a crew dressed up in sailor suits. Yet there is some redemption for the man. One of his crew that first year was Arnold Samuelson, an unemployed bum who had hitched down to Key West from depression-stricken Minneapolis and knocked on Hemingway's door. The writer took him in at once and promptly offered him a job. For all his image as a merciless swine, Hemingway had a warm and generous side to him. Samuelson recalled the interview:

> *EH: Of course, I don't know you very well, but you seem to be the sort of person that can be trusted. Do you drink?*
> *AS: Not much, just a little moonshine when I was a kid.*
> *EH: That's good, the owner is the only person who can get drunk aboard a boat.*

Pilar set sail for Cuba, where the wizened old fisherman Carlos Gutierrez and a younger Cuban, Gregorio Fuentes, bolstered her crew to three. Hemingway usually hosted a range of drinking buddies aboard during these trips, who he could booze, bully and brag with. On this first trip, however, he brought along a whole troupe of naturalists, hoping to analyse the Gulf Stream and the creatures of the deep therein. This may seem unusual, but Hemingway was actually deeply fascinated by the scientific side of the stream. Indeed, his methodical and thorough method of studying marlin – his endless notes on the habits of this fish are still extant – point to a man who wanted complete understanding of everything to do with this great, mysterious stream. Just as a deep understanding of the tides and reefs and wave formations of the break he rides aid the surfer, so Hemingway was using every ounce of knowledge he could lay his hands on to fish these mysterious waters to best advantage.

Yet, for all this fascination with the Gulf Stream, there was still the drinking and the guns and the lovers, all of were present aboard *Pilar*. These naturally grabbed the headlines. The guns really deserve some mention, for from day one there was always a rifle aboard *Pilar* and Hemingway was never far from the trigger. One particularly unpleasant incident is recounted by an ex-friend of his, Archibald MacLeish, who was invited out aboard *Pilar* for a spot of fishing in the early days. MacLeish hooked a sailfish and made rather a hash of reeling it in, probably not helped by Hemingway bellowing orders at him. Once the fish had escaped, Hemingway was so incensed that he vented spleen by firing at the terns that followed the boat. MacLeish was particularly scarred by the experience as seabirds plopped dismally into *Pilar's* wake, Hemingway bringing down the first tern with one barrel of the rifle and finishing off the grieving mate with the other. This is not the act of a budding naturalist. Anyone believing in karma, however, will be delighted to know that a year or so later, Hemingway managed to shoot himself in the leg after a bullet accidentally discharged from his pistol while he wrestled with a shark he was reeling in. The bullet hit something metal on *Pilar's* capping rail and rebounded into his leg, injuring him in the process. The guns were not really meant for shooting terns – or writers for that matter – at all. Their true purpose was to see off any sharks that might cluster round a stricken marlin before it could be gaffed and brought aboard. After a while, Hemingway decided that a mere rifle was never going to cut it, and therefore opted to buy a Thompson submachine gun. A female friend who went on one of his fishing trips around this time describes the drama the Tommy gun added thus:

> They [the sharks] come in like express trains and hit the fish like a planing mill – shearing off 25 pounds at a bite. Ernest shoots them with his machine gun rrrr – but it wont stop them – it's terrific seeing the bullets ripping into them– the sharks thrashing in blood and foam – the white bellies and fearful jaws – the pale cold eyes. I was aghast, but it's very exciting.

This extremely dangerous machine-gunning habit contributed to another deeply disturbing incident, which, again, was subconsciously going to help him write *The Old Man and the Sea*.

In 1935, his second season with *Pilar*, Hemingway took his command up to Bimini, another rich Gulf Stream fishing ground nestled on the western tip of the Bahamas. He hosted the usual selection of friends, kicking off with the old syphilitic ne'er do well and legendary big-game hunter Bror Blixen – now probably most famous for his earlier marriage to Karen Blixen who, under the name Isak Dinesen wrote *Out of Africa*. Back then though, he was big news in his own right. Hemingway made an impression in Bimini from the off. Making himself comfortable and well oiled at the *Compleat Angler* hotel and bar, he issued a standing challenge to all and sundry that he would take on all comers and pay out $200 to anyone who could go three rounds of boxing with him. His interest in pugilism wasn't confined to the ring, and it was in Bimini that the writer famously punched wealthy magazine publisher Joe Knapp in the face after the latter had called him a 'big fat slob'. This inspired the rather dire local ditty entitled 'Big Fat Slob'.

The big fat slob in Bimini
Is the night we had fun.
Mr. Knapp called Mr. Hemingway A big fat slob.
Mr. Hemingway balled his fist and gave him a knob.

Also among the party was an old friend from his Paris days, Mike Strater, an artist. There had always been a degree of rivalry between these two, but all went well until some weeks into the trip, when Strater hooked into a huge black marlin. The marlin was over 4m (13ft) long and Strater reckoned it weighed somewhere in the region of 450kg (1,000lbs). He later recalled:

As soon as I hooked him, I knew he was a big one. Then he came out of
the water walking on his tail and it was just like a metallic blue express
train bursting out of the water. Hem and I were both excited because it

was the first one we had hooked; the first big marlin anyone in Bimini
had snagged and we wanted very much to land him.

Both Hemingway and Strater had discussed tactics on landing a big marlin.
The problem was that if you played the fish for too long in order to tire him
out, the chances were that he would have bled sufficiently to attract sharks.
Bimini suffered with this problem more than most fishing spots and there
was a real risk that they would devour the marlin before it was landed. Strater
had therefore developed a strategy of putting his all into wearing the fish out
with a short, brutal fight. He put this strategy into play as he prepared to
do battle with this monster fish. All went well, and within an hour the fish
was close enough to the boat to be gaffed. This was to be Hemingway's job,
aided by paid hand 'Bread' Pindar. Sadly, the writer appears to temporarily
have lost his head. According to Strater, this is what followed:

Bread and I were still occupied with the marlin when suddenly Hem begins
to fire the gun off right behind us screaming 'sharks', 'sharks'. We could hear
the bullets going past our heads. Bread, who was being paid by the week
and not getting paid at all to get shot at, ran immediately to the other end of
the boat. If I hadn't had a record fish on my line, I would have run too.

Without Pindar's aid, the marlin was able to wriggle away and soon the line
was again screaming off the reel. An exasperated Strater yelled at his friend
to stop the shooting, and Hemingway responded by taunting him, shouting
that he, 'couldn't take the muzzle blasts'. Why did he act like this? Strater
has a theory:

The truth is that Ernest was overcome with jealousy because I had a record
marlin hooked and had brought it up in record time. He didn't want me to
be the one to catch the first big fish. In fact the fish was never in danger from
sharks because I had already brought it to gaff with no damage whatsoever.

There followed another hour of desperate wrestling with the giant fish
to land it again. This time, the blood from all that machine gunning had

definitely attracted the sharks and the anglers had to watch in horror as this giant, beautiful fish was attacked before their very eyes by the thrashing mass of bloodthirsty makos and tiger sharks, in a scene straight out of *The Old Man and the Sea*. Hemingway, over his moment of madness, was extremely helpful and eventually, at least two-thirds of the fish was landed on deck. *Pilar* returned to Bimini victorious.

It must be remembered that Mike Strater recalled this incident when Hemingway was long dead and unable to defend himself. That he caught a huge, half eaten marlin is beyond dispute, for there is a picture of Hemingway and Strater posing beside the great fish, its flanks clearly savaged by sharks. It must be said that Hemingway certainly has a slightly proprietary look about him as he stands by. It is possible that Strater was just sore about losing most of his record catch. Then again, he might be telling the truth. Later that evening, flushed with success, the crew of *Pilar* went out on the town and Strater was bought round after round of drinks by admiring anglers. At the end of the night, Hemingway's friend claims that his frustrated fellow fisherman slugged him in the guts. Hemingway had gathered some valuable source material for *The Old Man and the Sea*. He had also lost another friend.

I realise that this short story of Hemingway's sea experience is beginning to read like yet another character assassination of the great writer. I do not mean it to be. It is rather meant to be an illustration of his wonderfully nuanced relationship with the sea, which led him down the path to the *Old Man and the Sea*. And, of course, he must have had a sensitive side, but it is difficult to reconcile this bullet-spraying lunatic with that man. One person who understood him well was Gertrude Stein. Stein, a novelist and poet, had acted as mentor to the young Hemingway when he was in Paris, helping him develop his writing style. She was the godmother to his first son, Jack, but by 1934 Hemingway had long since fallen out with her, generally referring to her as 'the bitch'. She summed Ernest as follows:

When I first met Hemingway he had a truly sensitive capacity for emotion, and that was the stuff of the first stories; but he was shy of himself and started to develop, as a shield, a big Kansas City boy brutality about it, and so he was 'tough' because he was really sensitive and ashamed that he was. He went the way so many Americans have gone before, the way they are still going. He became obsessed by sex and death.

...then his agonising shyness escaped into brutality. No, now wait – not real brutality, because the truly brutal man wants something more than bullfighting and deep-sea fishing and elephant killing or whatever it is now, and perhaps if Hemingway was truly brutal he could make some real literature out of those things, but he is not, and I doubt he will ever again write truly about anything. He is skilful, yes, but that is the writer, the other half is the man.

And of course she was right, at least on one point. Hemingway, in addition to often being a brutal oaf, was also capable of being incredibly sensitive. Whatever Stein thought about his sport-fishing habits, there was no question that the sea brought out the softer side in him, even before *The Old Man and the Sea*. In 1934 he published *The Green Hills of Africa* – an experimental non-fiction piece about a hunting safari he had undertaken with his wife. Much of the book is a brutal catalogue of killing, but perhaps one of the finest passages relates to the Gulf Stream:

When, on the sea, you are alone with it and know that this Gulf Stream you are living with, knowing, learning about, and loving, has moved, as it moves, since before man and that it has gone by the shoreline of that long, beautiful, unhappy island since before Columbus sighted it and that the things you find out about it, and those that have always lived in it are permanent and of value because that stream will flow, as it has flowed, after the Indians, after the Spaniards, after the British, after the Americans and after all the Cubans and all the systems of governments, the richness, the poverty, the martyrdom, the sacrifice and the venality and the cruelty are all gone as the high-piled scow of garbage, bright-colored, white-flecked, ill-smelling, now tilted on its side, spills off its load into the blue water, turning it a pale green to a depth of four or five fathoms as the load spreads across the surface, the sinkable part going down and the flotsam of palm fronds, corks, bottles, and used electric light globes, seasoned with an occasional condom or a deep floating corset, the torn leaves of a student's exercise book, a well-inflated dog, the occasional rat, the no-longer-distinguished cat; well shepherded by the boats of the garbage pickers who pluck their prizes with long poles, as interested, as intelligent, and as accurate as historians; they have the viewpoint; the stream, with no visible flow, takes five loads of this a day when things are going well in La Habana and in ten miles along the coast it is as clear and blue and unimpressed as it was ever before the tug hauled out the scow; and the palm fronds of our victories, the worn light bulbs of our discoveries and the empty condoms of our great loves float with no significance against one single, lasting thing – the stream.

As the seasons ebbed and flowed, fishing and the Gulf Stream were giving Hemingway pause for thought, a certain spiritual outlook on life. His rapport with it was interrupted when he went off to report on the Spanish Civil War in 1938. He returned with his third wife and the material for his first critically acclaimed novel in almost a decade: *For Whom the Bell Tolls*, a book that deals almost exclusively with sex and death. Gertrude Stein must have loved it. In the meantime, Hemingway and his new wife bought a house, La Finca Vigia, located about nine miles out of Havana in the village of San Francisco de Paula. He seemed set up for life and was probably mildly irritated when World War Two came along to disturb him. His reputation as a hard-hitting reporter on big events such as these went before him and he would have felt the weight of expectation lie heavy on his shoulders. It didn't help that his wife, Martha Gellhorn, was a serious journalist who was champing at the bit to get involved with the seismic chaos going on in Europe. Gellhorn was a tough, chain-smoking journo who was almost as macho as Hemingway. She had no time for wimps and, if Hemingway had been half the man he portrayed himself to be, she would have been an ideal sparring partner. But Hemingway was now over 40, he was tired and he loved the stream and *Pilar* and that was where he wanted to be. While Gellhorn went off to cover the war deriding him for his lassitude and writer's block, Hemingway went to ground in Cuba to fight the demons in his own head. He was constantly aware that as a man of action he should be doing something, and his solution was simultaneously ingenious and pathetic: he obtained a commission from the office of Naval Intelligence to fit out the *Pilar* as an anti-submarine craft and took to the stream with serious intent to destroy German submarines with a 38ft wooden cabin cruiser.

The result was a kind of alcohol-fuelled Caribbean version of *Dad's Army*. Gathering together all of his most notorious drinking pals, Hemingway patrolled the stream with great diligence. *Pilar* was too small to mount proper machine guns, so she was kitted out with a couple of Tommy guns. To augment this armament, his drinks rack on the flying bridge was neatly filled with hand grenades. His crew included a millionaire polo player, a couple of Spanish musicians and an old Catalan sergeant who was a relic from the Spanish Civil War. There was only one professional among them, a marine communications expert named Don Saxon. This unlikely bunch chugged around Cuba apparently waiting for a submarine to surface in front of them. While they waited, they passed their time fishing, drinking and firing grenades at wooden targets roughly hewn into human form and named 'Hitlers' by the crew. A log entry at this time gives an insight into the kind of caper they were up to: 'Left Cabanas at 8:30. Out 6 miles for practice – Win[ston] erratic – Paxtchi same – Fernando N.G. [no good] Win bothered by gas in stomach – Fernando stood ground swell OK. Into Bahia Honda 1 pm.'

The *Pilar*'s motley crew did get one shot at glory. On 9 December 1942, they sighted a Spanish vessel moving slowly as if for a rendezvous. Peering through the glasses, the crew swore they could see the low outline of a sub approaching her stern. They moved in for the kill, trolling fishing lines in order to look as innocent as possible. Unfortunately, as they headed toward the mysterious craft, they suddenly got a bite, a barracuda, and while they battled to land the fish, the mysterious visitors disappeared. That was the only 'action' they were involved in, and in 1943 the *Pilar*'s orders ran out and the navy refused to renew them. One can only think of Don Quixote tilting at windmills. These activities were constantly lambasted by his wife who – engaged as she was in serious journalism – saw them as ridiculous. Some of the experiences, portrayed in a less ridiculous light, did find its way into *Islands in the Stream* a series of stories about the sea, which was published posthumously.

Eventually Hemingway *did* make it to Europe, as a leading reporter on the conflict for *Colliers* magazine. Many commented on his recklessness in the field, and he was heavily involved in the Normandy invasion. He also personally 'liberated' the Ritz Bar in Paris. This story has little to do with Hemingway and the sea, but it's just too priceless to leave out, recalled as it is by an eyewitness, Lucienne Elmiger:

> *He entered like a king, and he chased out all the British people who had arrived an hour earlier. He was dressed in khaki, but his shirt was open on his bare chest. He had a leather belt under his big stomach, with his gun beating against his thigh.*
>
> *Hemingway marched through the lobby and the restaurant, in a shouting match with his foes: 'I'm the one who is going to occupy the Ritz. We're the Americans. We're going to live just like in the good old days.'*
>
> *He barked at the British in the language of the former German occupiers: 'Raus, raus [get out, get out]!'*
>
> *Hemingway's rivals quickly gave up and fled, and he made a bee-line for the bar where he ordered drinks for the fellow correspondents who had conquered the Ritz with him.*

He and Martha Gellhorn divorced shortly after this exploit. Hemingway really needed a bit of care and softness and he settled on Mary Welsh, his fourth and final wife. They returned to the comfort of Cuba, *Pilar* and the stream and Hemingway retreated back into that horrible, uncomfortable myth of himself, which seemed to make him so miserable. His marital life descended into a sniping match with many ugly scenes and often the only solace Hemingway got was aboard his boat. By now his trustiest and most reliable companion had undergone numerous refits and ridden out many storms, including a full-blown hurricane that had wrought havoc on Havana. This reminiscence from 1949 clearly illustrates the satisfaction Hemingway gained from his fishing trips:

Coming out of the harbour I will be on the flying bridge steering and watching the traffic and the line that is fishing the feather astern. As you go out, seeing friends along the water front your feather jig is fishing all the time. Behind the boulevards are the parks and buildings of old Havana and on the other side you are passing the steep slopes and walls of the fortress of Cabanas, the stone weathered pink and yellow, where most of your friends have been political prisoners at one time or another.

Sometimes you will leave the gray green harbour water and as Pilar's bows dip into the dark blue water a covey of flying fish will rise from under her bows and you will hear the slithering, silk tearing noise they make when they leave the water.

He also wrote much of his next book, *Across the River and into the Trees* aboard *Pilar*. This was released a full decade after *For Whom the Bell Tolls* and was, by and large, mauled by the critics. Everyone concluded that the author had finally and completely 'lost it' – even Hemingway must have seriously pondered the possibility. He seethed – when his rapidly ailing health would allow it – and turned more and more to the bottle. In between bouts of taunting his wife by parading the prostitutes he used in front of her, Hemingway spent his time dreaming of Adriana Ivancich, his beautiful Italian 'daughter'.

This was the broken, disappointed man who sat down at his writing desk in 1951 and started a new story: 'He was an old man who fished alone in a skiff in the Gulf Stream and he had gone eighty four days now without taking a fish.'

Suddenly writing seemed to come to him easily again; the words flowed off the pen and onto the page. All those years out in the stream came to him and through him with such clarity, and the cruelty and beauty and futility of those years were all there in this one short novella. He seemed to shake off the disappointments and begin afresh, and while the style was unquestionably Hemingway, there was a softness, a lack of posture and toughness to his writing. The presence of the young Adriana was to be a key to this burst of inspiration, as he noted to his son, Gregory, in a letter:

God I feel strong and I don't even need to sleep, but Adriana is so lovely to dream of, and when I wake I'm stronger than the day before. And the words pour out of me. They come so fast I can't keep up with them and I don't want to stop, but force myself to, after five hours, because I know I must be getting tired.

So he went on, day after day pounding out this seminal story of the sea. He had carried the idea around in his head since he had first met Carlos Gutierrez back in the early 1930s. Back then, he had even mentioned in passing making a story out of it and recognised that it was important to 'make a good job of it'. He was doing just that. For the uninitiated, the story centres upon an old fisherman, Santiago, who, although he is hugely experienced, has been out at sea for 84 days without catching a fish. Santiago is based on the fishermen of Cuba, who used to drift for marlin in small, flat-bottomed sailing boats known as cuchuchas. These wooden craft were generally around 18ft long and were sailed out to the fishing grounds off the ports of Cabanas and Santa Cruz del Norte. Once out in the stream, the sails were lowered and the fisherman dropped his lines and lures and drifted gently eastward with the current in search of big fish to sell in the market in Havana. In the book, Santiago hooks into a giant marlin, which dives deep and proceeds to tow his skiff many miles offshore. Following an epic battle, Santiago manages to kill the giant fish, but, unable to bring the creature aboard for fear of swamping his boat, he then has to watch this beautiful creature be consumed by the rapacious sharks, which circle constantly as he sails agonisingly slowly back to the coast. When he reaches shore, half mad with grief and exhaustion, all that is left is the marlin's head and upper body, his bony spine stripped of its flesh, and its tail fin still attached, hanging forlornly. Just like that giant fish that Mike Strater landed all those years ago in Bimini.

It could be a macho story, but it isn't. True, Santiago is strong and resolute, 'A man can be destroyed but never defeated', Hemingway writes, but he is also a Zen-like figure, at one with the ocean, and this is a story full of empathy and softness. A story that overflows with the belief that man is at one with the sea.

He looked across the sea and knew how alone he was now. But he could
see the prisms in the deep dark water and the line stretching ahead and
the strange undulation of the calm. The clouds were building up now
for the trade wind and he looked ahead and saw a flight of wild ducks
etching themselves against the sky and water, then blurring, then etching ·
again and he knew that no man was ever alone on the sea.

Thus, this is a new Hemingway coming through with a distinct lack of ego
in the text. In the past, the hero could clearly be identified as Hemingway
himself on some level; Jake Barnes, Frederic Henry, Robert Jordan, all of
these tough men had thick strands of his own character on show. Yet Santiago
owes little to the easily-identified caricature of Hemingway. Yes, he is a very
strong man physically, but there is a softness to him.

He always thought of the sea as la mar *which is what people call her in*
Spanish when they love her ... Some of the younger fishermen, those who
used buoys as floats for their lines and had motorboats, bought when the
shark livers had brought much money, spoke of her as el mar *which is*
masculine. They spoke of her as a contestant or a place or even an enemy.
But the old man thought of her as feminine and something that gave or
withheld great favours.

Ultimately the book is about being at one with the sea, and Hemingway
– the veteran of all those years out in the stream – when stripped of his old
machismo and ego was able to convey this feeling of being part of something
that is bigger than us in a unique way.

In actual fact, the book was meant to be the final chapter of an ambitious
'sea' book that Hemingway had been planning to put together for years.
Other sections of this book can be found in *Islands in the Stream,* which was
posthumously published after his death. Yet Hemingway immediately saw the
potential of *The Old Man and the Sea* and published it as a standalone piece in
1952. The response was rapturous. All those years of stagnation, self-doubt and
critical savagery were washed away on a wave of rave reviews. The old master

was back at the top of his game, and the plaudits poured in thick and fast; first came the Pulitzer Prize for Fiction, followed by the Nobel Prize for Literature.

Yet the book was a final flourish, and, shortly after its completion there was another hammer blow to his battered psyche. Gregory Hemingway, a son from his second marriage, had developed a penchant for dressing up in women's clothes. Initially this was merely an embarrassment to his macho father, but in October 1951 he was arrested for entering a ladies toilet in a cinema dressed in drag. Hemingway's ex-wife Pauline called him to break the news and he hurled abuse at her down the phone. Later that night he received another call to tell him that his ex-wife had died of shock. He blamed his son, but must have known that he too was culpable. It was just another blow upon a bruise and another marker on the path of his seemingly inevitable demise. Between the *Old Man and the Sea* and the day Hemingway took his own life in 1961, he did not publish any new literature. He was spent, and his physical decline in those last years was alarming – certainly not helped by an extraordinary day out in Africa when he managed to be involved in two serious plane crashes in the space of a few hours. All those decades of hard living caught up with him with a vengeance in his later years. His last fishing trip aboard the *Pilar* was sometime in the spring of 1960, and shortly afterwards the Cuban revolution prompted the Hemingways to leave the troubled island and settle in a rather drab apartment in Idaho. A few months later he was dead. Meanwhile *Pilar* still lay at her anchor, awaiting her master's return. Mary Hemingway ordered that the boat be taken out into the stream and sunk. Thankfully, this did not happen, and the smart little cabin cruiser is still on view, sitting bolt upright on the tennis court of Hemingway's home, La Finca Vigia in Cuba, which is now a museum.

There is little doubt that *Pilar* was Hemingway's sanctuary: the swirling, dark water soothed him through his furies and took him out of the caricature of himself, allowing him the occasional moment of peace. Hemingway himself said that *The Old Man and the Sea* was the best of him in terms of writing, but it also conveyed the best of him as a person; deep down somewhere in that troubled man there was still something worthwhile and it all surged to the surface as this story flowed onto the written page. After all those years of fighting with himself and everyone else, it was to be the sea, *Pilar* and the stream that allowed him, at least for a while, to forget what he had become.

Jack London
The call of the sea

Few authors have written with greater abandon about the exhilarating freedom and sheer joy of being at sea than Jack London. To London, the sea was life and being ashore was a suffocating death. In everything he wrote on the subject he strove to convey this notion. This tenet was borne out time and again in London's own life and, ultimately, in his alcohol-ravaged death at the age of 40, when it seemed that life ashore had finally wrung out the last drop of vitality from his soul.

Jack London was an adventurous man of dash and dare, but he had escaped the grinding poverty of America's late nineteenth century underclass through the somewhat staid activity of writing literature. By 1903, he was the most successful author in America and devoted three hours of every day to composing new epistles with a skill and fluency that earned him the accolade of being America's best-paid writer. Yet it is telling that when London was at this peak, he reflected on his achievements and emphatically concluded that all of his literary plaudits meant little compared to those rare moments of total satisfaction derived from carrying out a practical activity with real finesse. As he summed up with his usual bravado: 'I'd rather win a water-fight in the swimming pool, or remain astride a horse that is trying to get out from under me, than write the great American novel.' And when he wasn't winning water fights or riding horses, this attitude generally brought him straight back to that great leveller, the sea. Seafaring and all of the brutish and manly values that used to come with a sailor's life cut right to the heart of the great paradox that was Jack London. Reflecting on this, when all the world lay at his feet, London wrote the following:

Possibly the proudest achievement of my life, my moment of highest living, occurred when I was seventeen. I was in a three-masted schooner off the coast of Japan. We were in a typhoon. All hands had been on deck most of the night. I was called from my bunk at seven in the morning to take the wheel. Not a stitch of canvas was set. We were running before it under bare poles, yet the schooner fairly tore along. The seas were all of an eighth of a mile apart, and the wind snatched the whitecaps from their summits, filling the air so thick with driving spray that it was impossible to see more than two waves at a time. The schooner was almost unmanageable, rolling her rail under to starboard and to port, veering and yawing anywhere between south-east and south-west, and threatening, when the huge seas lifted under her quarter, to broach to. Had she broached to, she would ultimately have been reported lost with all hands and no tidings.

I took the wheel. The sailing-master watched me for a space. He was afraid of my youth, feared that I lacked the strength and the nerve. But when he saw me successfully wrestle the schooner through several bouts, he went below to breakfast. Fore and aft, all hands were below at breakfast. Had she broached to, not one of them would ever have reached the deck. For forty minutes I stood there alone at the wheel, in my grasp the wildly careering schooner and the lives of twenty-two men. Once we were pooped. I saw it coming, and, half-drowned, with tons of water crushing me, I checked the schooner's rush to broach to. At the end of the hour, sweating and played out, I was relieved. But I had done it! With my own hands I had done my trick at the wheel and guided a hundred tons of wood and iron through a few million tons of wind and waves.

You only have to read that once to see the sort of life London aspired to as he sat in his comfortable study dictating stories to his wife. His refined existence was a million miles from that visceral, brutal storm off the Japanese coast, yet he clearly pines for that simplicity with every sentence he writes.

Growing up in Oakland, California no doubt gave the aspiring young sailor a head start in these matters, for the town's heart could be found down on the seedy wharves of this gold rush port. Jack would wander the bustling, vice-ridden streets trying to escape his poverty-stricken home life, and the bustle of ships and the swagger of the tarry old salts seemed to promise a life richer and stranger than his current existence: he wanted a part of it.

Jack was the illegitimate son of Flora Chaney, a headstrong woman who seemed to plunge from one crisis to another. Flora had originally come from a well-to-do Ohio family and had grown up used to luxury and comfort. Unfortunately, a bout of typhoid at a young age had stunted her growth, ruined her looks and left her bald. Inevitably this severely dented her chances of finding a suitable and respectable partner. Bored and disillusioned, she eventually stormed out of the family home at the age of 25 in search of a new life. She found little more than poverty and, after an ill-fated relationship with astrologer William Chaney, she fell pregnant with Jack. William Chaney rapidly disappeared and Flora was in a tight corner. Salvation came when she met John London, a Civil War veteran with a kind heart and ailing health. The pair married, but Flora's wilful, grasping personality ensured they would not be happy for long. She longed for the wealth and respectability she had enjoyed in her youth and bullied John into one poor business venture after another. Despite John setting up a successful smallholding, the London household was constantly overreaching itself financially and found itself gradually sliding into poverty. From a very early age, Jack was sent to work for a living, undertaking countless dreary jobs before and after school. Newspaper rounds, stuffing pickles in a cannery and working in a laundry: it all added up to one long round of drudgery.

Yet Jack was a lively boy, full of daring and with a keen sense of adventure. It was natural that he should be drawn to the sea that lay gleaming at his doorstep, beckoning him on to freedom. The first step was to scrape together enough money to buy a dinghy. By hiding some of his earnings from his mother, London was able to save enough to purchase a little 14ft sailing skiff with which he could explore San Francisco Bay. This was no mean feat, as the bay is as treacherous as it is beautiful. As Jack himself put it: 'No lustier, tougher, sheet of water can be found for small-boat sailing.' This huge natural harbour is a labyrinth of shallows, strong tides, fogs and brutal Pacific swells. It is no place for the novice and London learnt to sail his little vessel at the toughest of schools. With the basics mastered, he proceeded to drum up some extra cash for his ever-demanding family by running errands from ship to shore; whether it was working as a water taxi to some of the ships out at anchor in the bay, running messages or carrying supplies to and fro, London was always grateful for the extra income. All the while he was honing his sailing skills.

Ever since the first of the 49ers had passed through San Francisco's Golden Gate en route to the goldfields in 1849, the city had enjoyed a reputation for a certain reckless, lawless romance and wild living. In the 1850s the population of desperate prospectors and ne'er do wells had grown tenfold: lynch mobs roamed the ramshackle streets, and every now and again great swathes of the city would be destroyed by wildfire. The Barbary Coast area, crammed with prostitutes, drunks and thieves, gained a reputation that had barely diminished when Jack first started roaming its streets in the 1890s. Based across the bay in Oakland, he was positioned on the pulsing jugular of San Francisco's seediest suburb. Life was cheap, as the newly arrived Chinese and Italian Immigrants brawled and scrabbled about for their own slice of the American Dream. Young Jack was entranced and his adventurous soul was drawn to the gloomy bars that proliferated on the waterfront. He began to frequent Jonny Heinold's 'Last Chance' saloon, a dark, rundown bar made out of the rotting ribs of a long-forgotten whaling ship, all spit, sawdust and men who reeked of hemp, tar and spirits. It was here that he encountered some of the heroes of the Oakland waterfront; sailors who lived on the margins of society and often used their boats for illicit purposes in order to make ends meet. Jack was particularly entranced by an encounter aboard a sailing vessel by the name of *Idler*, which was rumoured to have operated as an opium smuggler. After ferrying a visitor across to the mysterious vessel, Jack was invited aboard and was immediately drawn into a world as heady and intoxicating to the young boy as the *Idler's* illicit cargo. He later recalled:

> *It was the first sea interior I had ever seen, the clothing smelled musty but what of it? Was it not the sea gear of men? Leather jackets lined with corduroy, blue coats of pilot cloth, sou'westers, sea boots, oil skins. And everywhere was in evidence the economy of space – the narrow bunks, the swinging tables, the incredible lockers. There were the tell tale compass, the sea lamps in their gimbals, the blue backed charts carelessly rolled and tucked away. The signal flags in alphabetical order, and a mariner's dividers jammed into the woodwork to hold a calendar. At last, I was living.*

Jack was clearly spellbound by the romance of the mariner's life and it is hardly a surprise that shortly after this encounter, he joined up with Oakland's desperate band of oyster pirates. The oyster pirates were very much a byproduct of the wanton avarice that was sweeping through North America during the late 1800s. This was a period branded by the novelist and satirist Mark Twain as America's 'gilded age' for beneath a veneer of glittering wealth, the rest of the country laboured, often in extreme poverty. Capitalism was king, and America was rapidly becoming a country divided between the haves and the have-nots. Jack fell firmly into the latter camp but he had sufficient fire in his belly to ensure that he was willing to redress the situation by any means available. In the oyster pirates, he saw an opportunity. San Francisco Bay was blessed with a wealth of marshlands and shallows, which were the ideal breeding ground for oysters. Traditionally the farming of the foreshore had been considered a public right, but gradually the richest areas had been leased out by landowners and were in the hands of private companies, who were very possessive of their investment. In turn, local fishermen, deprived of a valuable income stream, showed no compunction in raiding the oyster beds. These renegade fishermen became known as the oyster pirates and were often perceived as local heroes in the Oakland area due to the controversial manner in which the fishing grounds had been taken from the people. The risks of this pursuit were high, for the oyster fisheries had soon cottoned on to what was going on, and guards and watchmen were posted. The penalty for getting caught was often a bullet in the back or a lengthy stretch in San Quentin Prison. Yet the lure for young London was irresistible, as he later explained:

> *I wanted to be where the winds of adventure blew. And the winds of adventure blew the oyster pirate sloops up and down San Francisco Bay, from raided oyster-beds and fights at night on shoal and flat, to markets in the morning against city wharves, where peddlers and saloon-keepers came down to buy. Every raid was a felony. The penalty was state imprisonment, the stripes and the lockstep. And what of that! The men in stripes worked a shorter day than I. And behind it all, behind all of me with youth a-bubble, whispered Romance, Adventure.*

Fired up by his youthful exuberance, Jack persuaded one of his childhood mentors to stump up the $300 required for him to purchase an oyster sloop, the *Razzle Dazzle*. At the age of fifteen, he set about a new life as an oyster pirate. If the risks of the trade were high, so were the rewards and in a single successful night as an oyster pirate, Jack could earn as much as he would in a month or more of working in a cannery. He was soon able to pay off his $300 debt and also had plenty of spare cash for his family. In addition, there were more than enough risks associated with this hazardous trade to satisfy the youngster's thirst for adventure. In fact, he immediately fell foul of French Frank, the very man he had purchased *Razzle Dazzle* from. It appears that when London bought the sloop, he inherited her crew and this included a young girl called Mamie, who had earned the nickname 'The Queen of the Oyster Pirates'. French Frank was in love with this girl and was horrified when Mamie proceeded to seduce the new owner of *Razzle Dazzle*. According to London, he was taken aside by Whisky Bob, another member of the oyster pirates, and warned as follows:

Whisky Bob got me aside a moment. 'Keep your eyes open,' he muttered. 'Take my tip. French Frank's ugly. I'm going up river with him to get a schooner for oystering. When he gets down on the beds, watch out. He says he'll run you down. After dark, any time he's around, change your anchorage and douse your riding light. Savve?'

London did just that, and when he did finally encounter French Frank, he saw him off thus:

I stood on the deck of the Razzle Dazzle, *a cocked double-barrelled shotgun in my hands, steering with my feet and holding her to her course, and compelled him to put up his wheel and keep away.*

Many of his adventures in this esoteric trade are described picturesquely in his short story *The Cruise of the Dazzler,* a book that was aimed at youngsters, but can easily be appreciated by sailors of any age, as the narrative skims along with the ease and elegance of his former command. Much of the book is fiction, loosely based on fact, focusing on the adventures of the wild but kindly Frisco Kid, who bears more than a passing resemblance to London himself, and the well-to-do Joe Horton, a runaway who can't bear to be in school.

The description of the some of the pirate fleet gives a good insight into the boat he owned, while his whole relationship with the sea is perfectly encapsulated in this description:

There were four boats, and from where he sat he could make out their names. The one directly beneath him had the name Ghost *painted in large green letters on its stern. The other three, which lay beyond, were called respectively* La Caprice, the Oyster Queen, *and the* Flying Dutchman.

Each of these boats had cabins built amidships, with short stovepipes projecting through the roofs, and from the pipe of the Ghost *smoke was ascending. The cabin doors were open and the roof-slide pulled back, so that Joe could look inside and observe the inmate, a young fellow of nineteen or twenty who was engaged just then in cooking. He was clad in long sea-boots which reached the hips, blue overalls, and dark woolen shirt. The sleeves, rolled back to the elbows, disclosed sturdy, sun-bronzed arms, and when the young fellow looked up his face proved to be equally bronzed and tanned.*

All the romance of Joe's nature stirred at the sight. That was life. They were living, and gaining their living, out in the free open, under the sun and sky, with the sea rocking beneath them, and the wind blowing on them, or the rain falling on them, as the chance might be.

Oyster poaching in itself was something of an art. The little vessels would glide stealthily into the oyster grounds under cover of darkness, all running gear well oiled to ensure that no creaking block or squeaking pintle should betray them, navigation lights extinguished and the crew tiptoeing around as they handled sail. At the helm, skippers always kept one eye on where they were going and a weather eye out for the authorities. Sometimes skiffs with heavily muffled oars were used to land on the flats at low tide in order to pick the oysters by hand, at other times the sloops themselves towed dredges in order to pull up the oysters, which were then sorted on deck. This is tough enough work but bear in mind that San Francisco Bay has strong tides and is prone to severe fogs that can sweep in with little warning. Add in to that equation that the pirates were generally working in the dead of night and sailing their unpowered craft across shallows and bars, all the while trying to ensure that they were not detected, and you have some idea of the risks these sailors endured in order to bring home a catch. In *The Cruise of the Dazzler*, London has the French skipper sum up the unique relationship that these men gained with the bay itself:

'I feel ze tide, ze wind, ze speed,' he explained. 'Even do I feel ze land. Dat I tell you for sure. How? I do not know. Only do I know dat I feel ze land, just like my arm grow long, miles and miles long, and I put my hand upon ze land and feel it, and know dat it is there.'

This was true seamanship, and there is little doubt that London's skills as a sailor were honed by this experience in a manner that few modern sailors would dare to imagine. It is telling that *The Cruise of the Dazzler* concludes with a hair-raising escape from pursuing authorities by cutting across a shallow, storm-lashed bar to safety. Truly, London was living the macho life that he had aspired to, and he gloried in it in later years when he recalled:

> *There were the times I brought the* Razzle Dazzle *in with a bigger load of oysters than any other two-man craft; there was the time when we raided far down in Lower Bay, and mine was the only craft back at daylight to the anchorage off Asparagus Island; there was the Thursday night we raced for market and I brought the* Razzle Dazzle *in without a rudder, first of the fleet, and skimmed the cream of the Friday morning trade; and there was the time I brought her in from Upper Bay under a jib, when a rival burned my mainsail.*

For all his successes, the trade was always going to be a tenuous one and competition from other poachers was starting to put a squeeze on the young pirate. Troubles reached a head when his vessel was set on fire by a rival crew. From hereon Jack was compelled to work on someone else's sloop, and he chose the wildest and most daring character of them all, a youngster by the name of 'Scratch' Nelson whose *Reindeer* was noted for her sailing qualities, as Jack recalled:

> *I have never regretted those months of mad devilry I put in with Nelson. He COULD sail, even if he did frighten every man that sailed with him. To steer to miss destruction by an inch or an instant was his joy. To do what everybody else did not dare attempt to do, was his pride. Never to reef down was his mania, and in all the time I spent with him, blow high or low, the* Reindeer *was never reefed. Nor was she ever dry. We strained her open and sailed her open and sailed her open continually. And we abandoned the Oakland water-front and went wider afield for our adventures.*

It was during this relatively happy period of his life that Jack first became fully acquainted with alcohol. It was a relationship that was to bedevil him for the rest of his days and inspire his damning memoir *John Barleycorn*, which speaks both with fondness and disgust of the regular binges that took place in the 'Last Resort'. He later estimated that at one point he was drunk for a full three-week stretch. Perhaps the biggest wake-up call for Jack came after a very heavy session when, late at night and utterly intoxicated, he fell asleep on a jetty and unwittingly rolled into the waters of the Carquinez Strait, which runs out of the Suisun Bay. At certain points of the tide, this is a regular mill race, and there was little for it but to go with the flow, as Jack later recalled:

> *I was borne away by the current. I was not startled. I thought the misadventure delightful. I was a good swimmer, and in my inflamed condition the contact of the water with my skin soothed me like cool linen. Some maundering fancy of going out with the tide suddenly obsessed me. I had never been morbid. Thoughts of suicide had never entered my head. And now that they entered, I thought it fine, a splendid culminating, a perfect rounding off of my short but exciting career. I, who had never known girl's love, nor woman's love, nor the love of children; who had never played in the wide joy-fields of art, nor climbed the star-cool heights of philosophy, nor seen with my eyes more than a pin-point's surface of the gorgeous world; I decided that this was all, that I had seen all, lived all, been all, that was worth while, and that now was the time to cease.*
>
> *Next I discovered that I was very weary and very cold, and quite sober, and that I didn't in the least want to be drowned. I could make out the Selby Smelter on the Contra Costa shore and the Mare Island lighthouse. I started to swim for the Solano shore, but was too weak and chilled, and made so little headway, and at the cost of such painful effort, that I gave it up and contented myself with floating, now and then giving a stroke to keep my balance in the tide-rips which were increasing their commotion on the surface of the water. And I knew fear. I was sober now, and I didn't want to die. I discovered scores of reasons for living. And the more reasons I discovered, the more liable it seemed that I was going to drown anyway.*

Daylight, after I had been four hours in the water, found me in a parlous condition in the tide-rips off Mare Island light, where the swift ebbs from Vallejo Straits and Carquinez Straits were fighting with each other, and where, at that particular moment, they were fighting the flood tide setting up against them from San Pablo Bay. A stiff breeze had sprung up, and the crisp little waves were persistently lapping into my mouth, and I was beginning to swallow salt water. With my swimmer's knowledge, I knew the end was near. And then the boat came – a Greek fisherman running in for Vallejo.

This sobering incident seems to have ushered in a sort of new beginning for London: after a brief spell working for the fisheries authority trying to catch the very group of felons he had once worked with, Jack quit the oyster pirates for good. It was time to start a new chapter and, inevitably, London turned to the sea.

By now he was 17 and determined that he needed a deep-water passage to satisfy his lust for adventure. Using his waterfront contacts, he secured a berth aboard the sealing schooner, *Sophia Sutherland,* bound for the Northern Pacific, Japan, and the Bering Sea. Sealing was, in every sense, a different kettle of fish from life as an oyster pirate and, although it was legal, it was still a brutal and often tenuous existence. Sealers could be away from home for months at a time; a group of men all trapped together within the confines of a small ship. The *Sophia Sutherland* was a handsome three-masted schooner 90ft in length. The crew was divided into the hunters who were generally idle until the sealing grounds were reached and the sailors who ran the boat and handled the small narrow boats, or dories that were used for sealing once the grounds were reached.

With typical boldness, Jack signed up as an able seaman for the trip. The usual rank for a youngster was either ship's boy or ordinary seaman, but despite never having sailed beyond the Golden Gate, London bullied the captain into awarding him the higher rank. This, he knew, would lead to confrontation with some of the older hands but Jack, young and eager, was determined to make a good show of it.

I was an able seaman. I had graduated from the right school. It took
no more than minutes to learn the names and uses of the few new ropes.
It was simple. I did not do things blindly. As a small-boat sailor I had
learned to reason out and know the why of everything. It is true, I had to
learn to steer by compass, which took maybe half a minute; but when it
came to steering full-and-by and close-and-by, I could beat the average
of my shipmates, because that was the very way I had always sailed.
Inside fifteen minutes I could box the compass around and back again.
And there was little else to learn during that seven-months cruise, except
fancy rope-sailorizing, such as the more complicated lanyard knots and
the making of various kinds of sennit and rope-mats.

Given his indomitable confidence it is perhaps unsurprising that he acquitted himself extremely well and it is also evident that the life of a simple sailor brought him a great deal of contentment. In later years he seemed to look back on these months spent aboard the *Sophia Sutherland* as among his happiest. He was doing a manly job well in a healthy environment without any of his usual distractions of money concerns or alcohol. Nevertheless, he was left under no illusions that this was a tough existence. In the early days of the trip, he fell foul of a huge Swedish sailor by the name of Red John, who resented the youngster's rapid promotion to able seaman. At every turn he tried to make Jack's life a misery by bullying him into carrying out many of the more irksome tasks, which were in reality his own. From the first, Jack was unwilling to carry them out and realised that the only way to deal with this man was head on. Thus, despite Red John's far greater size and strength, London confronted him and when the big Swede took a swing at him with his lethal fists, London jumped on his back and proceeded to gouge at his eyes and face. Red John was completely taken aback by this approach and staggered around the low beamed fo'c'sle, smashing Jack into walls and braining him on the beams. Still London held on, shouting: 'Will y'let me alone? Will you?' Eventually Red John conceded defeat to the tenacious upstart, and from that moment on the *Sophia Sutherland*'s youngest able seaman had the respect of his elders.

Despite this, the voyage was tough and Jack saw life stripped down to the bare essentials. One incident, which unquestionably remained lodged in London's subconscious for many years to come was the death of a fellow seaman who was known as 'the Bricklayer'. This uninspiring character seemed to have almost no interest in anything around him, was a hopeless sailor and was deeply unpopular with his shipmates. Several weeks into the passage, the crew stopped talking to him entirely and London relates his final days and death in his short story, *The Dead Rise Up Never*:

We gave him the silent treatment, and for weeks before he died we neither spoke to him nor did he speak to us. And for weeks he moved among us, or lay in his bunk in our crowded house, grinning at us his hatred and malignancy. He was a dying man, and he knew it, and we knew it. And furthermore, he knew that we wanted him to die. He cumbered our life with his presence, and ours was a rough life that made rough men of us. And so he died, in a small space crowded by twelve men and as much alone as if he had died on some desolate mountain peak. No kindly word, no last word, was passed between. He died as he had lived, a beast, and he died hating us and hated by us. And now I come to the most startling moment of my life. No sooner was he dead than he was flung overboard. He died in a night of wind, drawing his last breath as the men tumbled into their oilskins to the cry of 'All hands!' And he was flung overboard, several hours later, on a day of wind. Not even a canvas wrapping graced his mortal remains; nor was he deemed worthy of bars of iron at his feet. We sewed him up in the blankets in which he died and laid him on a hatch-cover for'ard of the main-hatch on the port side. A gunnysack, half full of galley coal, was fastened to his feet. It was bitter cold. The weather-side of every rope, spar, and stay was coated with ice, while all the rigging was a harp, singing and shouting under the fierce hand of the wind. The schooner, hove to, lurched and floundered through the sea, rolling her scuppers under and perpetually flooding the deck with icy salt water. We of the forecastle stood in sea-boots and oilskins. Our hands were mittened, but our heads were bared in the presence of the death we did not respect. Our ears stung

and numbed and whitened, and we yearned for the body to be gone. But
the interminable reading of the burial service went on. The captain had
mistaken his place, and while he read on without purpose we froze our ears
and resented this final hardship thrust upon us by the helpless cadaver.
As from the beginning, so to the end, everything had gone wrong with the
Bricklayer. Finally, the captain's son, irritated beyond measure, jerked the
book from the palsied fingers of the old man and found the place. Again
the quavering voice of the captain arose. Then came the cue: 'And the body
shall be cast into the sea.' We elevated one end of the hatch-cover, and the
Bricklayer plunged outboard and was gone.

He remained haunted by the cold, brutal, emotionless manner of the
Bricklayer's departure from this world. It was a theme that he looked at
in depth in *The Sea Wolf,* one of his most successful novels, which draws
heavily on his experiences aboard the *Sophia Sutherland,* exploring the
relationship between the fey young writer Humphrey Van Weyden, who is
effectively kidnapped aboard the sealing schooner *Ghost,* skippered by the
brutal Captain 'Wolf' Larsen. The book explores in great detail the struggle
that clearly went on in London's own mind between his need to make a living
from writing and his great passion for the brutal simplicity of a sailor's life.

Haunted though he was by the death of the Bricklayer, he still took the
dead man's old bunk, which was a more comfortable one than his own,
although this was to have distressing consequences for London when he
stood his watch on deck that night. The vessel was hove to in rough seas and
it was traditional in these circumstances to only have one man on watch.
The night was wild, with great ragged clouds racing across the moon and, in
this solitude, Jack's imagination began to run riot. Soon, he was convinced
he could perceive a shadowy wraith flitting around forward, 'There, in the
dim light, where we had flung the dead man overboard, I had seen a faint
and wavering form. Six-feet in length it was, slender, and of substance so
attenuated that I had distinctly seen through it the tracery of the fore-rigging.'
The battle between Jack's steadfast reason and terror of this ghost went on
for some time, until, finally he plucked up the courage to confront the wraith

and, armed with a knife, he went forward, only to discover that it was a trick of the moonlight playing on the rigging and sails.

After a brief stop in the Bonin Islands off the coast of Japan, the *Sophia Sutherland* headed north to the Siberian coast to carry out her bloody trade. Sealing was a fascinating art in itself, which involved a good deal of risk. Every day the schooner would drop off dories, each loaded with a rower or 'puller' and a hunter armed with a shotgun. Jack was a rower and would have needed all of his strength to prove himself equal to the job. The schooner would then drop down several miles to leeward of its boats and wait to pick them up as evening fell. The icy sea was often rough, fogs could form quickly and by the end of the day, the dory, loaded down with seals, would become a liability to handle. Both oarsman and hunter lived with the constant threat of becoming permanently separated from the mother ship, which almost inevitably meant death. Once safely back aboard, sailors and hunters engaged in an orgy of blood and guts as the seals were skinned and salted down. This was the first step in a transformation from living creature to a fashionable piece of couture for the fine ladies of New York, Paris and beyond.

London described the work with relish: 'The deck was a slaughter-house, week in and week out ... We kept up a lively competition to see who would have the biggest number of skins salted down at the close of the season. It was wild, heavy work off the coast of Siberia, with no let-up weeks on end.'

Despite the nature of the work, London was truly in his element and there is little doubt that his experiences of the weeks with only dark sea and infinite heaven for company had a profound effect on his life and cemented his romantic view of the ocean.

In all, the *Sophia Sutherland* was away for three months and returned to San Francisco in 1893. London noted with some sadness that many of his shipmates were promptly fleeced out of their pay by the many crimps and criminals waiting in San Francisco on the lookout for any sailor out on a spree. By the end of a week's shore leave, many of the crew were once again penniless and had already signed up for the next voyage. Not so London, who dutifully handed over most of his earnings to his impoverished parents. In his absence, things had gone from bad to worse for his family. America was in the grip of a financial slump, and to exacerbate things the last shred of John London's health had failed and he was essentially an invalid. Jack became the main breadwinner for the family. He dutifully went back to work in a jute mill, working for ten hours a day for a pittance. The contrast between the wild freedom of the sea and the drudgery of life ashore could not have been starker.

Yet for some time London turned his back on sailing. No doubt he was further sobered by the news that most of his former Oakland Wharf associates were either dead or imprisoned. His closest friend 'Scratch' Nelson was in his grave, having been riddled with bullets following a barroom brawl. Jack's determination to make a fresh start was further bolstered by an unexpected windfall; after returning from the Pacific, he had written down his adventures in the great storm off the coast of Japan. Encouraged by his mother, he had decided to enter this piece into a writing competition and was elated when he won the first prize of $25. Even at the tender age of 17, Jack was more than capable of bringing the terrifying beauty of the storm alive:

It was on deck that the force of the wind could be fully appreciated, especially after leaving the stifling fo'castle. It seemed to stand up against you like a wall, making it almost impossible to move on the heaving decks or to breathe as the fierce gusts came dashing by. The schooner was hove to under jib, foresail and mainsail. We proceeded to lower the foresail and make it fast. The night was dark, greatly impeding our labor. Still, though not a star or the moon could pierce the black masses of storm clouds that obscured the sky as they swept along before the gale, nature aided us in a measure. A soft light emanated from the movement of the ocean. Each mighty sea, all phosphorescent and glowing with the tiny lights of myriads of animalculae, threatened to overwhelm us with a deluge of fire. Higher and higher, thinner and thinner, the crest grew as it began to curve and overtop preparatory to breaking, until with a roar it fell over the bulwarks, a mass of soft glowing light and tons of water which sent the sailors sprawling in all directions and left in each nook and cranny little specks of light that glowed and trembled till the next sea washed them away, depositing new ones in their places. Sometimes several seas following each other with great rapidity and thundering down on our decks filled them full to the bulwarks, but soon they were discharged through the lee scuppers.

No doubt his success in getting the piece published spurred the youngster on and, determined to better himself, he set about putting himself through high school, despite the fact he was now four years older than his classmates. After a brief stint back at school, he crammed for the entrance exams to Berkeley University and passed with distinction. All this time he was still paying his way through odd jobs, and after four months of living a double life of student and wage slave, he was forced to quit and return to a full-time job in a laundry.

Yet he was far from beaten and his next adventure was just around the corner. This time it was not the call of the sea he answered, but the call of the wild. In 1896 gold was discovered in the barren wastelands of the Yukon in Northern Canada. By 1897, gold fever had taken full grip and hopefuls travelled from all over the world in search of untold and generally elusive wealth. Among them was Jack London. Although he barely found a speck of gold, his adventures in this harsh white wasteland left him more determined than ever to become a writer. He was fortunate, for the American public was hungry for stories of exploits from the goldfields and his subsequent narration of these adventures for various magazines and journals helped him to make a name for himself. In the meantime, he married Bess Maddern, a lady he liked but certainly did not love, and they settled down to have a family.

Everything was to change when he scored his big breakthrough with the publication of *The Call of the Wild*. This novel based around the Yukon brought him fame and fortune. From hereon the man who always relished the simple pleasures of working with his hands would make his living pushing a pen. The next time he contemplated the sea, it would be not to support himself and his family but from the privileged position of a yachtsman. It is telling that his first act on hitting the big time was to purchase *Spray*, a small yacht in which he explored some of his old oyster-raiding haunts from the new perspective of a wealthy man. Sailing around San Francisco was not London's only use for the *Spray*: he also used her snug cabin to seduce a number of ladies from the Bohemian set he had begun to hang around with as a successful writer. This fact underlines that, despite Bess bearing Jack two daughters, all was not well with their relationship. Jack had married Bess in order to prove his theory at the time that it was better to make a cold-headed decision on finding a partner based on compatibility than forging a match based on passion and true love. Whatever the merits of this theory, Jack seemed hell-bent on proving himself wrong at the expense of his wife. Jack and Bess skirted around this issue until he met Charmian Kitteridge, a vivacious lady some five years his senior. Like Jack, she was red blooded, bold and adventurous. She was more than a match for him whether they were sparring verbally or indulging in a spot of boxing, a hobby the pair enjoyed greatly. The couple embarked on a passionate affair and the ultimate conclusion was Jack's permanent separation from Bess.

While all of this was going on, Jack was completing his second novel, *The Sea Wolf*, in which he returned to his first love, the sea. The tale leans heavily on Jack's own adventures on the *Sophia Sutherland* for its inspiration, and his new romance with Charmian certainly influenced the second part of the book, which features a rather nauseating romance, written in such a prudish and hidebound fashion that it almost ruins the latter stages of the book. In Jack's defence, he was utterly hemmed in by the social mores of the period and it is doubtful that a publisher would have sanctioned any of the kind of fiery romantic prose that Jack was certainly more than capable of putting together on this subject.

Charmian's influence was to be even more profound when it came to London's next seafaring adventure:

It began in the swimming pool at Glen Ellen [London's home at the time]. Between swims it was our wont to come out and lie in the sand and let our skins breathe the warm air and soak in the sunshine. Roscoe [Eames, Charmian's uncle] was a yachtsman. I had followed the sea a bit. It was inevitable that we should talk about boats. We talked about small boats, and the seaworthiness of small boats. We instanced Captain Slocum and his three years' voyage around the world in the Spray.

We asserted that we were not afraid to go around the world in a small boat, say forty feet long. We asserted furthermore that we would like to do it. We asserted finally that there was nothing in this world we'd like better than a chance to do it. 'Let us do it,' we said ... in fun.

Then I asked Charmian privily if she'd really care to do it, and she said that it was too good to be true. The next time we breathed our skins in the sand by the swimming pool I said to Roscoe, 'Let us do it.'

I was in earnest, and so was he, for he said: 'When shall we start?'

The reference to Captain Slocum is interesting: in 1899, Joshua Slocum had kick-started what we now know as 'blue water cruising' by sailing single-handed around the world on his 36ft ketch, *Spray*. London was clearly inspired by his adventures – the name of his own yacht at the time clearly illustrates this – and it played a big part in his decision. There was more, however: as always it boiled down to London's persistent plea that a life of adventure was truly living and everything else was just a slow death. He explained:

There is also another side to the voyage. Being alive, I want to see, and all the world is a bigger thing to see than one small town or valley. We have done little outlining of the voyage. Only one thing is definite, and that is that our first port of call will be Honolulu. Beyond a few general ideas, we have no thought of our next port after Hawaii. We shall make up our minds as we get nearer, in a general way we know that we shall wander through the South Seas, take in Samoa, New Zealand, Tasmania, Australia, New Guinea, Borneo, and Sumatra, and go on up through the Philippines to Japan. Then will come Korea, China, India, the Red Sea, and the Mediterranean. After that the voyage becomes too vague to describe, though we know a number of things we shall surely do, and we expect to spend from one to several months in every country in Europe.

Thus the decision was made to build a brand new vessel, *Snark*, with the express intention of sailing around the world. Named after one of Lewis

Carroll's nonsense poems, she was a 44ft-long ketch that would be the last word in cruising design, featuring an early petrol engine for auxiliary power and promising to be extremely comfortable. Such a craft was ideal for cruising the world, or so it seemed.

From the start, the project seemed almost cursed. It didn't help that London was trying to get the vessel built in the aftermath of the San Francisco earthquake of 1906. The city had been devastated and one of the effects of the rebuild was that materials and tradesmen were in extremely short supply. London found himself facing endless delays and extortionate fees for basic work to be carried out. It didn't help that he chose the aforementioned Roscoe Eames, Charmian's uncle, to oversee the project. Eames proved himself to be utterly incompetent and did a great deal to hamper work on the *Snark*. London wanted everything on the yacht to be of the best possible quality, yet under Eames' supervision the vessel's frames were laid up in pine rather than oak, making the yacht fundamentally weaker and therefore less seaworthy. Many other aspects of the fitting-out were botched and all the while the cost of building the *Snark* soared beyond expectation. The press started to nickname the boat 'London's folly'.

It is a scenario that almost anyone who has commissioned a new yacht will identify with and *Snark* was months overdue when she was finally launched. Even then things went far from smoothly: shortly after the launch, the Londons and their entourage took the *Snark* for a test sail and were well satisfied. The yacht was then left under the watchful eye of crewmember Martin Johnson. Unfortunately during the night the *Snark* drifted and became trapped between two large lumber scows that were also at anchor and which dragged down on to the yacht during the night. The *Snark* was severely crushed in the middle of this sandwich and her hull was seriously distorted and leaking heavily by the time she was pulled back out of the water at the boatyard. At this point, further catastrophe occurred; as the yard workers were lowering the vessel back into the water following her repair job, the slings they were using to lower her into the water parted, and the yacht was unceremoniously dumped into the mud of Oakland Harbour. In the process, the mountings for the much-vaunted engine sheared and this was left totally disconnected and disabled. London was utterly exasperated. By now, the endless delays and London's own high profile were turning his vessel and his dream into a laughing stock. San Francisco newspapers would run snide daily bulletins proclaiming: 'The Snark will sail ... Soon.' Ultimately he took drastic and rather reckless measures: lashing down the useless engine and staunching *Snark*'s leaky hull as best he could, London and his entourage departed San Francisco for Hawaii with the vessel in bits. It seemed the only way to escape.

In addition to London and Chairman, now his wife, *Snark* carried Roscoe Eames as skipper. Quite how Jack mustered the patience to bear this incompetent has not been recorded, but it must have come as little surprise when it was discovered that Eames could not even navigate. The crew was completed by London's personal assistant Nakata, a chef named Martin Johnson, and another deckhand. From the first the trip was fearful: the vessel leaked dreadfully and the supposedly watertight tanks containing all of the petrol for her useless engine also leaked, meaning that the boat reeked of petrol and sloshed her flammable liquid around with every roll and scend. The *Snark* soon encountered high winds and at this point it was discovered that the wretched craft could not be persuaded to heave to. This was a real blow, as in heavy weather it is very important for a boat to lie safely with her bows to the oncoming seas. All of the crew were fearfully sick and became frightened for their lives. London remained cool, however. In his memoirs of the voyage, Martin Johnson recalls that his own nerve gave out after several days of terrible battering by the seas. He confided his fears in London, who replied: 'Nonsense Martin, we're only two miles from land at present.' When Martin asked where the land he spoke of was, London replied with admirable *sang froid*: 'Straight down, Martin, Straight down.'

Eventually, *Snark* emerged from the storm and the crew resumed their haphazard progress to Hawaii, teaching themselves navigation and succumbing to frequent bouts of seasickness as they went. To everyone's surprise, the island of Oahu was finally located and *Snark* was once again put in the hands of the repair men. At this point Roscoe Eames was finally dismissed after again neglecting to maintain the vessel. A new captain was appointed – a convicted murderer as it happened. From here, *Snark* made the lengthy and hazardous voyage to the Marquesas. It was typical of Jack's devil-may-care approach to sailing that he chose to make such a trip, for it was popular knowledge that to run from Hawaii to the Marquesas was folly, as you were obliged to go against the prevailing winds and currents. The trip was therefore a trying one for the crew of the *Snark;* Captain Warren distinguished himself by trying to throttle the cook for allegedly stealing his favourite pot of honey, and tensions cannot have been soothed when they ran out of water after one crewmember managed to carelessly empty most of their supply into the bilges. After several days of extreme thirst, the tanks were replenished following a torrential rainstorm and normality returned. *Snark* was finally anchored Taiohae Bay on the island of Nuku Hiva after a truly epic passage of 60 days. This was a magical moment for Jack for this was the island where Melville's legendary novel *Ty-pee* was set (see pages 233–238). This autobiographical tale of two sailors who desert their whaling ship and take refuge in the savage valley of Ty-pee was one of the books that had been pivotal in inspiring the young London to go to sea. The thrill of making the fabled island aboard his own yacht was great, and was only matched by the sadness and disappointment in discovering that the populace of Ty-pee Valley had been all but wiped out since Melville's time by western diseases such as typhoid and tuberculosis. As Charmian noted, 'It is as if a curse had fallen upon it spreading over it a choked jungle of burao, damp and unwholesome, on the edges of which, near the river, unkempt grass houses stand upon the lordly pae-paes of decayed affluence.'

The Londons must have made quite an impression on what remained of the islanders and the colonials living there, for they took to swanning around in Japanese kimonos, which must have looked most curious to all, although doubtless they were very cool in the hot climate. From Nuku-Hiva, the *Snark* headed for the Paumotus, or Dangerous Islands, and just as Stevenson in the *Casco* had conspired to get hopelessly lost (see page 317), so too did the *Snark*, for the low atolls of the Paumotus are as alike as belaying pins and extremely hard to tell apart. In addition, cross currents make them exceedingly difficult to navigate with any great accuracy without a GPS. Soon Captain Warren, *Snark*'s navigator, was totally befuddled and it did not help that he was the sort of pig-headed old mariner who would not admit he was wrong. After many, many hours of drifting about and arguing, Jack took the decision to head straight to Tahiti, where he had mail waiting.

The maddening nature of this exploit was later adapted to form the story of *The Seed of McCoy*, which featured in Jack's *South Sea Tales* and is the true story of the large four-masted barque, *Pyrenees*, which turned up off Pitcairn Island with its cargo on fire. Her captain was searching for a beach to run his vessel ashore, with an eye to salvage once her cargo had burned, and enlisted the help of one McCoy, a distant relative of one of the *Bounty*'s mutinous crew, who settled on Pitcairn. The story essentially relates the extreme difficulty of making one of these awkward atolls and the *Pyrenees*, laden with a fiery cargo, endures all manner of close calls before finally coming to rest on the pristine sandy beach of an atoll.

Leaving the Paumotus untouched in her wake, *Snark* blazed a trail through the islands of the South Pacific, which these days are familiar to many cruising yachtsmen: Tahiti, the Society Islands and Samoa are all relatively mainstream destinations, but back then the London entourage were deep in the heart of unknown territory. Tensions were now building between the crew and the irascible Captain Warren. One of the hands had jumped ship in Tahiti, having had enough of the skipper's temper, and Jack was beginning to lose patience with him, as Charmian relates after a bungled attempt at anchoring in Pago-Pago, Samoa:

And here we are, disgusted, and keenly disappointed with our messy arrival in Pago Pago, after our bright beginnings. Jack said gloomily: 'I really think, when all's said and done, I've got more sailor-pride than all the rest of them put together even if I don't talk about it; and just look at the spectacle we've made of ourselves this morning!' I feel so sorry for him; he spares nothing in order to have things as they should be, and seldom gets what he pays for. And the one and only thing in the world in which he fights for style, is his boat.

This fractiousness culminated in Captain Warren's discharge in Suva, Fiji, by which time the miserable and morose captain had earned the nickname of 'the blight' and was loathed by one and all. His culminating catastrophe was to get hopelessly lost amid a maze of corals and reefs off the coast of Fiji and for many hours it was touch and go as to whether the *Snark* would extricate herself from the trap. Once she did, it was no surprise that Warren was hastily dismissed and was later described by London as: 'So crooked he could not hide behind a corkscrew.' After this, Jack wisely took charge of the *Snark* himself.

The turnover of crew was leading to all kinds of wild rumours back home, with tall tales spreading around that London was the embodiment of Wolf Larsen, captain of *The Sea Wolf*, the sort of brute who treated his crew roughly. London did no such thing, and further refuted the claim in the *Log of the Snark*:

> *When I discharged an incompetent captain, they said I had beaten him to a pulp. When one young man returned home to continue at college, it was reported that I was a regular Wolf Larsen, and that my whole crew had deserted because I had beaten it to a pulp. In fact the only blow struck on the* Snark *was when the cook was manhandled by a captain who had shipped with me under false pretences, and whom I discharged in Fiji. Also, Charmian and I boxed for exercise; but neither of us was seriously maimed.*

As they pressed on into the unknown, they remained haunted by the ghosts of some of Jack's childhood literary heroes. First it was Melville in the Marquesas, then, in Samoa, the Londons made a point of visiting the home of Robert Louis Stevenson, marvelling at the great house that he had built. They were some years too late in paying their visit, for Stevenson had died in 1892 and his wife, Fanny, had sold the house a couple of years later to a German Governor. The group visited his grave, high on the hill above his last home, and Jack murmured, 'I wouldn't have gone out of my way to visit the grave of any other man in the world.'

Still the Londons pressed on, deeper into the unknown. The next destination was to be the Cannibal Islands of the South Pacific. In 1906, many of the inhabitants of these beautiful yet savage islands still knew the taste of human flesh and as the *Snark* threaded her way through the New Hebrides to the Solomon Islands, things rapidly went from the exotic to the plain terrifying. Photos of Jack and Charmian ashore show them mingling with the locals in a friendly manner, but carrying pistols at their waists. This was a very prudent measure and Jack kicked himself for not installing a machine gun aboard the *Snark* as he had originally planned to do.

If one incident illustrates how fraught with risk their lives had become, it is perhaps their adventures aboard the trader *Minota*. *Snark* fell in with this vessel while at anchor off the island of Penduffryn. The vessel was a 'blackbirder'; little more than a glorified slave trader, transporting labour between islands. Her captain, Jansen, invited the Londons to accompany him on a cruise through the Malaitian Islands and the pair eagerly agreed. By now they were deep in the heart of darkness, for it soon came to light that the previous captain of the *Minota* had been murdered by a marauding group of islanders. 'The hatchet-marks were still raw on the door of our tiny stateroom advertising an event of a few months before. The event was the taking of Captain Mackenzie's head', London noted with strange relish. Despite this, the Londons seem to have been not in the least dismayed, and Charmian described their first night aboard the vessel as follows:

> *There was not a single moment of silence on the* Minota *that long sweltering night. And yet it was wonderful to lie there, pistols and extra cartridges under our pillows a rifle apiece alongside us on the couch, realizing the slashing riskiness of our situation. Nothing between us and danger except our wardfulness and our lucky stars.*

Matters took a turn for the worse off the island of Malu in the Solomons. The *Minota* was nosing her way back out into open water through a gap in the reef, when a windshift forced her off her course and, to the horror of everyone, the vessel was hard aground and pounding her hull to pieces in the Pacific swell. Within an instant, the vessel was surrounded by native canoes, as Jack relates:

When the Minota *first struck, there was not a canoe in sight; but like vultures circling down out of the blue, canoes began to arrive from every quarter. The boat's crew, with rifles at the ready, kept them lined up a hundred feet away with a promise of death if they ventured nearer. And there they clung, a hundred feet away, black and ominous, crowded with men, holding their canoes with their paddles on the perilous edge of the breaking surf. In the meantime the bushmen were flocking down from the hills armed with spears, Sniders [rifles], arrows, and clubs, until the beach was massed with them. To complicate matters, at least ten of our recruits had been enlisted from the very bushmen ashore who were waiting hungrily for the loot of the tobacco and trade goods and all that we had on board.*

Squall after squall, driving wind and blinding rain, smote the Minota, *while a heavier sea was making. The* Eugenie *[a fellow blackbirder] lay at anchor five miles to windward, but she was behind a point of land and could not know of our mishap. At Captain Jansen's suggestion, I wrote a note to Captain Keller, asking him to bring extra anchors and gear to our aid. But not a canoe could be persuaded to carry the letter. I offered half a case of tobacco, but the blacks grinned and held their canoes bow-on to the breaking seas. A half a case of tobacco was worth three pounds. In two hours, even against the strong wind and sea, a man could have carried the letter and received in payment what he would have laboured half a year for on a plantation. I managed to get into a canoe and paddle out to where Mr. Caulfield [A missionary friend from Malu] was running an anchor with his whale-boat. My idea was that he would have more influence over the natives. He called the canoes up to him, and a score of them clustered around and heard the offer of half a case of tobacco. No one spoke.*

'I know what you think,' the missionary called out to them. 'You think plenty tobacco on the schooner and you're going to get it. I tell you plenty rifles on schooner. You no get tobacco, you get bullets.'

At last, one man, alone in a small canoe, took the letter.

Three hours from the time our messenger started, a whale-boat, pressing along under a huge spread of canvas, broke through the thick of a shrieking squall to windward. It was Captain Keller, wet with rain

and spray, a revolver in belt, his boat's crew fully armed, anchors and
hawsers heaped high amidships, coming as fast as wind could drive – the
white man, the inevitable white man, coming to a white man's rescue.'

Ultimately, the *Minota* was saved and the Londons survived to sail onward. Yet the incident illustrates just how far they had come and how close to the bone their adventures were. Many of the encounters from this period are related in London's *South Sea Tales*, a collection of short stories which capture more acutely than any other the uneasy beauty of these savage islands and how vital and visceral life was among them. Perhaps most astute are his observations about the unsavoury relationship between the relentlessly avaricious white colonisers, pious yet misguided missionaries, and the local population. This period was probably the high point of the Londons' cruise, for as the *Snark* progressed through the South Sea islands toward Australia, London and his crew began to suffer the ill effects of months at sea in strange lands. Many were laid up with fever and, most disturbingly of all, London's hands became horribly afflicted by a mysterious skin disease. At times they swelled up to twice their normal size, and huge chunks of peeling skin would fall from them. In addition, his toenails grew to such an extent that they were almost as thick as they were long. All of this was gruesome and baffling to the doctors and London, without the use of his hands, was utterly incapable of writing. Jack was further unnerved by a rumour that the crew of his former vessel, the *Sophia Sutherland*, had been completely obliterated in the South Seas around this time by a skin disease rather fittingly known as 'scratch scratch'. Another theory was that he had contracted leprosy from a visit to a leper colony in Molokai, Hawaii in the early stages of the voyage. This proved to be unfounded and the doctors argued it was a stress-related ailment. Nevertheless, London could no longer earn a living at all and he made the difficult decision to take a steamer from the island of Guadalcanal to Sydney, Australia where he and his sickly crew could receive some proper medical attention. After a brief period of convalescing, London was presented with a devastating prognosis. The doctors concluded that life in a tropical climate combined with the basic rations aboard the *Snark* was responsible for his ill health and decreed that

London should return to California in order to regain his vigour. It was an agonising decision for London to have to take, as he was finally forced to make the gut-wrenching choice between his literary career and all the life-affirming challenges that the sea offered. Weakened by illness, he chose the former and turned his back on the cruise. Charmian was devastated, as Jack recalled, 'In hospital when I broke the news to Charmian that I must go back to California, the tears welled into her eyes. For two days she was wrecked and broken by the knowledge that the happy, happy voyage was abandoned.'

The *Snark* was sailed to Sydney by some of the remaining crew and laid up there. She was later sold and remained trading – ironically as a 'blackbirder' – in the South Seas for many years before finally being wrecked off the coast of Vanuatu.

Thus ended one of the most offbeat and pioneering cruises ever. In the process, London had ensured that he would not only be noted as one of the foremost American storytellers of the early twentieth century, but that he would also go down as a yacht-cruising pioneer, who blazed a trail now so well trodden by blue water yachtsmen. Yet for London, the disappointment of not concluding the round the world voyage was severe. His return to land seemed to stifle him and he fell far too easily into a life of heavy drinking and smoking, egged on by his many bohemian friends, acquaintances and hangers on. In his twilight years, he dabbled with yachting again, heading down to his beloved San Francisco Bay aboard a new yacht, *Roamer* and it was aboard her that Charmian and Jack seemed to enjoy some of the happiest and most intimate moments of these latter years of their relationship. It was during one of these trips that he penned the following paean to the joys of sailing:

> *Once a sailor, always a sailor. The savour of the salt never stales. The sailor never grows so old that he does not care to go back for one more wrestling bout with wind and wave. I know it of myself. I have turned rancher, and live beyond sight of the sea. Yet I can stay away from it only so long. After several months have passed, I begin to grow restless. I find myself day-dreaming over incidents of the last cruise, or wondering if the striped bass are running on Wingo Slough, or eagerly reading the newspapers for*

reports of the first northern flights of ducks. And then, suddenly, there is a hurried pack of suit-cases and overhauling of gear, and we are off for Vallejo where the little Roamer lies, waiting, always waiting, for the skiff to come alongside, for the lighting of the fire in the galley-stove, for the pulling off of gaskets, the swinging up of the mainsail, and the rat-tat-tat of the reef-points, for the heaving short and the breaking out, and for the twirling of the wheel as she fills away and heads up Bay or down.

Jack was also particularly thrilled when one of the voyages resurrected one of the ghosts from his oyster pirate days. A trip up an obscure backwater led to an encounter with his old enemy 'French Frank', the jealous former keeper of *Razzle Dazzle*. The aged man was a shadow of his former self, but the meeting prompted more fond reminisces from Jack.

This was 1911. Jack was still only in his late 30s and he had packed in enough adventure to last most a lifetime. This was fortunate, for the shadows were lengthening on his life. He had only three years left to live and he spent much of that time trying to destroy himself and his liver with booze and other drugs with which he had begun to self medicate. His health was failing by this time, which came as a supreme blow to a man who had always viewed himself as almost indestructible. His main problem was, without doubt, alcohol and the litres of rotgut he had consumed in his sailor days down on Oakland Wharf were starting to take their toll on his body. Jack had always suffered from severe bouts of depression and by 1912 he seemed to be plunging headlong into the abyss.

Inevitably it was the call of the great wild open ocean and all the unknown vicissitudes within that pulled him back from the edge and he made one final foray back into the sea. Sensing that he desperately needed to dry out, London realised the best place to do this was aboard a ship. In 1912, he and Charmian undertook a voyage aboard one of the last Cape Horn windjammers, the *Dirigo*, on her voyage from New York to San Francisco, rounding the dreaded Cape Horn along the way. Despite the hardship of the voyage, the Londons enjoyed it greatly and Jack, who had spent a winter deep in the slough of a seemingly neverending hedonistic binge, seemed to rally, writing *Mutiny of the Elsinore* as a result. In addition to this, he laid out the bare bones of another book, *John Barleycorn: an Alcoholic Memoir*. This autobiographical piece was a stinging condemnation of the evils of alcohol and gathered together every single incident of his wild youth to illustrate the dangers of over-consumption. In addition to being deeply entertaining, the book proved to be a huge hit with the prohibitionist movement, who trumpeted Jack as a leader of their campaign to ban alcohol from sale.

The sad reality was that even as he was being lauded for this confessional, London returned to the bottle as soon as he stepped off the decks of *Dirigo*. The trip around Cape Horn proved to be a final futile attempt to escape the inevitable. Two years later, aged 40, London was dead; a combination of heavy living, persistent illness and a cocktail of different medicines combined with booze had wrung the last drop of life out of him. On the night of his death, 22 November 1916, he turned in early, telling Charmian that he was 'absolutely worn out'. He did not wake up from his drug-induced coma. It is telling that the book he put down on that last night was entitled *Around Cape Horn: Maine to California in 1852 by Ship*. His last written words formed a letter to his daughter inviting her to go sailing with him the following weekend. The sea and sailing remained two of his great passions right up to the final stroke of his pen. They always brought out the best in him. Just as the land never ceased to strangle him. So it was that the man to whom adventure was everything had died the most prosaic of deaths, many miles from the sea at his comfortable California ranch. Today, however, we still remember him as one of the few writers who can convey the raw thrill of venturing across oceans and raising mysterious and savage lands over the horizon with exhilarating sharpness. For that alone, Jack London's sailing exploits and the literature that accompanied them deserve to be remembered and these words, written in his later years, form a fitting epitaph.

And if a man is a born sailor, and has gone to the school of the sea, never in all his life can he get away from the sea again. The salt of it is in his bones as well as his nostrils, and the sea will call to him until he dies. Of late years, I have found easier ways of earning a living. I have quit the forecastle for keeps, but always I come back to the sea.

Captain Marryat

A forgotten hero of the Royal Navy

Browse any bookshop in the UK for nautical literature and you will generally find that most of this section is devoted to fictional tales of Nelson's navy and the period of the Napoleonic Wars. The shelves groan with swashbuckling stories of Horatio Hornblower, Lieutenant Ramage and a host of other disturbingly patriotic and worryingly chiselled young men hell-bent on saving the Royal Navy from the fiendish Frenchman. What is curious is that, among these books, you rarely find any publications by Captain Frederick Marryat, even though his stories formed the template for much contemporary naval fiction. Here was not only a writer more witty than any of his successors, but one who understood the navy during this period better than any of his imitators, having served with great distinction as an officer during the Napoleonic era.

The fading of Captain Marryat and his books from the public consciousness is a shame, for his novels on the subject remain as fresh today as they did when they were first published in the 1830s. His ability to bring a naval scene to life is pretty much unparalleled, and his wit remains as relevant as ever. At his peak, he stood alongside Charles Dickens as the most popular novelist of his day, and his writing has entered into our culture: 'It's just six of one and half a dozen of the other' is a phrase coined by Marryat. These days he is largely remembered as a writer of children's literature: *The Children of the New Forest* and *Masterman Ready*, but he was much more than that. He was one of the grandfathers of nautical literature, and many of his successors (Melville, Conrad, and Masefield among others) touched on the profound influence of his books on their own writing.

Before he was a writer, Marryat was a sailor and here his career followed a similar pattern. Despite his heroism afloat – he served bravely in many notable actions of the Napoleonic Wars and also personally saved at least three people from drowning during his naval career – he was never knighted and felt strangely overlooked even in his own lifetime. It is telling that one of his last acts before his death in 1848 was to burst several blood vessels during a particularly violent argument with the Admiralty over this lack of recognition.

If his lack of renown is hard to explain, his life itself is also hard to unravel, for Marryat never wrote a complete autobiography, although he conceded that much of his fiction was reality, thus creating a tangled web of suppositions and intrigue. The bare facts of his upbringing can be sketched out thus: he was born in London in 1792 and came from a family of great wealth: his father, Joseph, was a hugely successful trader, with substantial holdings in the West Indies. His American mother, Charlotte had been a Boston society girl with a reputation for great beauty and had met Joseph while he was travelling abroad. It appears that Frederick's early years were typified by the emotional detachment between parent and child that the English upper classes specialised in. Certainly he had a nanny, and any depiction of family life in his later novels generally portrays the father as a rather distant, cold sort of a chap and the mother as simpering and pathetic.

At a young age he was sent away to a boarding school at Ponders End in Essex, which seemed to specialise in flogging. Young Marryat was clearly something of a free thinker and undoubtedly a bit of a wit, not to mention a troublemaker. Marryat's daughter, Florence, had a crack at her father's biography and described his schooldays:

Learning with great facility, he forgot his tasks with equal readiness and, being of a genial temperament, he preferred play to lessons and was constantly flogged for inattentiveness and idleness.

His master was heard, on more than one occasion, to declare that he and the late Charles Babbage (his classmate) could never come to any good, or be otherwise than dunces, seeing how little heed they paid to his instructions.

The true irony of this statement can only be fully appreciated when you realise that Babbage later went on to become one of the greatest thinkers of his time and is often considered the father of the modern computer. Nevertheless, there is little doubt that Marryat was a hugely disruptive influence at school. One classmate recalled walking in on the youngster to find him balancing on his head, while placidly reading a book, 'dignified but graceful'. When asked what he was up to, Marryat replied: 'Well, I've been trying to learn it for three hours on my feet, but I couldn't, so I thought it might go in easier if I was to learn it on my head.' That kind of attitude was never going to go down particularly well at a Victorian school for gentlemen and it is no surprise that Marryat was almost perpetually running away, generally with the plan of going to sea. In actual fact, his father had little objection to this plan, provided it was done in good time. Frederick was his second son and did not stand to inherit the estate. As such he presented the family with a bit of a dilemma career-wise, particularly as he seemed to be such a loose cannon. Following Frederick's fourth attempt at escape, his father relented and agreed to sign him up as a midshipman in the Royal Navy. Frederick was delighted and turned his back on school without a second thought. He later summed up the whole affair thus:

What fool was it who said that the happiest times of our lives is passed at school? There may, indeed, be exceptions, but the remark cannot be generalised. Stormy as has been my life, the most miserable part of it (with very little exception) was passed at school; and my mind never received so much injury from any scenes of vice and excess in after-life, as it did from the shameful treatment and bad example I met with there.

Marryat felt he had escaped, and was thrilled when his father informed him that he had been able to use his influence in order to attain him a position aboard the HMS *Imperieuse*, a 38-gun frigate. In this he was indeed fortunate, for she was commanded by Thomas Cochrane, who was newly appointed to the ship and a man who was to go down in the annals of naval history. Cochrane was a fiery Scotsman, very charismatic and exceedingly daring. His voyages in the HMS *Speedy, Pallas* and *Arab* had already made his name as a maverick and a man of uncommon dash and dare, and he had left a swathe of devastation in his wake. For Cochrane the thrill of naval action was irresistible and service aboard a ship commanded by him was always going to be an incident-packed affair. In addition to being an excellent captain, Cochrane was the archetypal renegade and his outspoken views were a permanent thorn in the side of the Admiralty. He had already sparked an international incident in 1803 when he had attacked an American merchant ship despite the countries not being at war. This was the forum within which young Marryat was to complete his schooling and, if it was a brutal and dangerous one, it was also rewarding, as Marryat was about to discover.

Before we get to the action, however, it is important to take a look at the state of the Royal Navy itself. Marryat joined in 1806, a watershed year for the service. Three years into the Napoleonic Wars with France, the navy was taking stock following the previous year's glorious victory at Trafalgar in which Nelson, the service's great talisman, had perished. In the process, he had shattered the French Navy and her allies and for the remainder of the war it was largely accepted that Britain enjoyed naval superiority over the French and this was a position that was rarely challenged. Much of the fleet therefore spent their time blockading French ports, keeping the enemy fleet at bay in Toulon and generally waiting for something to happen, which it rarely did. What this did mean was that the coast of France and the Mediterranean as a whole was basically a giant playground for the British Navy, and the main aim of vessels such as the *Imperieuse* was in 'cutting out' or capturing any traders or privateers allied to the French. Not only was this exciting work, it was also very profitable to both captain and crew, who could expect to keep a share of the spoils of any captured vessels.

Despite the clear superiority of British naval power, the service was certainly not without serious faults: In losing Nelson, the navy had lost its most dynamic commander, who was replaced by the more sedate Admiral Collingwood. The service was bloated with some 140,000 men in its employ at the peak of the Napoleonic Wars and many men had been forced, or press-ganged, into the service to make up the numbers. The navy could also be infuriatingly inflexible, while dominance of the waves brought complacency, incompetence and more than a hint of corruption. It was for these reasons that Cochrane opted to stand as MP for Honiton in 1806, the very year Marryat joined his ship. He was infuriated by certain aspects of the service and sought to place some of the bungling practices of the Admiralty under the spotlight. He was successfully elected and, in common with many MPs today, saw nothing unusual in pursuing his full-time job alongside the minor task of helping to run the country. The Admiralty were furious with him.

It was against this backdrop of mutual contempt that Frederick Marryat sallied forth to Plymouth in order to board the *Imperieuse*. He was only 14 years old and as proud as any youngster could be. He arrived in Plymouth and spent his first night in an inn trying on his service uniform as he later recalled:

One of the red-letter days of my life was that on which I first mounted the uniform of a midshipman. My pride and ecstasy were beyond description. I had discarded the school and school-boy dress, and, with them, my almost stagnant existence. Like the chrysalis changed into a butterfly, I fluttered about, as if to try my powers; and felt myself a gay and beautiful creature, free to range over the wide domains of nature, clear of the trammels of parents or schoolmasters; and my heart bounded within me at the thoughts of being left to enjoy, at my own discretion, the very acmé of all the pleasure that human existence can afford.

But to return to my uniform. I had arrayed myself in it; my dirk was belted round my waist; a cocked-hat, of an enormous size, stuck on my head; and, being perfectly satisfied with my own appearance at the last survey which I had made in the glass, I first rang for the chambermaid, under pretence of telling her to make my room tidy, but, in reality, that she might admire and compliment me, which she very wisely did; and

I was fool enough to give her half a crown and a kiss, for I felt myself quite a man.

Thus attired, the young midshipman strutted out to find his ship and blundered straight into the Port Admiral, a Mr Young, who was returning with a group of officers from a court-martial. Here, the young officer was severely rebuked after he failed to touch his hat to Young and it was only after it was clear that the officers were rebuking the greenest officer in the service that he escaped being confined to the *Imperieuse* until she had left port. Smarting from this dressing down, Marryat sought out his captain, although this short stroll was not without further incident as he later recalled:

During the remainder of my walk, I touched my hat to every one I met. I conferred the honour of salute on midshipmen, master's mates, sergeants of marines, and two corporals. Nor was I aware of my over complaisance, until a young woman, dressed like a lady, who knew more of the navy than I did, asked me if I had come down to stand for the borough? Without knowing what she meant, I replied, 'No.' 'I thought you might,' said she, 'seeing you are so damned civil to everybody.' Had it not been for this friendly hint, I really believe I should have touched my hat to a drummer.

Further chastened, he met with Cochrane and shortly afterward was rowed out to HMS *Imperieuse*, which was lying at anchor in Mutton Cove, down on the banks of the River Tamar. If the morning had been a trying one for the youngster, it was about to get worse, for stepping aboard his new vessel, his home for the next few years, he was faced with the grim reality of life aboard a man-of-war. The ship was fitting out and was in a dreadful mess; workmen were hammering oakum into the deck seams and the ship was strewn with wood shavings and general detritus. A recent heavy shower completed the depressing scene and for the first time it occurred to Marryat that perhaps school wasn't such a bad place after all. Nevertheless, he steeled himself and headed below to his new quarters in the midshipman's mess and received another dispiriting blow, which he described as follows:

We descended a ladder, which brought us to the 'tween decks, and into the steerage, in the forepart of which, on the larboard side, abreast of the mainmast, was my future residence – a small hole which they called a berth; it was ten feet long by six, and about five feet four inches high; a small aperture, about nine inches square, admitted a very scanty portion of that which we most needed, namely, fresh air and daylight. A deal table occupied a very considerable extent of this small apartment, and on it stood a brass candlestick, with a dip candle, and a wick like a full-blown carnation. The black servant was preparing for dinner, and I was shown the seat I was to occupy. 'Good Heaven!' thought I, as I squeezed myself between the ship's side and the mess-table; 'and is this to be my future residence? Better go back to school; there, at least, there is fresh air and clean linen'.

The work of fitting out the ship continued for a further three weeks. Eventually, however, Cochrane was piped aboard and the ship prepared to head out to sea. The beginning of the voyage did not augur well for anyone aboard the *Imperieuse*, as Cochrane had returned from a stint in the House of Commons in an utterly foul mood and not without good reason. The Admiralty were thoroughly fed up with him, and his well-directed broadsides at them while he sat in the Commons made them all the more determined to be rid of this troublemaker. Cochrane was therefore ordered to the *Imperieuse* and told he must depart despite the fact that the vessel was some days away from readiness. In vain her captain argued with Admiral Young that he needed more time, but to no avail and Cochrane was eventually compelled to leave in a terrible state of disorganisation: stores were not stowed, rigging was unfinished and many of her guns were not shipped on to their carriages, and those that were had not been lashed to their ringbolts. Early on the morning of departure, a signal gun was fired from the shore, denoting that the *Imperieuse* must sail. Cochrane chose to ignore this and all through the day the signal gun boomed with increasing exasperation, yet it would not be until early evening that Admiral Young had the satisfaction of finally seeing the frigate slip out of the bay. 'Damn his eyes! There he goes at last! I was afraid the fellow should have grounded on his own beef bones before we got him out!' the Admiral was reported to exclaim with some satisfaction. The *Imperieuse* did not go far, and brought up in a bay just outside Plymouth where Cochrane oversaw the loading of powder and ammunition and made extra efforts to ensure all the cannon were lashed down. The weather was already looking menacing and a badly-secured cannon rattling around below decks during a gale could cause untold damage. Besides, what with Marryat and Cochrane himself, there were probably already quite enough loose cannons onboard already.

This hasty departure – and the unnecessary risks that came with it – entailed Marryat's first encounter with the kind of administrative inflexibility and pigheadedness that had already riled Cochrane to such an extent that he was willing to stand as MP. Marryat was less than impressed, particularly when they resulted in near fatal consequences, as he later recalled:

A few hours more would have enabled us to proceed to sea with security, but they were denied; the consequences were appalling, they might have been fatal. In the general confusion, some iron too near the binnacles had attracted the needle of the compasses; the ship was steered out of her course. Midnight, in a heavy gale at the close of the month of November, so dark that you could not distinguish any object, however close, the Imperieuse *dashed upon the rocks between Ushant and the Main.*

The cry of terror which ran through the lower decks; the grating of the keel as she was forced in; the violence of the shocks which convulsed the frame of the vessel; the hurrying up of the ship's company without their clothes; and then the enormous waves which again bore her up and carried her clean over the reef, will never be effaced from my memory.

Our escape was miraculous: with the exception of her false keel having been torn off the ship had suffered little injury; but she had beat over a reef, and was riding by her anchors, surrounded by rocks, some of them as high out of water as her lower yards and close to her. How nearly were the lives of a fine ship's company, and of Lord Cochrane and his officers, sacrificed in this instance to the despotism of an admiral who must be obeyed.

This was a pretty rough – not to mention terrifying – introduction to life aboard a naval vessel and it doubtless didn't help that Frederick suffered from seasickness, which must have made this first night even more of an ordeal; he was unwell, bewildered, and very much out of his depth. Yet he rapidly got to grips with things. As midshipman, he was essentially a trainee officer: separate from the seamen, but still expected to work alongside them in order to learn how to handle a ship correctly. This involved going up the rigging to set sails, general maintenance, and errand running. In addition to this, as a trainee who one day hoped to make the rank of lieutenant, the midshipman would be expected to learn the art of navigation and take command of some of the smaller open boats from time to time. If a midshipman was really fortunate, he might also be asked to take command of a captured prize and bring her to the safety of a neutral port.

As already noted, the midshipman's mess was a bit of a pit and, being filled with as many as ten young gentlemen, it was far from a pleasant or wholesome environment. Bullying was rife and there was a very clear hierarchy, with youngsters having to submit to the 'oldsters' as Marryat described them, going on to depict life as 'severe' and 'demoralising'. He was therefore fortunate that the dominant force within his mess was William Napier, a man who later found fame as a politician and diplomat. At the time when Marryat met him, he was master's mate, a kind of halfway house between midshipman and lieutenant, and in this role he seemed to offer the youngsters some protection.

If Napier helped to keep peace in the midshipman's mess, there was no preventing Lord Cochrane making things extremely interesting on deck. The *Imperieuse* had been dispatched to patrol south-west France where a squadron of naval vessels had been tasked with blockading La Rochelle and the ports surrounding it. It was winter, and this storm-tossed section of Atlantic coastline was a truly intimidating place to operate a ship of war. As a frigate, the *Imperieuse* enjoyed a degree of freedom and was generally despatched to the south on patrols of the coast. She would have endured many hazards on this stormy, unforgiving coast, but Cochrane was undeterred by the weather and Marryat's diary is a litany of attacks and seizures of craft. It was a very educational period for young Marryat: unquestionably he must have been scared at times, for many of the actions were brutal and violent, yet the young sailor was far from dismayed, as this later recollection reveals:

The cruises of the Imperieuse were periods of continual excitement, from the hour in which she hove up her anchor till she dropped it again in port; a day that passed without a shot being fired in anger, was with us a blank day; the boats were hardly secured on the booms than they were cast loose and out again; the yard and stay tackles were for ever hoisting up and lowering down. The expedition with which parties were formed for service; the rapidity of the frigate's movements, night and day; the hasty sleep, snatched at all hours; the waking up at the report of the guns, which seemed the only key-note to the hearts of those on board: the beautiful precision of our fire, obtained by constant practice; the coolness and courage of our captain, inoculating the whole of the ship's company; the suddenness of our attacks, the gathering after the combat, the killed lamented, the wounded almost envied; the powder so burnt into our faces that years could not remove it; the proved character of every man and officer on board, the implicit trust and the adoration we felt for our commander; the ludicrous situations which would occur even in the extremest danger and create mirth when death was staring you in the face, the hair-breadth escapes, and the indifference to life shown by all – when memory sweeps along those years of excitement even now, my pulse beats more quickly with the reminiscence.

Marryat was quickly learning about the harsh reality of war. Life was certainly cheap, but the youngster did not seem to care. Nevertheless, it must have come as something of a relief when the *Imperieuse* made her return to home waters, anchored off Plymouth, and was finally at rest. Marryat was allowed some leave and it was natural that the youngster swaggered home overflowing with tales of bravery, bloodshed and glory. Given that he revelled in the excitement of the service, it was perhaps fortunate that he had accrued a good stock of it, for the *Imperieuse*'s next cruise was singularly devoid of incident.

The problem was that Cochrane had become too preoccupied with politics and, as a result, a Captain Skene was put in charge of the frigate on a temporary basis. His period of command was as uneventful as the preceding cruise had been dramatic and Marryat noted:

> *Our guns were never cast loose or our boats disturbed out of their booms.*
> *This was a repose which was however, rather trying to the officers and*
> *ship's company, who had become accustomed to an active life.*

Skene remained in command for five months, but in September 1807, Cochrane returned and officers and men once more looked forward to relentless action. Down in the mess room, Marryat was being forced to endure action of a different kind, for the arrival of a new midshipman by the name of William Cobbett, son of the famed reformer of the same name, had changed the heretofore peaceful dynamic of the mess, and bullying became severe. Although barely 15, Marryat was already a voluble force within the mess room and he was clearly unafraid to back up his sharp tongue with physical violence if required. He and Cobbett frequently came to blows and much of this long-running battle was recounted in his later works, particularly his first novel, the semi-autobiographical *Frank Mildmay*. One particularly vicious incident involved the cutting of hammock ropes, a foolish prank, which sends the slumbering victim crashing to the deck amid much hilarity. Having fallen victim to Cobbett, Marryat determined to pay back the compliment, but took the further step of ensuring the sharp corner of a trunk was positioned just under Cobbett's head. The consequence of this was that Cobbett was laid up for many days recovering. Marryat was clearly not one to be trifled with.

If the occupants of the mess room had entered into more stormy waters, the same could not be said of the *Imperieuse*, which had been dispatched to the Mediterranean at the head of a convoy of trading vessels. Once the convoy had dispersed without incident, she proceeded to Valetta on the island of Malta to receive further orders. There was much excitement aboard the frigate, for the officers and men were thrilled at the opportunities that awaited them. Considering the amount of damage they had managed to inflict on the storm-tossed Atlantic coast the previous winter, they realised the potential was all the higher in the calmer waters of the Mediterranean. Unfortunately the first serious action they were involved with was an unmitigated disaster.

Cruising along the coast of Corsica, a large, heavily armed polacca, square-rigged on the main but with lateen sails on the fore and mizzen, was spotted cruising the coast. Although she was flying British colours, the officers aboard the *Imperieuse* thought her worthy of further investigation as a possible prize. The weather being calm, several of the frigate's boats were lowered, manned and armed in order to pay the stranger a visit. Marryat was in a boat commanded by William Napier, and it was as they approached that matters turned truly unpleasant. Napier hailed the polacca, asked her business and requested permission for the navy to step aboard and inspect the vessel. The captain of the mysterious ship replied that she was Maltese and therefore an ally but he would not allow any of the men aboard to inspect his ship as he did not believe they were naval officers. This was all the provocation that was required and the men in the boats prepared to board, surging forward with a cheer. They were met with a volley of grapeshot and the air was soon alive with the crackle of gunfire as the *Imperieuse*'s boats ranged alongside. Eager cutlasses slashed through the nettings of the polacca and soon the adversaries were engaged in a desperate hand-to-hand battle as the men of the *Imperieuse* desperately sought to get a footing aboard the stranger. Marryat was in the thick of the action, launching himself on deck to grapple with the errant crew. For ten breathless minutes, which must have seemed to last for hours, blood ran red on the polacca's deck. All the while the sun shone down benevolently on the shimmering sea, the boarded vessel rolling gently in the greasy swell while men aboard her toiled and struggled and died. Ultimately it was the men of the *Imperieuse* who came out on top, but the tally of two dead and thirteen wounded was a high one for a single prize. The price seemed all the higher when it was ascertained that the captured vessel was indeed a Maltese privateer and therefore, at least theoretically, an ally.

Cochrane was dismayed and knew he would have to vindicate himself in front of the court of the Admiralty in Valetta. He was relieved that he had been in the right to attack the vessel when he made enquiries on arriving in Malta and discovered that the polacca was in fact a pirate ship and that there was a bounty of £500 for her capture. He presented this case to Court of the Admiralty, assuming he would be duly praised and rewarded. Unfortunately, the Maltese authorities were notoriously corrupt and a number of members of the court had a financial interest in the polacca and her activities. As a result, Cochrane was fined £500 and left the court even more embittered than before.

Thus chastened, the *Imperieuse* returned to her patrolling, and ranged almost the entire scope of the Mediterranean in her search for prizes and glory. It was the capture of a small trader that was to lead to the next really significant piece of action, as one of the captives aboard hinted that a large French privateer was currently anchored in the Spanish port of Almeria Bay. This vessel had already beaten off the frigate HMS *Spartan* with great loss of life and Cochrane made for the Spanish coast with due haste in order to intercept the ship and exact revenge. In the early hours of 21 February 1808, the *Imperieuse* ghosted into Almeria Bay flying the neutral American flag from her rear mast. The assignment was a tricky one; the port was heavily fortified, with several batteries of guns trained upon the shipping in the bay. In addition to the French privateer, there were five smaller vessels, all armed and hostile to the British. Cochrane dropped his anchor in the midst of these boats and within range of the batteries of Almeria. It was a bold move, and the daring captain took the wise precaution of setting up springs on the anchor chain. These meant that the frigate could be quickly hauled around to allow her guns to be trained on various targets. At the same time her boats were launched, and all were fully prepared for an epic battle. Marryat was in a boat commanded by First Lieutenant Caulfield. This vessel was first away and received the full force of the French broadside as they ranged alongside. Many of Marryat's companions fell back into the boat dead. Immediately, the bay erupted into life with the thunder of cannonballs and the cries of men. The garrison manning the battery was suddenly well aware of the intruders and brought cannon to bear on the *Imperieuse*. The frigate was far from caught unawares, however, and Cochrane used his anchor springs to good advantage, swinging the big frigate back and forth and raking the enemy vessels with shot. This tactic proved highly effective and it was not long before the British were on top. In a mere eight minutes they had overwhelmed their adversaries.

For Marryat, however, the action was extremely brief, for he had been crushed under the weight of men who had fallen back into the boat during that first valiant assault. To his horror, he discovered that he was being suffocated by the corpse of his valiant commander, Caulfield. Badly wounded himself, he passed out at this point and remembered no more. He regained consciousness back on deck, and describes the scene thus:

> *The first moments of respite from carnage were employed in examining the bodies of the killed and wounded. I was numbered among the former, and stretched out between the guns by the side of the first lieutenant and the other dead bodies. A fresh breeze blowing through the ports revived me a little, but, faint and sick, I had neither the power nor inclination to move; my brain was confused; I had no recollection of what had happened, and continued to lie in a sort of stupor, until the prize came alongside of the frigate, and I was roused by the cheers of congratulation and victory from those who had remained on board.*

It was at this point that Marryat's hated adversary, Cobbett, spotted his lifeless body and could not bring himself to be magnanimous, even in the face of death. Gently kicking at the lifeless body, he then exclaimed: 'Here is a young cock that has done crowing! Well, for a wonder, this chap has cheated the gallows.'

Yet the young midshipman was not dead, and Cobbett was in for a rude shock, as Marryat recalled:

> *The sound of the fellow's detested voice was enough to recall me from the grave, if my orders had been signed: I faintly exclaimed, 'You are a liar!'*

which, even with all the melancholy scene around us, produced a burst of laughter at his expense. I was removed to the ship, put to bed, and bled, and was soon able to narrate the particulars of my adventure; but I continued a long while dangerously.

It was indeed some weeks before Marryat had fully recovered from this ordeal and it was shortly after his convalescence that he made the first in a remarkable series of rescues. Marryat was a strong swimmer at a time when many in the navy could not swim at all, so when the cry of 'man overboard!' rang through the ship one day while the *Imperieuse* was anchored off Malta, Marryat did not hesitate to jump in and rescue his shipmate, who turned out to be Cobbett, his hated enemy. The water was warm and the ship was not moving, but Cobbett could not swim and was on the verge of death when Marryat saved him. It was a selfless act for which he was roundly praised. As for Cobbett, the hatchet was well and truly buried and Marryat wrote to his mother: 'From that moment I have loved the fellow as I have never loved before. All my hate is forgotten, I have saved his life.'

The adventures continued thick and fast and much of Marryat's career reads like pure fiction, but it is backed up by Admiralty reports. The next scrape involved a small brig in young Marryat's charge. Cochrane had ranged far and wide in his search for prizes and each time he took one, he had to man it with some of the *Imperieuse*'s crew, already depleted by injury and death at the hands of the enemy. By the time a small brig laden with wine was captured, he had little choice but to give the command to Marryat, and ordered him to sail the vessel back to Gibraltar. The trip turned out to be a catastrophe. Cochrane could only spare Marryat three hands and this was not enough to handle the ship properly. Not that Marryat was worried: 'I was so delighted with my first command, that, I verily believe, if they had only given me a dog and a pig I should have been satisfied', he later recalled.

Once clear of the *Imperieuse*, Marryat shaped a course simply by following the coast, as he had limited navigational knowledge. The freshening wind started to develop into a gale and the crew struggled to take in her upper sails. It was soon clear there would be no means of shortening the big lower sails with so few crew, so the vessel raced on before the gale at breakneck speed. It was unfortunate for Marryat that the prize was loaded with wine, for the sailors soon perceived that here was an excellent opportunity to get drunk and duly broached the cargo. Marryat takes up the story with a dryness clearly not present at the time:

> We got on pretty well till about two o'clock in the morning, when the man at the helm, unable to wake the other two seamen to fetch him a drop of wine, thought he might trust the brig to steer herself for a minute, while he quenched his thirst at the wine-cask: the vessel instantly broached to, that is, came with her broadside to the wind and sea, and away went the mainmast by the board. Fortunately, the foremast stood. The man who had just quitted the helm had not time to get drunk, and the other two were so much frightened that they got sober. We cleared the wreck as well as we could, got her before the wind again, and continued on our course. But a British sailor, the most daring of all men, is likewise the most regardless of warning or of consequences. The loss of the mainmast, instead of showing my men the madness of their indulgence in drink, turned the scale the opposite way. If they could get drunk with two masts, how much more could they do so with one, when they had only half as much sail to look after? With such a rule of three there was no reasoning; and they got drunk, and continued drunk during the whole passage.

It was in this pickled state that the vessel approached Europa Point, the entrance into Algeciras Bay and the safety of Gibraltar. Marryat ordered the anchor to be attached to its hawser and made the fatal mistake of believing his men when they said it had been done. With the wind blowing fresh into the bay, the disabled vessel sped in at a fair pace amid urgent hails from the surrounding craft at anchor to shorten sail post haste. Unfortunately, his inebriated crew were unable to obey this order and the vessel ran on until she collided with a fishing smack. This brought down her foremast and solved the problem of shortening sail. Unfortunately the travails of the young midshipman were not yet over, for his next move was to give the order to let go the anchor, which was done smartly enough by his drunken crew, but it was soon clear that, although they had claimed to have tied the hawser onto the end of it, they not done so. The anchor therefore kissed the mud of Algeciras Bay, and no doubt held well, but the completely dismasted ship, now anchorless, drifted on until she finally came to a standstill by running afoul of a troop ship, whose crew were kind enough to assist, bringing the brig to rest.

Thus ended a disastrous journey and Marryat must have awaited with some trepidation the arrival of the *Imperieuse* and Cochrane. Yet he needn't have worried, for once Marryat had explained himself, his captain was very understanding and actually praised the boy for bringing the boat to safety in the face of such adversity.

It was now 1808 and Marryat had been two years in the service. During that time he had seen more adventure than most saw in a lifetime and could count himself extremely lucky to be alive. Yet there was much more action to come, for in February of that year the French turned on their erstwhile allies, the Spanish, and attempted an invasion of the Iberian Peninsula. In the process, Britain gained a new ally, which Marryat recalled was greeted with disgust by many aboard *Imperieuse*, as it meant there was far less scope for capturing prizes. If this was a loss to some, it meant that the frigate's work became much more varied and Cochrane was to distinguish himself again. His most notable achievement during this period was his service during the siege of Rosas, where he holed up his forces within a fort which was 'little more than rubble' and proceeded to play a key part in holding up the advancing French army for over a month. As Marryat noted: 'In this instance a mere handful of seamen detained the whole French army for more than six weeks. In this long contest we lost only seventeen men of our ship's company killed and wounded.'

Marryat also draws a wonderful picture of Cochrane during this siege as he strolled through the battlefield apparently immune to the many sharpshooters who had been stationed to pick off the British within the fort. Despite the danger, Cochrane did not deem it necessary to increase his pace, to the dismay of Marryat:

I felt bound in honour as well as duty to walk by the side of my captain, fully expecting every moment that a rifle-ball would have hit me where I should have been ashamed to show the scar. I thought this funeral pace, after the funeral was over, confounded nonsense; but my fire-eating captain never had run away from a Frenchman, and did not intend to begin then. I was behind him, making these reflections, and as the shot began to fly very thick, I stepped up alongside of him, and by degrees brought him between me and the fire. 'Sir,' said I, 'as I am only a midshipman, I don't care so much about honour as you do; and therefore, if it makes no difference to you, I'll take the liberty of getting under your lee.' He laughed, and said, 'I did not know you were here, for I meant you should have gone with the others; but, since you are out of your station, I will make that use of you which you so ingeniously proposed to make of me. My life may be of some importance here; but yours very little, and another midshipman can be had from the ship only for asking: so just drop astern, if you please, and do duty as a breastwork for me!'

Cochrane and his men finally quit their stronghold at the fort after most of the port of Rosas had been reduced to ruins and the Spanish forces in the town had surrendered. Nevertheless, the delay caused to the French army would play a key part in how the war played out, as it gave the Spanish a chance to galvanise their forces in Barcelona.

Shortly after this dramatic event, the *Imperieuse* turned her back on the conflict and made her way home to England, dropping the hook in the familiar waters of Plymouth Sound in February 1809 and allowing all aboard a welcome respite from the rigours of war. But this was to be a mere prelude to the final piece of serious action that Marryat would see against the French: the battle of Basque Roads, a skirmish so bewildering that even though it ended in victory for the British, it forced Cochrane to resign his post and led to the Commander, Lord Gambier, being labelled as unfit for his post and court-martialled.

The premise behind the conflict was simple enough: the French fleet had been able to gather together an impressive array of warships, which had joined forces at Rochefort. The size of the fleet gathered was seen as a threat to British national security, and the channel fleet, under the command of Lord Gambier, was despatched to blockade them into the Basque Roads, which is the entrance to Rochefort and was overlooked by the guns of the Ile d'Aix. It was a well-protected haven and the only real risk came from fire-ships being sent into the bay. In order to protect against this, the French had rigged up a boom across the channel entrance, made up of huge pieces of timber lashed together and anchored in place. Lord Gambier declared the barrier impassable. He was therefore happy to sit out to sea and maintain the blockade. This stalemate continued for several weeks, and many senior captains were incensed by Gambier's somewhat passive approach. The decision was therefore taken by the Admiralty to dispatch the *Imperieuse* to the area and see if Cochrane and his men could find a means of breaching the boom and destroying the French fleet. Cochrane's quick mind rapidly saw a way through.

His plan was simple: he proposed to rip apart the barricade with thirteen 'explosion vessels', little more than very primitive floating mines. With the barricade blown, a stream of fire-ships would follow in and wreak destruction on the fleet trapped within. All Cochrane needed was a north-west wind, a favourable tide and the cover of darkness. All these factors conspired in his favour on the night of 2 April, and Marryat volunteered his services for a place in one of the explosion vessels. I can do no better than quote his own account of what ensued:

> The night was very dark, and it blew a strong breeze directly in upon the Isle d'Aix, and the enemy's fleet. Two of our frigates had been previously so placed as to serve as beacons to direct the course of the fire-ships. They each displayed a clear and brilliant light; the fire-ships were directed to pass between these; after which, their course up to the boom which guarded the anchorage was clear, and not easily to be mistaken.
>
> I solicited and obtained permission to go on board one of the explosion vessels that were to precede the fire-ships. They were filled with layers of shells and powder, heaped one upon another: the quantity on board of each vessel was enormous. Another officer, three seamen, and

myself, were all that were on board of her. We had a four-oared gig, a small, narrow thing [nick-named 'a coffin' by the sailors], to make our escape in. Being quite prepared, we started. It was a fearful moment; the wind freshened, and whistled through our rigging, and the night was so dark that we could not see our bowsprit. We had only our foresail set; but with a strong flood-tide and a fair wind, with plenty of it, we passed between the advanced frigates like an arrow. It seemed to me like entering the gates of hell. As we flew rapidly along, and our ships disappeared in the intense darkness, I thought of Dante's inscription over the portals: – 'You who enter here, leave hope behind.'

Our orders were to lay the vessel on the boom which the French had moored to the outer anchors of their ships of the line. In a few minutes after passing the frigates, we were close to it; our boat was towing astern, with three men in it – one to hold the rope ready to let go, one to steer, and one to bail the water out, which, from our rapid motion, would otherwise have swamped her. The officer who accompanied me steered the vessel, and I held the match in my hand. We came upon the boom with a horrid crash; he put the helm down, and laid her broadside to it. The force of the tide acting on the hull, and the wind upon the foresail, made her heel gunwale to, and it was with difficulty I could keep my legs; at this moment the boat was very near being swamped alongside. They had shifted her astern, and there the tide had almost lifted her over the boom; by great exertion they got her clear, and lay upon their oars: the tide and the wind formed a bubbling short sea, which almost buried her. My companion then got into the boat, desiring me to light the port-fire and follow. If ever I felt the sensation of fear, it was after I had lighted this port-fire, which was connected with the train. Until I was fairly in the boat, and out of the reach of the explosion – which was inevitable, and might be instantaneous – the sensation was horrid. I was standing on a mine; any fault in the port-fire, which sometimes will happen; any trifling quantity of gunpowder lying in the interstices of the deck, would have exploded the whole in a moment: had my hand trembled, which I am proud to say it did not, the same might have occurred.

Only one minute and a half of port-fire was allowed. I had therefore no time to lose. The moment I had lit it, I laid it down very gently, and then jumped into the gig, with a nimbleness suitable to the occasion. We were off in a moment: I pulled the stroke oar, and I never plied with more zeal in all my life: we were not two hundred yards from her when she exploded. A more terrific and beautiful sight cannot be conceived; but we were not quite enough at our ease to enjoy it.

The shells flew up in the air to a prodigious height, some bursting as they rose, and others as they descended. The shower fell about us, but we escaped without injury. We made but little progress against the wind and tide; and we had the pleasure to run the gauntlet among all the other fire-ships, which had been ignited, and bore down on us in flames fore and aft. Their rigging was hung with Congreve rockets; and as they took fire they darted through the air in every direction, with an astounding noise, looking like large fiery serpents.

In actual fact, this daring plan was almost scuppered by the indiscipline of those manning the fireships. Marryat refers to having to row back through these ships as they exploded, because the sailors aboard had lost their nerve and abandoned their combustible charges far too soon, leaving them to drift out of control and miss their target. Fortunately, the French vessels within the anchorage panicked at this pyrotechnic display and promptly cut their anchor cables in a desperate attempt to escape the perceived danger. With wind and tide against them, they soon ran afoul of the mudbanks off Rochefort and by morning they were high, dry and helpless as they awaited the flood tide to refloat them. Cochrane saw the opportunity for total destruction of the fleet and proceeded to bring the *Imperieuse* in close in order to rake the French with gunfire. Unfortunately for the captain, repeated requests for backup from Gambier's Channel Fleet, some 14 miles out to sea, were ignored and the *Imperieuse* was actually ordered to return to safety. All aboard the frigate knew that there were only a few hours before the French refloated and were anxious to destroy them in the meantime. To this end, Cochrane took the desperate measure of drifting within range of the French Batteries on the Ile d'Aix and then signalling that he needed help. This finally spurred Gambier to allow Cochrane two frigates, which worked with the *Imperieuse* to destroy several of the French ships. After a couple of hours, however, they were once more called off. As dusk fell the *Imperieuse* reluctantly returned to the main fleet and was promptly despatched back to England. All aboard were utterly infuriated at witnessing the opportunity to obliterate the French fleet being wilfully thrown away.

Back home, the action was initially seen as a roaring success, but soon the outspoken Cochrane made it clear how much more significant the victory should have been. The upshot was that the Admiralty was compelled to court martial Gambier, but it was in the interests of nobody within the Royal Navy to humiliate this high ranking man and, in order to save embarrassment, the Admiralty took the pragmatic route and cleared him of any wrongdoing. In the circumstances, they also thought it wise to dispense with the services of the troublesome Cochrane, who went on to serve in the Chilean and Greek navies and was finally reinstated to the British Navy in 1832.

Marryat's final cruise with Cochrane was evidently as dramatic as anything he had seen before, and there is no doubt that during the three years Marryat worked for him he was well aware that he was rubbing shoulders with one of the greats. Marryat never felt anything other than devotion and admiration for the brilliant commander who became the template for several of his fictional captains in later novels. With Cochrane's departure, some of the fire also left Marryat's life, and the wistfulness for those three glorious years of intense action must have spurred him on in his evocative portrayals of a heroic era.

Marryat's time aboard the *Imperieuse* was also nearly up. His final act aboard was an abortive mission to the Dutch Scheldt that ended in embarrassment for the Admiralty and a bout of Walcheren fever (a combination of malaria and typhoid) for Marryat who was invalided home. This was the end of his service aboard the *Imperieuse*.

It was now the summer of 1809 and, given the incident that had already been crammed in to Marryat's short life, it is hard to believe that he had only just turned 18. By now he was a strongly built lad, certainly more capable of looking after himself than most. He had gone to sea a tearaway and a worry to his family, but the service was moulding him into a reliable officer and a sailor who feared very little. In his personal life there are clear hints that, with his sharp wit, good looks and gentlemanly demeanour, he was something of a ladies man. Sadly any romantic liaisons were carefully expunged from his records by Florence Marryat, his daughter and first biographer.

He was not to receive his promotion to lieutenant until 1813 and spent most of that time in the Caribbean and the US. He initially returned to the Mediterranean aboard the *Centaur*, where he again distinguished himself by jumping overboard to rescue a man who had fallen from aloft. After this, he was solidly occupied on various duties protecting the colonies in the Caribbean and latterly playing a part in the American conflict of 1812, wherein the powerful American frigates cut quite a dash in a number of ship–to–ship battles that made the British Navy question – for the first time in many years – just how effective their officers and ships really were. While stationed in Halifax, Nova Scotia, Marryat yet again swam to the rescue of a man who was drowning in the harbour and for this he received a special commendation.

The most notable incident of these years occurred while he was serving aboard the HMS *Aeolus*, a 40-gun frigate commanded by Captain Townshend. In September of 1811, the *Aeolus* was cruising along the American coast when she was caught up in a hurricane and received such a savage pounding that all seemed lost, for the vessel was pinned over on her beam ends by the sheer power of the wind, and for a time it looked certain that she should founder. It was while the ship and crew were trapped in this desperate corner that Marryat was able to exhibit every ounce of his uncommonly high stock of courage. The first crisis came when one of the anchors came adrift and proceeded to swing around madly, threatening to smash the bow of the ship in. Marryat was alert to the danger and was daring enough to venture forward into the maelstrom of water and order it to be cut away. On the forecastle he found the men 'clinging to the rigging and crying like children', realising that this was not the time for hysterics he headed back to find his captain. The ship still lay over on her side to an alarming extent and Townshend realised the masts must be cut away. I will leave Marryat to relate the reminder of the tale:

The danger of sending a man aloft was so imminent, that the captain would not order one on this service; but calling the ship's company on the quarter-deck, pointed to the impending wreck, and by signs and gestures, and hard bawling, convinced them that unless the ship was immediately eased of her burden, she must go down. At this moment every wave seemed to make a deeper and more fatal impression on her. She descended rapidly in the hollows of the sea, and rose with dull and exhausted motion, as if she felt she could do no more. She was worn out in the contest, and about to surrender, like a noble and battered fortress, to the overwhelming power of her enemies.

No man could be found daring enough, at the captain's request, to venture aloft, and cut away the wreck of the main top-mast, and the main yard, which was hanging up and down, with the weight of the top-mast and topsail-yard resting upon it. There was a dead and stupid pause, while the hurricane, if anything, increased in violence. I confess that I felt gratified at this acknowledgment of a danger which none dared face. I waited a few seconds to see if a volunteer would step forward, resolved, if he did, that I would be his enemy for life, inasmuch as he would have robbed me of the gratification of my darling passion – unbounded pride. Dangers, in common with others, I had often faced, and been the first to encounter: but to dare that which a gallant and hardy crew of a frigate had declined, was a climax of superiority which I had never dreamed of attaining.

Seizing a sharp tomahawk, I made signs to the captain that I would attempt to cut away the wreck, follow me who dared. I mounted the weather-rigging; five or six hardy seamen followed me; sailors will rarely refuse to follow where they find an officer lead the way. The jerks of the rigging had nearly thrown us overboard, or jammed us with the wreck. We were forced to embrace the shrouds with arms and legs; and anxiously, and with breathless apprehension for our lives, did the captain, officers, and crew gaze on us as we mounted, and cheered us at every

Erskine Childers' wife Molly (left) and co-conspirator Mary Spring Rice (right) aboard the Childers' beautiful Colin Archer-designed yacht *Asgard* during her daring gun-running trip into Howth. The guns are German Mauser rifles and the aim was to provide armed support for the Irish rebels. (Photo © The Board of Trinity College, Dublin)

Erskine and Molly Childers aboard their yacht *Asgard*. Erskine was one of the true pioneers of yacht cruising and his trail-blazing voyage through the North Sea to the Baltic in 1897 was an integral part of the plot of *The Riddle of the Sands*. (Photo © The Board of Trinity College, Dublin)

The clipper barque *Otago*, Conrad's first and only command. He described her as 'an Arab steed in a string of cart horses'. Certainly she was an elegant little ship, built by the famous Glasgow shipbuilder Alexander Stephen. She survived intact until 1937 and some of her ribs are still visible at her final resting place near Hobart, Tasmania. (Photo © The State Library of Victoria)

Joseph Conrad later in life. He retired from the sea in 1892 but often toyed with the idea of returning, at one point coming close to buying a rather decrepit old tall ship. Common sense eventually prevailed. (Photo © New York Public Library)

James Fenimore Cooper during his time in the US Navy. Like many other Americans, he had been outraged by the British Navy's treatment of American sailors who were seized and press-ganged to fight in the Napoleonic Wars with alarming regularity. He had experienced the injustice of this treatment while serving aboard the merchant vessel *Sterling* and this voyage not only inspired him to join the US Navy, but later provided him with a rich source of inspiration when writing his nautical novels. (Engraving courtesy of Wikimedia Commons)

The dramatic battle between the HMS *Shannon* and the USS *Chesapeake*. This was one of the few British successes of the war of 1812. Cooper had previously served under Captain Lawrence of the *Chesapeake*, who died in this battle. (Painting © Christopher Wilhelm Eckersberg/Villy Fink Isaksen)

Ernest Hemingway poses with a giant marlin he landed during the 1934 season. For those who are not *au fait* with sports fishing, the rather obscene-looking codpiece hanging from his waist is his 'fighting belt' where the fishing rod is secured while you battle with the fish.

(Photo © National Archives and Records Administration)

Hemingway poses aboard his yacht, the *Pilar*, with a gun. A mixture of automatic weapons and booze made fishing with Hemingway an interesting pursuit. On one occasion he was hospitalised after shooting himself in the leg. Hemingway generally used the machine gun to keep sharks at bay while reeling in marlin, but the upshot was sometimes simply a bloodbath.

(Photo © National Archives and Records Administration)

Hemingway aboard *Pilar* in later life looking suitably dazed and confused. He was never the same after his double aeroplane crash in 1954, and his last trip on *Pilar* took place in 1960.
(Photo © National Archives and Records Administration)

Jack London and his wife Charmian in Honolulu. London took up the fledgling sport of surfing during his stay on Hawaii and got so badly sunburnt that he became seriously ill.
(Photo courtesy of Wikimedia Commons)

Jack London the young writer poses at his desk at his home at Glen Ellen, California, in 1905. It was around this date that the grand plan for a world cruise aboard the *Snark* was formulated. (Photo © Century Company, New York)

The building of the *Snark*, or 'London's Folly' as she was labelled by the press. Here London is seen inspecting her frames, which were supposed to be of oak but somehow ended up being pine. (Photo © Century Company, New York)

The battle of Basque Roads in which young Frederick Marryat played an important role. In this picture, the French fleet lies aground and utterly helpless while Marryat's ship *Imperieuse*, with Lord Cochrane in command, waits for reinforcements to come and finish them off. The reinforcements never came. (Painting © Louis Philippe Crepin, courtesy of World Imaging)

Determined, self assured and extremely charming, Frederick Marryat as a young man.
(Painting © John Simpson, courtesy of Wikimedia Commons)

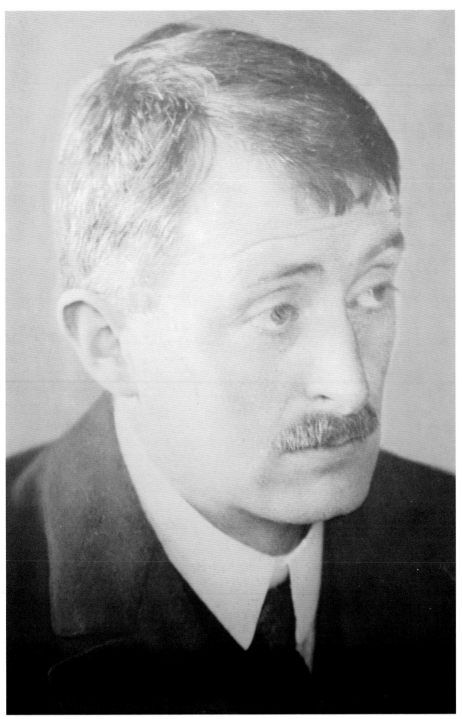

John Masefield in 1916 aged 38 when he was already a successful author and had long since turned his back on the sea. He always felt something of a fraud when it came to the sea, but his short ocean-going career gave him plenty to work with for the rest of his subsequent literary career. (Photo © Library of Congress)

The four-masted barque *Gilcruix*. It was aboard this big iron ship that Masefield served his apprenticeship and here that he learned to love and hate the sea in equal measure. On Masefield's voyage, the *Gilcruix* took a terrible battering and was over a month getting around Cape Horn. Owned by the White Star Line, she was later sold to the Germans and renamed *Barmbek*. She was broken up in 1923. (Photo © State Library of Victoria)

A whaling crew do battle with a sperm whale, demonstrating precisely the kind of risks men such as Melville had to take in order to secure their prize. (Print from the author's collection)

Herman Melville in 1860. By this time, his biggest hit *Ty-Pee* had been in print for well over a decade. Melville cut a disillusioned figure, frustrated at the lukewarm reception of his later works, among them *Moby Dick*. When the latter was published in 1851, he was convinced it would be a huge success and was left bitterly disappointed. It was only after his death that the book received the acclaim it deserved. (Photo © Library of Congress)

Arthur Ransome: fisherman, sailor and foreign correspondent. By 1923, when he took to the
sea in earnest, Ransome was so fed up with politics that all he really wanted to do was escape.
(Photo © Arthur Ransome Society)

Tobias Smollett: fiery, irritable and generally armed with a pen as sharp as a razor blade. He used this to good effect to pour scorn upon the Royal Navy after serving as surgeon during the catastrophic siege of Carthagena. (Painting © Culture Club/Getty)

Robert Louis Stevenson painted in 1892 when he had settled in his final resting place of Samoa. He died there two years later aged 44. Stevenson was dogged by illness throughout his entire life and spent much of his time at death's door. The artist has conveyed his frailty very successfully. (Painting © Girolamo Nerli, courtesy of ArtMechanic)

stroke of the tomahawk. The danger seethed passed when we reached the catharpings, where we had foot room. We divided our work; some took the lanyards of the top-mast rigging; I, the slings of the main yard. The lusty blows we dealt were answered by corresponding crashes; and at length, down fell the tremendous wreck over the larboard gunwale. The ship felt instant relief; she righted, and we descended amidst the cheers, the applauses, the congratulations, and, I may add, the tears of gratitude of most of our shipmates.

The work now became lighter, the gale abated every moment, the wreck was gradually cleared away, and we forgot our cares. This was the proudest moment of my life, and no earthly possession would I have taken in exchange for what I felt when I once more placed my foot on the quarter-deck. The approving smile of the captain – the hearty shake by the hand – the praises of the officers – the eager gaze of the ship's company, who looked on me with astonishment and obeyed me with alacrity, were something in my mind, when abstractedly considered, but nothing compared to the inward feeling of gratified ambition – a passion so intimately interwoven in my existence, that to have eradicated it the whole fabric of my fame must have been demolished. I felt pride justified.

So the ship was saved and Marryat's bravery was once more displayed to all. In 1812 he was sent home from America in order to sit his examination for commission as lieutenant. In January of the following year he was appointed second lieutenant aboard HMS *Espiegle*, commanded by Captain Taylor and bound for the Americas. Marryat made haste from his father's home to Spithead, where he observed his new ship 'a most beautiful vessel. She mounted 18 guns, and sat on the water like a duck'. It was a proud moment for Marryat; the reward for many years of danger and hardship, but his elation was to be short lived. Even as he surveyed his new vessel he noted with surprise that she flew a pennant signifying that punishment was being carried out aboard. On alighting her deck, he found that one of her crewmembers was receiving an extremely severe flogging for what he discovered was a minor offence, and he eyed Captain Taylor with concern. His worries proved to be well founded, for the skipper soon proved himself a crass, uncouth bully and tyrant. What must have grated most with Marryat was that he was a coward, as demonstrated shortly after arrival on the opposite side of the Atlantic, when Taylor, through a mixture of bad seamanship and indolence, completely failed to catch the USS *Hornet*, a sloop of war which attacked and sank the HMS *Peacock* within sight of the *Espiegle*. Taylor was ashore at the time and delayed his departure to such an extent that he seemed to deliberately allow the *Hornet* to escape. When the *Espiegle* finally started out in apparent pursuit of the *Hornet*, it was soon clear that the course set meant the two vessels were actually slowly diverging away from each other. On this occasion, Marryat felt he had to speak up and asked Taylor if he should consider changing course; he was told in no uncertain terms to hold his tongue.

Shortly after this, Marryat again found himself in the drink rescuing another hapless colleague who had fallen in the water. Unfortunately for Marryat, the *Espiegle* was moving at pace when the incident happened and Captain Taylor handled her clumsily in his reluctant efforts to retrieve both crewmember and second lieutenant. By the time a boat arrived, Marryat had been compelled to let the drowning seaman slip from his grasp and was all but finished himself, having resigned himself to death when he was fished out. Shortly after the *Espiegle*'s arrival in Barbados, Marryat was invalided out of the ship after bursting two blood vessels in his lungs. This was doubtless a result of the overexertions he had endured during his failed rescue attempt, but it did at least mean he escaped from the tyranny and incompetence of Captain Taylor. Marryat was doubtless delighted when, shortly after his departure, Taylor was court martialled and dismissed due to his brutal treatment of his crew and the complete failure of his half-hearted pursuit of the *Hornet*.

After the incompetence and brutality of the loutish Captain Taylor, Marryat now experienced incompetence of a more refined nature, for shortly afterwards he joined the company of the HMS *Newcastle*, a 58-gun frigate commanded by Lord George Stuart, who Marryat later recalled:

> *... had a very good opinion of himself; proud of his aristocratic birth, and still more vain of his personal appearance. He had been many years at*

sea, but, strange to say, knew nothing, literally nothing, of his profession. Seamanship, navigation, and everything connected with the service, he was perfectly ignorant of.

Although this man was not a coward, he must have been utterly infuriating to work for, for he had a cold aristocratic bearing, which didn't ride well beside his complete lack of knowledge of the sea. He was also a very vague man, as illustrated by the following recollection:

One day he went on deck, and actually gave me the following very intelligible order: 'Mr What's-his-name, have the goodness to—what-do-ye-call-'em – the – the thingumbob.' 'Ay, ay, my lord!' said I. 'Afterguard, haul taut the weather main-brace!' This was exactly what he meant.

His chilly indifference to his officers was very nearly the end of Marryat. While cruising off the American coast in the winter of 1814, Stuart despatched Marryat ashore to retrieve his gig (or thingumbob, as he referred to it), which had broken adrift and floated into Boston Bay, enemy territory, where it had naturally been seized. This was a far from necessary mission, but Marryat was obliged to take it up. He did, however, ask for his party to be armed, which Stuart refused, stating that it was all a misunderstanding and the townspeople would give his gig back once they realised their mistake. Marryat rightly deduced this might not be the case and covertly armed his company before they headed out into the lacerating cold. On arriving in Boston Bay, they were met with a hostile reception. There was no sign of the gig and Marryat determined to 'cut out' some shipping anchored off. This was successfully achieved, the original crew was split between the two seized vessels, and the pair of boats headed offshore back to the *Newcastle*. The weather worsened to an onshore gale with blizzard conditions and one of the prizes and her eleven crew were driven ashore and lost. Marryat and his men were compelled to anchor in this vulnerable spot and, after a night of extreme privation, all aboard knew they had little option other than to run the boat ashore and surrender, or die where they were. They chose the former but just as they were within striking distance of the shore they were saved by a wind shift, which drove them helplessly offshore again. Salvation was some distance away, however, for the *Newcastle* had not even bothered to await their return. On finally chasing down the frigate, Marryat immediately went below to report the various mishaps and the unfortunate death of eleven seamen.

I was mad with hunger and cold, and with difficulty did we get up the side, so exhausted and feeble were the whole of us. I was ordered down into the cabin, for it was too cold for the captain to show his face on deck. I found his lordship sitting before a good fire, with his toes in the grate; a decanter of Madeira stood on the table, with a wine-glass, and most fortunately, though not intended for my use, a large rummer. This I seized with one hand and the decanter with the other; and, filling a bumper, swallowed it in a moment, without even drinking his lordship's good health. He stared, and I believe thought me mad. I certainly do own that my dress and appearance perfectly corresponded with my actions. I had not been washed, shaved, or 'cleaned,' since I had left the ship, three days before. My beard was grown, my cheeks hollow, my eyes sunk, and for my stomach, I leave that to those fortunate Frenchmen who escaped from the Russian campaign, who only can appreciate my sufferings. My whole haggard frame was enveloped in a huge blue flushing coat frosted like a plum-cake with ice and snow.

As soon as I could speak, I said, 'I beg pardon, my lord, but I have had nothing to eat or drink since I left the ship.' 'Oh, then you are very welcome,' said his lordship; 'I never expected to see you again.' 'Then why the devil did you send me?' thought I to myself.

With such remarkable commanders as these, it is a wonder a diligent and headstrong officer like Marryat was able to stick with the service. What is perhaps unsurprising is that he was once again struck down with the same respiratory problem that had afflicted him aboard *Espiegle* and was invalided back to Britain in February 1815, where he made a full recovery.

In June of the same year, he achieved the rank of captain. Finally he had scaled the peak that his years of diligent service merited. Yet it was to be something of a pyrrhic victory for Marryat: the Napoleonic Wars, which had propelled his career along with such speed, ended abruptly with the Battle of Waterloo just days after he received his promotion. Given that the conflict with the US had also been settled, the British Government suddenly found itself with an utterly bloated navy. If Marryat was hoping for a ship, he was going to have to compete with the 800 or so out-of-work captains who were currently laid up on half pay with little prospect of getting to sea again. It would be five years before Marryat was given his coveted first command – and he could count himself fortunate to gain that, for unemployment was still high within the navy. In this prolonged interval between ships, Marryat was not idle ashore, publishing his signalling codes, which provided a universal set of flags for merchant vessels to communicate both to the shore and also with other ships. This system proved to be a big success and was still widely in use as late as the 1880s.

He was already entertaining himself by reminiscing over his life as a midshipman, and lampooning some of its absurdities in a popular series of caricatures entitled *The Midshipman's Progress, or the life of Mr Blockhead*, engraved by his friend, George Cruikshank. Marryat was far from an accomplished artist, but his caricatures had enough vigour and wit to chime with the British public and they became very popular. In addition to this, Marryat had married the rather dour Catherine Shairp in 1818. This union with a somewhat puritanical Scotswoman might seem to indicate that he was preparing to settle down. In direct contradiction of this he became increasingly close to London's bohemian set, who loved his ready wit and general swashbuckling air. Marryat also had the sailor's traditional inability to look after his money and, being a wealthy man, he was boundlessly generous. It is likely that this combination of rambunctiousness and wastefulness made his wife supremely relieved to see him embark aboard the HMS *Beaver*, although she was probably alarmed that he had been despatched to St Helena, where she would be engaged in patrolling the waters of Napoleon Bonaparte's last home.

The *Beaver* was supposed to ensure that no insurgents were able to gain access to Bonaparte as he sat in exile on this lonely Atlantic island. There was still a fear that someone might smuggle him away to create further mischief, but the reality was that Napoleon was on his last legs. On 5 May 1821, he passed away. There was something rather poetic about the fact that Marryat, veteran of so many battles of the Napoleonic era, should be on hand when he died, and it is a shame his personal thoughts on witnessing the end of this little man, who had made such profound shockwaves throughout Europe, have not been preserved. Nevertheless, Marryat's somewhat dubious artistic skills were now brought into action again and his rendering of Napoleon on his deathbed is still extant. Marryat returned to Britain in command of the HMS *Rosario*, bringing with him the dramatic news of Bonaparte's death.

His next assignment was less exotic and closer to home, working to try and curb the rash of smugglers who operated along the British coastline. This could often be exciting work, involving epic chases and plenty of detective work, but Marryat plainly did not relish the task. This was probably because it involved going to war with fellow countrymen and sailors who were noted for their fine seamanship. If this was the case, he wasn't detained too long in the process, for in 1822 the *Rosario* was found no longer fit for service and Marryat was back ashore on half pay. He must have looked back dewy eyed at his glory days with Cochrane at this point and wished he could be employed in some slightly more active service. In the meantime, he used all of his years of experience within the navy to publish two pamphlets, which were widely respected at the time. One was on methods of preventing smuggling and the other looked at serious reforms to the navy and in particular turned the spotlight on the unpopular policy of impressment.

While he was busy with this, he was further buoyed by news that he had been given command of the 28-gun frigate HMS *Larne*, which was to be despatched to Burma in order to help put down the uprising in this troublesome corner of the empire. Eight years after gaining his position of captain, Marryat was set to return to the battlefield. In reality, his role was limited but heroic, providing support for the British troops as they waged a war with the Burmese over control of territories inland of Rangoon.

Marryat's main task was patrolling steamy swamps and rivers and involved frequent skirmishes with Burmese war canoes, and a number of epic battles focused on the fortifications that lined the Irawaddy river. In the course of one such battle, victory came only at the price of 76 British lives, giving some indication of the intensity of the fighting.

Marryat was acquitting himself very well, but in the sweaty, tangled mangrove swamps of Rangoon and its environs, the British were very vulnerable to disease and it was to be this that finally defeated Marryat. Midway through the campaign he wrote this letter to his brother, which brings across some of the suffering he and his crew endured:

The Larne, with the remnants of a fine ship's company, is at last removed from the scene of action, where perhaps, in the course of five months they have undergone a severity of service almost unequalled. I should still have been there, but the men had been on salt provisions since February last, and the scurvy broke out and made such ravages that it was impossible to stay longer without sacrificing the remaining men. I am not ill, but my head is so shattered with the fever which I have had, that it swims at the least exertion, and I am obliged to lay my pen down every four or five lines.

Despite this, Marryat returned to the battlefield for another stint and it would be several months more of this sweltering purgatory before he finally made his departure for home. This strenuous piece of action was to be his last real engagement with enemy forces, for with Napoleon gone and Britain fully established as the world's leading power, peace and prosperity were the prevalent forces throughout the world, and *Pax Britannica* was only to be shattered on a large scale with the outbreak of World War One, many years distant. In the meantime, naval officers would have to satisfy themselves with more mundane tasks, and this was the fate to which Marryat resigned himself when he took command of the *Ariadne*, a 28-gun frigate, in 1828. He had now attained the rank of post captain and, if his career prospects looked rosy, his fortunes looked all the better. Following the death of his father in

1824 he had inherited £250,000, a sum of money that would make you the equivalent of a multi-millionaire in today's terms. To add to his cup of happiness, he had a growing family, based in his plush home in London, and a lively group of friends from the bohemian set.

Yet it is clear that he was not satisfied and that, with so many adventures and achievements behind him, Marryat was starting to yearn for something else. Perhaps it was a pining for the golden days of his youth, when adventure had been a daily occurrence that made him turn to his writing desk and pick up his pen.

He had started making up some vague plans for a novel many years earlier when he was serving aboard HMS *Beaver* off St Helena. Slowly but surely these plans distilled into what was to become his first novel, entitled *The Naval Officer; Adventures in the life of Frank Mildmay*. He completed the final chapter aboard HMS *Ariadne* and the book was published anonymously in 1829. The novel essentially recounted his own naval adventures, drawing heavily on his experiences under Cochrane and some of the later, less competent captains. Interwoven with this was a portrayal of Frank Mildmay, a young tearaway and relentlessly vindictive philanderer who still somehow triumphs in the end. He is one of the first anti-heroes to be portrayed in modern fiction and his creation was a brave step by Marryat, with unforeseen repercussions. The problem was that by interweaving his own adventures with fictional romantic conquests and acts of spitefulness on the part of Mildmay, it was easy to assume that this was a straightforward confessional autobiography of a cad and a bounder. The book may have been published anonymously, but the events related – including the Basque Roads adventure – were too high profile for Marryat not to be identified. Although the action scenes were often compelling, the book also rambled somewhat, and generally received a mixed reception.

In later years Marryat sought to clarify matters, explaining that although the 'sea adventure' scenes in the book were 'materially true', the hero of the book was fictitious, Marryat owning that, 'Had I run the career of vice of the hero of the Naval Officer at all events I should have had sufficient sense of shame not to have avowed it.' He also defended the slightly chaotic writing style by explaining that this was his 'first attempt' at a novel and that, 'It was written hastily and before it was complete I was appointed to a ship. I cared much about the ship and little about the book.'

The ship in question was the *Ariadne* and if Marryat cared for her to start with, he was to become disillusioned, finding the life of a captain in peacetime relentlessly dull. His first task was to endeavour to find a submerged rock that had been reported off Ireland, or as he later put it in more forceful terms: 'Searching for a rock in the Atlantic which never existed except in the terrified or intoxicated noddle of some master in the merchant navy.' He made use of this time to make a start on his next novel, *The King's Own*. This new account was more fictitious than the last but still drew very heavily on his own experiences and the stories he had heard from others. He was also developing the clear, conversational style that would run through all of his novels. To read a Marryat naval tale is like sitting down in a low-beamed tavern and listening to some old mariner spin a yarn, frequently deviating from the original storyline, and heading down some amusing and dangerous cul-de-sac. His books were peppered with his unique brand of lacerating wit and endless adventure. *The Kings Own* is a particularly salt-stained example of his work, for at one point he actually transports you aboard the *Ariadne* and to his writing desk, where he sits, his ship being tossed by a gale, and he clinging to his table attempting to write, his feet hooked into the table's lashings to keep him from pitching over, and a river of water streaming across the deck above him. Such moments let you know you are in the hands of a real sailor. *The King's Own* was also innovative for its time in that it does not have a happy ending. Marryat was already starting to make waves in this new forum.

In 1830 he resigned the command of the *Ariadne*, a move not looked upon favourably at a time when there were captains queuing up for a commission, and it was arguably this rash move that ensured he never again achieved a command in the Royal Navy, though he sometimes missed the service. The 1830s were to be typified by restless wanderings as Marryat desperately sought to find his niche. He tried his hand as editor of the *Metropolitan* magazine, dabbled with becoming an MP, travelled to the US and enjoyed many revels with London's artistic community, becoming firm friends with his literary rival Charles Dickens in the process. All the while the list of books he published continued to grow, as did his fame. *Newton Forster, Peter Simple* and *Mr Midshipman Easy* were perhaps the best works of these years and all feature swashbuckling tales, rambling plotlines and rapier wit. They were each major hits, making him one of the top-selling authors of his era.

He never returned to the sea, although he often seemed poised to do so. By the 1840s his stock of tales was running dry. He had other problems too: his marriage was not a particularly happy one, this despite – or perhaps because of – the couple having five children. Another problem was money: like many a sailor before him, he was generous to a fault and seemed to run through his substantial fortune at a rate of knots. It was time for a reinvention, and after adventure in North America and a year spent in Brussels, Marryat returned to his country home in Langham, Norfolk after agreeing to separate from his wife. Here he indulged in the simple pleasures of life in the country surrounded by his children. Mounting his favourite horse, Dumpling, he would spend his days surveying his property and dreaming up elaborate methods of wasting his dwindling fortune. He took to writing children's stories and proved himself very adept. His *Children of the New Forest* and *Masterman Ready* have both stood the test of time.

Marryat had much to be proud of as he reflected back over his turbulent life, yet even then he seems to have had a sneaking suspicion that history would overlook him to some extent. He had already endured the chagrin of seeing his friend and rival Dickens overtake him as the dominant novelist of the era. In naval terms, Marryat also felt thwarted: for all his heroism as a youth, history had dictated that he could never achieve the greatness of Cochrane and he felt that the Admiralty had for many years passed him over. The event that finally broke his health and led to his death was a visit to the Admiralty in London in 1847 to enquire about the possibility of a new command, or some kind of pension, or at least further recognition of his services, particularly in Burma. His requests were brushed aside and Marryat was so livid that he lost his temper, bursting several blood vessels and suffering an internal haemorrhage. This was a recurrence of the old complaint that had laid him up many years before while serving on the *Espiegle* and *Newcastle*. Weakened by many years of overexertion, it was now to prove fatal. His health and spirits took a further tumble when his eldest surviving son Frederick, who was serving as second lieutenant aboard HMS *Avenger*, was lost when the vessel was wrecked in the Mediterranean. This was a final shattering blow for Marryat Senior and he returned to Langham, where he died in August 1848.

News of his death was largely greeted with indifference by the British public, who had come to view him as little more than a writer of children's books and adventure novels, and his memory gradually faded to the point where he is merely a literary footnote. Yet time and fashion have been unjust to Marryat; and the resurgence of naval literature covering this era has highlighted what a talented chronicler he was of this heroic age. His characters, the action he depicts and the bitter cynicism he uses to describe it are all so unquestionably real that his novels are not only hugely entertaining, but vital pieces of British history, which serve to preserve and bring alive a fascinating period of war in a manner no one has been able to do since.

Perhaps what really sets Marryat apart is the fact that although he loved the navy and served it faithfully, he certainly did not love the service blindly and many years of witnessing the blundering incompetence of his seniors sharpened his ready wit to the keenness of a dagger. He also saw that lionhearted heroism and absurdity went hand in hand and this made his depiction of the navy far more 'real' than later, more glamourised novels. It is perhaps best to close this chapter with a passage from *The King's Own*, which perfectly encapsulates Marryat's cynicism and affection for the service in equal measure. You can easily visualise his sneer as he penned these lines:

The squadron of men-of-war and transports was collected, the commodore's flag hoisted, and the expedition sailed with most secret orders, which, as usual, were as well known to the enemy, and everybody in England, as they were to those by whom they were given. It is the characteristic of our nation, that we scorn to take any unfair advantage, or reap any benefit, by keeping our intentions a secret. We imitate the conduct of that English tar, who, having entered a fort, and meeting a Spanish officer without his sword, being providentially supplied with two cutlasses himself, immediately offered him one, that they might engage on fair terms.

The idea is generous, but not wise. But I rather imagine that this want of secrecy arises from all matters of importance being arranged by cabinet councils. In the multitude of counsellors there may be wisdom, but there certainly is not secrecy.

On the arrival of the squadron at the point of attack, a few more days were thrown away, – probably upon the same generous principle of allowing the enemy sufficient time for preparation.

John Masefield

The seasick sailor

I must go down to the sea again, to the lonely sea and the sky,
And all I ask is a tall ship and a star to steer her by,
And the wheel's kick and the wind's song and the white sail shaking,
And a grey mist on the sea's face and a grey dawn breaking.

Masefield's *Sea Fever*

Surely no poetry or prose ever written evokes the great beauty, mystery and romance of the sea with more pith and elegance than John Masefield's classic poem 'Sea Fever'. Since its publication in 1903, this short verse has become almost a mantra for sailors from all walks of life and its beautiful depiction of an almost irresistible call of the sea must have seduced many a hesitant landsman out onto the water for the first time. The poem is perhaps Masefield's best-remembered work, yet he penned many other poems, novels and short stories and, as often as not, he returned to the theme of tall ships and the sea for inspiration, often with great success. His narratives of day to day life at sea in the twilight of the tall-ship era bring the subject matter to life in a way that many have struggled to do either before or since: the roughness, simple humour and superstition of sailors are more closely observed and lifelike than anything many more celebrated writers of maritime literature ever managed. He was also able to convey the joy of a ship underway, and the utter misery of actually serving aboard that same vessel, better than almost anyone else.

With this in mind, it is perhaps understandable that one would have expected Masefield to be a crusty old sea dog. The kind of leathery-skinned old sailor who, having rounded the Horn a score of times and more, had retired to some rustic fisherman's cottage, reeking of Stockholm tar and hemp, in order to scribble down his musings. Yet this was not the case. Masefield only ever undertook a single tall-ship passage from Cardiff to Iquique, Chile in 1894 during which he was violently seasick and often desperately unhappy. At the conclusion of the passage he was invalided home from Valparaiso and, despite much pressure from his family to return to the sea, he fled the water, and home for that matter, going on the run in the US and becoming a vagrant, then a barman, then working as sweated labour in a carpet factory in Yonkers, upstate New York.

Despite these hardships ashore, the young Masefield still successfully managed to evade the call of the sea, and it was only when he settled to writing a couple of years after these adventures that the oceans beckoned him once again. By the 1900s his poetry and prose on the subject were beginning to bring him great acclaim and the British public looked up to see who this champion poet, sailor and salt-encrusted spinner of yarns really was, at which point Masefield felt himself very much at a disadvantage. As he reflected in 1907, when his career was taking off: 'I am, quite frankly, a fraud and have very little sea experience'. It is perhaps this that explains his reticence when it came to writing, or talking, about his own short seafaring career. He often dismissed his early life by simply describing it as 'squalid', yet by dismissing it, he did himself an injustice and, in some circles, allowed a fallacy to be perpetuated. One only has to read some of Masefield's seafaring tales to realise that here is a man who understood the sea and ships thoroughly: from the technicalities of sailing a tall ship through to an appreciation of the sea itself.

Masefield may never have commanded ships like his contemporary Joseph Conrad, but his alienation from the subject meant that he could convey, better than perhaps anyone, the great contradiction of life at sea: the constant knife-edge between beauty and brutality; exhilaration and terror;

the excitement and utter tedium that make up a sailor's existence. Indeed, perhaps unwittingly, Masefield himself had become a perfect microcosm of that contradiction. To understand why, we must learn more about the man and his connection with the sea.

Masefield was born in 1878, the third of six children. His father was a solicitor and the family lived in something of a rural idyll near the town of Ledbury, in Herefordshire, many miles from the sea. John was a naturally dreamy child and the beautiful countryside ably abetted his lively imagination. Although he was far inland, it was to be the waterways surrounding the area that first captured his vivid imagination, as he later recalled:

Of all the countless beauty spread before me, in childhood, the ponds, the springs, the brooks, the varying lovely river with its bewitching mill stream, were among the most dearly loved.

Masefield was also fascinated by the canal, which ran close to his house, and watched with wonder at the boats passing by his home, the leisurely horse ahead of the barge and the captain busy about the decks. He also recalls being rather traumatised when the canal was closed and the narrow waterway filled with rubble. It was the first of many rude shocks for the youngster, as in 1885 his mother died rather suddenly following a bout of pneumonia. Following this, John and his five siblings were placed under the supervision of a nanny, who John loathed and once stabbed with a fork. Only six years later, his father, who had spiralled into a terrible mental and physical decline after his wife's death, followed her to an early grave, leaving six orphans. With both parents gone, such extravagances as a nanny were out of the question, and the Masefields were fortunate to be taken into the care of Uncle William, his father's brother and his wife, Aunt Kate. Although the couple were evidently generous to take on such a burden, Kate had little tolerance for John.

Now aged 13, John was a sensitive soul and already harboured dreams of becoming a writer. To Kate, such a tenuous profession was beyond the pale and she was often aggressively dismissive in her attempts to discourage the boy. It was perhaps in an endeavour to crush the youngster's literary tendencies that, in the summer of 1891, the decision was taken to sign Masefield up as an apprentice aboard the HMS *Conway*, a school ship lying on the River Mersey and set up expressly to prepare young men for a seafaring career. Masefield, however reluctantly, went down to the sea for the first time.

The HMS *Conway* almost deserves a book in her own right. Indeed, a number have been written, not least by Masefield himself. The *Conway* was permanently stationed in the river and had been converted to a school ship after serving for many years in the Royal Navy as a ship of the line under the name HMS *Nile*, an old relic of Nelson's navy. She was eventually destroyed after grounding in the Menai Straits in 1956. Masefield came to know her intimately in the two and a bit years he served aboard her from 1891–93. She was set up expressly to educate youngsters who wished to become officers in the Merchant and Royal navies and, to this end, classes were given with an emphasis on navigation, meteorology and seamanship. In addition to this, the usual tasks of running a ship, such as pumping, swabbing and polishing brass were also carried out. At the end of the working day, pupils remained aboard the ship, sleeping in hammocks slung up in the 'tween decks and taken down every morning. It was unquestionably rather a strange and claustrophobic existence and it is perhaps understandable that Masefield didn't take to it at first, 'The tone of the ship was infamous. Theft, bullying, barratry, sodomy, and even viler vice were rampant.'

This is a fairly damning assessment, and given that Masefield was the youngest pupil aboard when he first joined, things must have been even more miserable. His experiences are recalled in his book *New Chum*, a short autobiographical piece that almost puts the teeth on edge it is so painful to read, as Masefield recalls the bewilderment, loneliness and systematic bullying that came his way in his first few weeks aboard. Perhaps what is most sad is that it marks the beginning of Masefield's love/hate relationship with the sea, for even as he documents this miserable existence, he tries to put a brave face on things, does his best to fit in and works hard to please. Thus, after a depressing first meal where he is vilified by his messmates for allowing the butter to be stolen, he still manages to remain strangely optimistic as he looks out upon the river:

> *My heart was still young enough to bounce up after coming down. The river was exquisitely new and beautiful, the most interesting thing I had ever seen. The fact I was on a ship, in a mess, on a gun deck, one of a ship's company, was overwhelming.*

Newcomers to this singular institution were known as 'new chums' and were treated with utter disdain by their superiors, yet gradually Masefield began to find his feet aboard the *Conway*. He was fortunate to be befriended in the first few days by an older boy, HB Meiklejohn, whom he idolised. HB slept in the hammock next to him and always asked Masefield to tell him a ghost story after they had turned in. This was a source of great pleasure to Masefield. He also enjoyed going aloft into the rigging of the *Conway* whenever he got the chance, and he loved the solitude of the cross trees. It was during one of these forays aloft that his imagination was first fired by the sight of a tall ship, the *Wanderer*, which he described as:

> *... much the finest ship now in dock. It struck into my mind as a name of beauty, as a sort of seagull of grace there. The* Wanderer, *the more I thought of the name, the more wonderful it seemed. It suggested skies of desolation, with a planet; seas of loneliness with that ship in sail.*

It was the *Wanderer* that was to provide young Masefield with the first hint that there was an even crueller, harsher yet more beautiful world outside the *Conway*, for a couple of weeks later she left the Mersey on her maiden voyage. That night the wind blew fearfully from the north, and Masefield lay in his hammock aboard the *Conway* as she groaned and strained at her anchor, all the while fearing the worst for the beautiful *Wanderer*, battling gallantly into the teeth of this equinoctial gale in the Irish Sea. The following day, his fears were confirmed, for the *Wanderer* was back in the Mersey, her masts badly damaged and her skipper dead after being hit by a falling yard.

Masefield described the scene of her return with awe:

> *At an instant, the fog in the lower Sloyne went, and the river there brightened. The* Wanderer *came out of the greyness into sunlight as a thing of such beauty as the world can seldom show ... She had been lopped of her upper cross trees and the wreck of her upper spars was lashed in her lower rigging. As she turned, her tattered sails (nearly all were tattered) suddenly shone all over her; her beautiful sheer, with its painted ports shone. I had seen nothing like her in all my life and knew, then, that something had happened in a world not quite ours.*

Afterwards the ship was always labelled an unlucky or 'hoodoo' ship in sailor's terms and she was dogged by death, wreck and misfortune throughout her life. Given the powerful impression she had made on the youngster, it is perhaps unsurprising that she provided the inspiration, and title, for one of Masefield's best-known poems in later years.

In the meantime, Masefield continued to adjust to life aboard the *Conway* and prepare for his own seafaring career. There were other consolations too. As time went by, Masefield became well acquainted with one of his seamanship instructors, Wally Blair. Blair was a true seadog who had served for many years aboard the China tea clippers, and he could sometimes be persuaded to spin a few yarns of the saltiest sort from his time at sea, transporting his young audience to the hazy shores of the Min River or skimming before the south-east trade winds down to Mauritius, stunsails set alow and aloft. Such tales would hold young Masefield entranced, and a number of them were included or adapted in his later works. For a time, things looked promising for the aspiring sailor, although the unconventional life aboard the *Conway* began to envelop the youngster to the detriment of his literary ambitions, as Masefield himself noted:

> *I have not been able to tell of the effect the ship made on me. It was profound; it was translation to another world utterly unlike anything before known, read of, or imagined. I had been plucked up by the roots*

and pitched endways, to strike root or die; now the roots were trying to catch something.

I had been fond of stories of all kinds, and had read and invented many; with some thought even that some day I might write stories. My coming to the ship put what I now call 'a stopper over all' upon any such thought. Stories, reading and invention were shut suddenly away. I had to learn a new language and a new life, word by word, task by task; my past was dead, my present, not made.

Masefield felt himself bending to the will of the sea and it looked like his aunt's ambitions for him might well be fulfilled, but of course the ultimate test was to come: a real life sea voyage. The omens were not necessarily good: as an apprentice aboard the *Conway*, Masefield and his shipmates were occasionally given what was known as 'Liverpool leave', a day's liberty to go into the famous port and look over the ships. The traditional pursuit was to go aboard some of the tall ships and get to 'know the ropes', so to speak, and for Masefield the results were distinctly mixed. At first, he was thrilled to be able to assist in some work aloft aboard a barque, which had become entangled in the rigging of another ship, but this satisfying experience was muted by an utterly dispiriting visit to the fo'c'sle of a steamer not long docked. Masefield was utterly dismayed at her accommodation, describing it as:

a small frowsy bare iron box with a wet floor and a few wooden shelves. The ship had probably taken a sea aboard while crossing the bar that morning. I know that my young heart sank at the thought that that box was the home of many men for days together and that those wooden shelves were their resting places, after their battling with the sea. I had seen many dogs and many pigs better housed.

This was hardly an encouraging view for a sensitive young boy preparing for a life at sea, and the sight of that miserable little fo'c'sle had a profound effect on him at the time, as he reflected:

Ships were beautiful to me. Their building and rigging wonderful. It was, however, clear to me that something was amiss somewhere; there was too much grab, too much snatch, and I knew very well I did not want to belong to it. I wanted to be clear of the type of man who gave iron walls and a shelf and a little daily offal in exchange for a life's work.

Thus, Masefield's battle between the beauty and the grim cruelty of ships and the sea was already well defined when, in March of 1894, he signed up as an apprentice aboard the four-masted barque *Gilcruix* bound around Cape Horn to Iquique on the west coast of South America. He was 15 years old, but when he stepped aboard the *Gilcruix,* he entered a man's world.

The barque was lying in Cardiff docks loading a cargo of patent fuel – essentially compressed coal dust. She was a 289-foot iron ship with a tonnage of 2,304. Twenty years previously she would have been viewed as a huge ship, but by the 1890s she was about par for the course. She was a relatively new vessel, having been built in 1885 by the Whitehaven Shipbuilding Company in West Cumberland. Her name reflected her Cumbrian heritage, as Gilcrux is a small village nestled on the edge of the Lake District. Her owners, the White Star Line, also owed a lot to West Cumberland, as one of the founding members of the company, Thomas Ismay, hailed from the Cumbrian town of Maryport. By 1891, the White Star Line was already famous for its fast and luxurious transatlantic passenger service, which reached its peak, and also nadir, with the launch and disastrous maiden voyage of the *Titanic* in 1912. In the 1890s, however, the company was still happy to run a mixed fleet of steamers and windjammers.

The *Gilcruix* represented the final evolution of commercial sail, being built with a good cargo capacity in mind above all else. By 1891, the golden age of sail was over. The clipper ships of the 1850s, 60s and 70s were being driven off the seas by the advent of more efficient steamships which, slowly but surely, were supplanting sail. By the time Masefield joined the *Gilcruix,* most clippers had been laid up, scrapped or sold to foreign interests. The *Cutty Sark* and the *Thermopylae,* the most famous of the earlier clippers, were both sold abroad in the early 1890s and tramped the oceans in increasingly threadbare condition barely scraping a living. Newer, more efficient sailing ships such as the *Gilcruix*, 'windjammers' as they were scornfully called, still had many years left to run, and there was still a sizeable fleet of these big, steel vessels plying the seas up until the outbreak of World War Two. The last of the windjammers could survive in certain trades simply because their sails, on long voyages, were more economical when pitted against the coal-guzzling steamships. This was particularly true on long-haul trips over the wilder stretches of ocean. This meant that the trades into which windjammers were being forced were generally bulk cargoes to or from far-flung destinations where speed of dispatch was not the primary concern. Grain, timber and fossil fuels were favoured cargoes. To this end, tall ships continued to serve in the grain trade with Australia where the intimidating stretch of the Southern Ocean, where the infamous Roaring Forties with their endless howling westerly winds, kept the steamship at bay for the time being.

The other decent money-spinner for windjammers prior to the opening of the Panama Canal in 1914, was the nitrate trade between Europe and the west coast of South America. Sailing ships made reasonable profits from battling out to ports such as Callao, Valparaiso and Iquique with general cargoes, returning loaded with the rich deposits of guano, or nitrates as they were termed, which were used in Europe as fertiliser or to make explosives.

The outward leg of this trip was most feared by sailors as it frequently included an epic battle with the dreaded Cape Horn. Lurking at the southernmost tip of South America this uncompromising headland lies right down among the icebergs and great storms that ravage this area. Plunge down to 40 degrees south, and the Southern Ocean is unrestricted by any great landmasses. Thus the great westerly winds whirl around this section of the globe unfettered, often building up enormous menacing seas in the process. In order to get into the Pacific from the North Atlantic, sailing vessels had to butt straight into these prevailing winds and huge swells, often battling for weeks at a time to make enough westing in order to 'turn the corner' and make the run up the Pacific into more clement latitudes.

John Masefield had all of this before him as he boarded the *Gilcruix*, where she lay loading in Cardiff docks. At the time, the vagaries of Cape

Horn seemed a far distant concern. A ship is never at her best when loading, covered in the grime and filth of a port, she can often look rather forlorn. There is little doubt that Masefield's heart must have sunk as he lugged his trunk aboard. Nevertheless, he will have admired the barque's tall spars and modern appearance. After more than two years aboard the *Conway*, he was able to look over the *Gilcruix* with an expert eye. She was a four-masted barque, meaning she carried square sails on her fore, main and mizzen masts and a fore and aft sail on her fourth mast (or 'jigger' as it was known). This evolution of square-sail rig had proven the most efficient, and by the 1890s vessels such as the *Gilcruix* were being handled by crews of fewer than 30 men. Contrast this with the 1852 voyage of the racing clipper *Sovereign of the Seas*, which carried a crew of 106, and you get some idea of how manageable the last tall ships had become – or how parsimonious owners were becoming, depending on your perspective. Certainly, labour-saving devices were in surprisingly short supply, and most tall ships still had a fairly appalling safety record. Frederick Wallace was a master of one of the big Cape Horners of this period and gave the following withering assessment of the windjammer fleet:

> *In the designing and building of sailing ships, the humanitarian aspect has generally been neglected. The comfort of the crew was hardly considered and seemingly very little was done to reduce the peril of the work. Life in the sailing ship may be heroic, but it was often desperately cruel and unnecessarily harsh, and that largely because nobody bothered to make it less so. If anything, the latter day sailers, huge switch backed cargo tanks, are the worst ever built as far as sailor's comfort is concerned.*

Masefield was one of six apprentices serving aboard the *Gilcruix*. The rest of the 33 crew was made up of captain, first, second and third mates, steward, cook, carpenter, sailmaker, bosun, 'donkeyman' (engineer) and a fo'c'sle made up of able and ordinary seamen. Able seamen were more experienced sailors than ordinary seamen and therefore received slightly more pay. The apprentices, also known as brassbounders, lodged in the half deck, separate from the fo'c'sle and were essentially trainees who were 'bound' to the ship by a premium paid by the apprentices' family. In addition to undertaking all the same maintenance, sail handling and cleaning work that the sailors did, apprentices were also expected to learn the rudiments of navigation and meteorology in preparation for sitting their officers' exams after a couple of years at sea. Thus, although the work was incredibly tough for apprentices, the intention was that these passages made men of them and set them up for a bright future. It was in this frame of mind that young Masefield headed down to Cardiff Docks and reported aboard the *Gilcruix*. He recalled his first impressions of the ship some years later:

As I went down to the docks I felt, I remember, strangely at one with the sun, strangely hopeful and confident, telling myself rosy yarns and conscious of the nobility of a sailor's life.

I had heard of my ship, the Gilcruix, *from the lads who had seen her and sailed in her, and I had a fine picture painted in my brain of myself in a brass bound suit walking her quarter deck. She lay in mid-dock, and it was a proud moment for me when I paid the boy who carried my gear, and hailed her from the grimy pier head, '*Gilcruix *ahoy!'*

A filthy youth in dungarees put in from her gangway in a dinghy. He was a Conway *boy of my time and one morning's work had altered him strangely from the neat midshipman I had known a month before. He tumbled my gear into the stern sheets and I jumped in and I took the oars from him and pulled alongside.*

When I reached the deck, a little pock marked man with a limp and a sallow face came shambling to me. He was in shirt sleeves and smoked a foot of clay.

'So you're another of 'em?'

He had 'mate' written all over him, so I touched my cap and said, 'yes sir.'

'Go forrard to the half deck and shift your duds [change clothes] and come on deck an' turn to [get to work].'

This was the salubrious start to Masefield's seagoing career. If it was a bit of an anticlimax, worse was to come when he entered the half deck, where he and the five other apprentices were to be lodged for many months to come. He recalled:

> The Gilcruix *was loading patent fuel and the black blocks of compressed coal dust were sliding down the hatches at a rate of, roughly speaking, 200 tons a day. One hatch was just abaft the half-deck door, and though fuel is tolerably clean, it had spread in fine particles through the closed edges of the skylight and the chinks of the door, till the half deck was like a colliers pantry. As I opened the door to enter, the desolation of the place came over me like a bad dream, for it was in a state of litter and disorder quite indescribable. It was not a large place (its measurements were twelve feet square by eight feet high), and the hurried unpacking of five boys had strewn it two feet deep in clutter and scattered clothes. Chests and sailor's bags, sea bedding, pannikins and dungarees were flung 'all how' under the bunks and all over the floor and lockers. I had never seen such a dissolute sight and the rough discomfort of the place made me sick to be there.*

That evening he retired to the half deck utterly disillusioned and got his first taste of ship's supplies. It was a shock to a lad used to the relatively pleasant fare aboard the *Conway.*

> This meal consisted of a sodden mess of 'dry hash' [minced meat], which fell with a most unreassuring 'plunk' when helped onto a plate. We had also some broken portions of a loaf, a block of rancid butter, some moist salt and a kettleful of ship's 'tea'. Coming to six hungry lads who had been doing the hardest kinds of manual labour all day, and who were fresh from the pleasant refinements of the* Conway, *this disgusting mess was at once an injury and an insult. Food at sea is bad always, but to give food not so much bad as vile when in dock in inexcusable. The very pigs in the sty refused it. We hove it into the pigs' platter and supped on some Bovril, a few buns, a little jam and some tobacco.*

Sadly, the fare which so outraged Masefield was pretty standard among windjammers of this period. Eric Newby, a fellow voyager in one of the last of the windjammers, the *Moshulu*, recalled being delighted to receive fresh fish for breakfast on his first morning at sea. He was curtly informed by a fellow crewmember that it was actually rancid bacon and he had little choice but to throw it over the side, where a seagull picked it up and hastily dropped it again. Ship's captains seemed to pride themselves on scrimping on supplies. This was largely because shipowners insisted on fully stocking their ship for a round voyage in her home port, possibly because they did not trust the captain to do it sensibly and without getting ripped off once aboard. This did not take into account any unexpected stopovers, delays, or failure to secure a cargo later in the trip and meant that, right from the outset, captains were obliged to save supplies and serve up the kind of muck that clearly disgusted Masefield greatly. There were a few exceptions to this rule, but they were few and far between. James Holmes, captain of one of the last wool clippers, *Cimba,* in the 1890s, clearly had the trust of his owners, A. A. Nicol, and was one of the few skippers able to correctly victual his ship. This led to him gaining huge popularity with his crews. He recalls one set of men giving him a rousing three cheers at the end of a voyage and skippers and officers from nearby ships running to the scene, fearing that the crew must be about to lynch him.

Returning to the *Gilcruix*, and an increasingly depressed and hungry Masefield: there was a round of rather bawdy shanty singing among the boys, at the end of which Masefield was able to crawl into his bed, reflecting bitterly on his disillusionment with seafaring life:

On my first night of my new life, these wretched ballads, heard in the unaccustomed squalor of a half deck, gave me a disgusted loathing for the sea and all connected with it. I was fifteen years old and I had looked forward to a life rough in the main but withal courtly. Instead I found a life as brutal as that of a convict, a life foul, frowsy, whose one refinement was that of a low tavern by the dock.

It was not a good start and clearly Masefield's romantic nature clashed horribly with the grim reality of life aboard, and the weeks of waiting while the vessel loaded proved to be immeasurably tough. Aside from the officers, there were no men aboard the ship yet, as they were paid by the day. This meant that any labour fell upon the six apprentices, and they followed a brutal routine that started at 5.30am with the night watchman tumbling them out of their bunks in order to start work at 6am. Aside from lunch and tea breaks, the boys were kept hard at it until 7pm. Masefield describes one particularly tough day:

We trooped out on deck just as the clock over the warehouse was showing six. It was chilly on deck, and comfortless, but we were not there for comfort. We were marched aft to the sail locker in a body and there to 'wrastle out' staysails to bend [attach to the rigging] before breakfast. I was put to bend the main topmast and main topgallant staysails, a piece of work which necessitates a nice sense of balance in the performer. The bender goes aloft, say, a hundred and twenty feet, and seats himself astride on a cruel hard wire about as thick as a broomstick. He then has to lean gingerly forward and work, with both hands and every muscle above his belt, at a heavy sail dangling underneath him. When you come down from aloft after bending staysails you wonder why you left home.

The remainder of this particular day was devoted to the incredibly laborious work of loading the stores aboard the ship from 'lighters' or barges that ranged alongside. This was backbreaking work, which completed a very long day of toil.

Our hands were full of splinters, bleeding at the finger tips and quite raw down the palm. I don't know how I did what I did that afternoon, but I suppose it was just the sense of duty that had been drilled into me till it was habit. Soldiers and sailors are like that, I think; they have a collective wisdom of sheep, the unquestioning mind of the running guinea pig. Tell them to do a thing, they will do it, and keep on doing it until they drop.

It seems a goodish quality in print. In life it is only goodish for those doing the telling. When we cast loose the last lighter that afternoon we sank gasping against the fife rail. 'Great snakes' roared the second mate, 'what are you knocking off for? Get the brooms along and man the head pump, two of you.'

Towards seven o'clock that evening, six utterly tired lads sat upon chests and blinked at each other stupidly in the twilight. They were too fagged to eat, or to wash, or to sing, or to undress and turn in. They sat there stupidly for twenty minutes, not saying a word, blinking at each other like owls. They had looked labour in the face and the exceeding glory of her countenance had struck them dumb.

One begins to get an insight into why Masefield entertained such mixed feelings about life at sea. One blessing was that he was not afraid of heights, so the tall spars of the *Gilcruix* held little terror for him. This was just as well, for there were no safety harnesses, and it was very common to lose a sailor or two falling from aloft on a voyage. Given the hard work the apprentices were enduring as the ship loaded, the actual departure date must have been hotly anticipated, and after three weeks of misery the *Gilcruix* was readied for sea. To this end, a motley bunch of sailors was procured, all hungover to hell – with many still drunk – and the ship was all set for a sea passage. Here, finally, was some of the romance that Masefield loved so dearly:

The whole stately fabric of the Gilcruix *seemed to quiver and sway, and I glanced over the focs'le rail and saw a line of bubbles spreading, spreading, whitening away from her bows. We were off.*

... From down the docks came a confused noise of cheering.

'So long the Gilcruix. *Hip! Hip! Hip! Hooray!'*

Very presently we were at the pier head, passing slowly, slowly through the narrow passage which led to the wide seas – the wide seas I had read about in Marryat. Such a crowd to give us a send off. Dock officials in peaked caps, customs men, boarding house runners, old sailors, lumpers, riggers, stevedores, ships husbands, crimps and what-not.

And one man there, dressed in thin dungaree slops, barefooted, hatless, sleeveless in that bracing cold wind, stood at the dock's edge ready for what is called the 'pier head jump'. We were one man short and the mate signed to him and he sprang aboard of us in the fore chains.

Then all the long-shore company took off their hats and shouted 'So long the Gilcruix. Hip! Hip! Hooray!'

The little pockmarked mate uncovered.

'Three cheers for the pier head,' he cried, adding, under his breath, 'Three cheers for the bloody stay at homes,' and I passed into blue water leaning over the rail, waving a ragged cap and cheering, cheering.

Now we were clear of the docks and busy with the towing gear on the focs'le head. Busy getting our port anchor inboard, bustling and heaving and getting my ears singed generally.

I was outside England. England lay astern and to the port hand, stretching ahead, all bright in the sun, screamed over by gulls and kittiwakes – was the dancing, tossing channel.

From this point onwards, Masefield kept a diary of his trip, although it ends rather suddenly once the *Gilcruix* is off the pitch of the Horn. Compared with his later reminisces his writing style is short and terse. The first entry is typically understated, simply saying:

Was very sick while passing Bull Point and felt very ill indeed until I went below at 9pm. Coming on deck at 12pm I took the poop watch and was very sick all watch. Captain and Mate were very kind.

This describes a period of two days, which must have been nothing short of a world of misery. As the *Gilcruix* was towing out of the Mersey she would not have set any sails, meaning her motion would have been most uncomfortable and this had an immediate effect on the youngster:

A strange deadly feeling, like a cold cloth laid suddenly over the heart, an uncanny giddiness and lassitude; I was faint, clammy, helpless, weakly wishing for death or dry land.

He was most fortunate that the officers treated him kindly during these first two days of seasickness. He was the youngest crewmember aboard and this seemed to bring out the protective side of these men of iron, for, after a bit of lighthearted chaffing from each of them in turn, he was generally sent to his bunk or ordered to go and vomit over the side, whichever seemed more suitable. This was fortunate indeed, and not at all typical. In many tall ships, much rougher and crueller treatments were often doled out. James Bissett, a contemporary of Masefield who served aboard the barque *County of Pembroke* and went on to become captain of both the Cunarders *Queen Mary* and *Queen Elizabeth*, recalled the mate aboard the *County of Pembroke* curing his seasickness by manhandling him out of his bunk and forcing him to drink seawater scooped from the scuppers. After this – and a good deal of vomiting – he was set to work.

The gentler treatment John received was a real blessing and, over the course of the passage, he admitted that he 'grew to worship' the captain, stating that all of the first voyagers would have gladly 'oiled his boots with their weekly whack of butter.' After two days of utter misery, Masefield found his sea legs and was able to report more effectively for duty. By now the *Gilcruix* was clear of land and heading out into the broad sweep of the North Atlantic, and Masefield was able to get into the routine of life aboard. His first task aloft seemed to carry with it an omen, as he recalled:

One bell had been struck and I was lounging about the poop when the old man [the captain] came on deck for a turn in the sun before he went to breakfast.

With that sailor's second nature, he went aft for a squint at the compass, then forrard to the break for a look aloft. Something was not altogether right. 'Jan,' [Masefield refers to himself as 'Jan' in these reminisces] 'I see you got some nice rope yarns in your belt.'

'Yes sir.'

'You see that mizzen to'gallan' yard?'

'Yes sir.'

'There's a buntline aloft that needs overhaulin' about a fut n' a half

an then stoppin'. Now, let me see how you kin run aloft after all them
nice pickles I seed you eat yesterday.'

   'Ay ay, sir.'

   I flung the buntlines off the pin and overhauled them through the fair
lead and up I trotted to the swaying topgallant mast. It was the first time
I had been aloft since we left the dock.

   The sea air and seasickness had freshened me up into a hearty state
of health. If this is sea life, I thought, as I laid out on the yard, I shall
do alright after all. Just then the foot of the topgallant sail lifted slightly
and brushed my cap from my head. It fell slowly, hitting the bunts of the
topsails, hanging a second in one of the crojick leech lines, then flopping
into the sea with a gentle splash.

   It was a common sea incident, but happening just then it came to me
like a rebuke. I was superstitious as any in blue water and I felt it a bad
omen. The blow fell later on, announced or unannounced, and knocked
the poor tune clean out of me.

Bad omens aside, these first days gave Masefield a chance to settle in and also
assess his shipmates. It was soon clear to him that of the five other apprentices
he housed with, there was only one he actually got on with particularly well,
and he was in the opposite watch. The two boys in his own watch, Hely and
Shaw, were both first voyagers out of the *Conway* like himself and he already
knew from his time on the school ship that he disliked them and, as often
as not, he tried to separate himself from them. He recalled that they both
viewed him as 'an odd fish' and 'a bit uncongenial' as well as being 'a damned
innocent etc etc'. He was also unfortunate that he was denied his favourite
habit of yarn spinning as one of the senior apprentices saw it as his domain
and would not tolerate usurpers. The company of the ordinary sailors was
also denied to the apprentices, for although they were expected to do the
same work, they were separated off otherwise, and it was made clear to them
that, as officer material, it was unacceptable to have much to do with the
men. It was a strange and isolated existence, and his recollections of coffee
break aboard illustrate this:

There was no ships biscuit to eat with it, and ships sugar to eat with the ship's biscuit, dirty tin pannikins to drink from and two shipmates whom I loathed (and loathed me) to drink with.

After I had been at sea a while I used to keep poop watch after watch so as to escape the society of Hely and Shaw. And especially did I keep the morning poops, partly in order that I might watch the sunrise, partly that I might escape that comfortless cup of devilled water.

Despite this lack of companionship, one big consolation of life afloat was that the work was somewhat less backbreaking than it had been ashore. Aside from night watch, when the boys were set the rather pointless task of 'lee poop watch' (essentially acting as an extra lookout and general runner of errands) the largest part of his work was cleaning, scrubbing, polishing, and chipping rust from the hull. It was while engaged in this last activity that Masefield was again laid low with 'a slight touch of sun'. If this got him out of chipping rust, then it was a good thing, for this activity was undoubtedly the most loathsome aboard. Iron ships of a certain age accrue rust internally at an alarming rate, and this must be chipped from the hull for hour after hour. Eric Newby gives an excellent insight into the full misery of this activity in *The Last Grain Race*, his account of life aboard a Finnish windjammer:

The rust got in our eyes and blinded us, trickled down our sleeves and down the backs of our necks, setting up violent itching.

As always when engaged in 'Knacka Rost' [the Finnish term for this activity] I tried to think of nothing at all, but only succeeded in conjuring up visions of failure, bankruptcy and death from painful diseases brought on by this monstrous occupation, all the fears that beset civilised man.

Although much of the work was tedious and punishing, out in the Atlantic, bowling along before the trades, life aboard was often very comfortable and pleasant. Masefield's relationship with the officers remained good and the mates indulged him. He recalls playing a game of chess with the first mate and, halfway through backing his superior officer into a corner that could only end in checkmate, he realised his error and subtly allowed his boss to defeat him. Then there was the sailing of the ship which, as she thrummed before the steady breezes, was always satisfying and at other times truly exhilarating. The *Gilcruix* was no flier – she had been easily outpaced by the *Cutty Sark* when the pair had fallen in together in 1890 – yet she was still a big, powerful vessel and could log up to 15 knots in favourable conditions. This may not sound like much in modern terms, but aboard a windjammer powered only by her towering sails, it feels like flying. Off the coast of South America, the *Gilcruix* showed what she could do, as Masefield recalled joyously many years later:

We were at sea off the River Plate, running south like a stag. The wind had been slowly freshening for twenty four hours, and for one whole day we had whitened the sea like a battle ship. Our run for the day had been 271 knots, which we thought a wonderful run, though it has, of course, been exceeded by many ships. For this ship it was an exceptional run. The wind was on the quarter, her best point of sailing, and there was enough wind for a glutton. Our captain had the reputation of being a 'cracker on', and on this occasion, he drove her till she groaned. For that one wonderful day we staggered and swooped and bounded in wild leaps and burrowed down and shivered and anon rose up shaking. The wind roared up aloft and boomed in the shrouds, and the sails bellied out as stiff as iron. We tore through the sea in great jumps – there is no other word for it. She seemed to leap clear from one green roaring ridge to come smashing down upon the next.

I have been in a fast steamer – a very fast turbine steamer – doing more than twenty knots, but she gave me no sense of great speed. In this old sailing ship, the joy of the hurry was such that we laughed and cried aloud. The noise of the wind booming and the clack, clack, clack of the sheet blocks, and the ridged seas roaring past us and the groaning and whining of every block and plank, were tunes for a dance. We seemed to be tearing through it at ninety miles an hour. Our wake whitened and broadened and rushed away aft in a creamy fury. We were running here and hurrying there, taking a small pull of this and getting another inch of that, till we were weary. But as we hauled we sang and shouted. We were possessed of the spirits of the wind. We could have danced and killed each other. We were in an ecstasy. We were possessed. We half believed that the ship would leap from the waters and hurl herself into the heavens, like a winged god. Over her bows came the sprays in showers of sparkles. Her foresail was wet to the yard. Her scuppers were brooks. Her swing ports spouted like cataracts. Recollect too that it was a day to make your heart glad. It was a clear day, a sunny day of brightness and splendour. The sun was glorious in the sky. The sky was of a blue unspeakable. We were tearing along across a splendour of sea that made you sing. Far as one could see there was the water shining and shaking. Blue it was, and green it was, and of dazzling brilliance in the sun. It rose up in hills and in ridges. It smashed into a foam and roared. It towered up again and toppled. It mounted and shook in a rhythm, in a tune, in a music. One could have flung one's body to it as a sacrifice. One longed to be in it, to be a part of it, to be beaten and banged by it. It was a wonder and a glory and a terror. It was a triumph it was royal to see that beauty.

And later, after a day of it, as we sat below, we felt our mad ship taking yet wilder leaps, bounding over yet more boisterous hollows and shivering and exulting in every inch of her. She seemed filled with a fiery unquiet life. She seemed inhuman, glorious, spiritual. One forgot that she was man's work. We forgot that we were men. She was alive, immortal, furious. We were her minions and servants. We were the star dust whirled in the train of the comet. We banged our plates with the joy we had in her. We sang and shouted and called her the glory of the seas.

Few before or since have managed to convey with such fervour the sheer delight of the sea. Here was the consolation, and here was the crux of Masefield's relationship with the sea. Those sentences convey great love, just as much as his other reminisces of the voyage convey despair and depression. Such writing and memories can be seen in many of his later descriptions of ships running well, most particularly in *The Bird of*

Dawning, which conveys the exhilaration of sailing swiftly in a tall ship with almost as much fervour and feeling as this. There was more too: Masefield's diary describes with wonder many of the strange sights that to the seasoned sailor eventually become everyday. He speaks of the great beauty of a night watch spent among phosphorescence as 'a cloud of spray coming over the bows like a shower of sparks'.

Slowly the *Gilcruix* edged her way down the Atlantic, thrumming through the north-east trade winds and then flogging and ghosting her way through the doldrums. There was real labour here, for once out of the trades, the entire suit of over 30 separate sails had to be switched over and replaced with an older set. This was to minimise the expense of the chafe caused by the constant flogging of sails as the ship drifted through the doldrums. Once through this belt of calm, the process was reversed. To write about two changes of sail takes a couple of sentences and does little to convey the world of hard, backbreaking effort required to complete the task. Nevertheless, the consolations for this tough life kept presenting themselves to Masefield in all sorts of ways, and he was particularly moved by the sight of a fellow tall ship passing them by. This was the four-masted barque *Glaucus*, owned by Carmichael's 'Golden Fleece' line of fast sailers. All of these vessels had a reputation for speed and beauty and the sight of the *Glaucus* slipping by in the first glow of dawn had a profound effect on the young sailor, as he later recalled:

> *When I saw her first there was a smoke of mist about her as high as her foreyard. Her topsails and flying kites had a faint glow upon them where the dawn had caught them. Then the mist rolled away from her, so that we could see her hull and the glimmer of her red sidelight as it was hoisted inboard. She was rolling slightly, tracing an arc against the heaven, and as I watched her the glow upon her deepened, till every sail she wore burned rosily, like an opal turned to the sun, like a fiery jewel. She was radiant, she was of an immortal beauty, that swaying delicate clipper. Coming as she came, out of mist into the dawn, she was like a spirit, like an intellectual presence. Her hull glowed, her rails glowed;*

there was colour upon the boats and tackling. She was a lofty ship (with skysails and royal staysails) and it was wonderful to watch her blushing in the sun, swaying and curvetting. She was alive with more than mortal life. One thought that she ought to speak. She came trembling down to us, rising up high and plunging; showing the red lead below her waterline, then diving down until the smother bubbled over her hawse holes. She bowed and curvetted, the light caught the skylights on her poop; she gleamed and sparkled; she shook the sea from her as she rose. There was no man aboard us but was filled with the beauty of that ship.

The old mate limped up to me and spat and swore. 'That's one of the beautiful sights of the world,' he said. 'It's beauty and strength.'

All the while, the great menace of Cape Horn lay ahead, creeping up on them day by day. To make matters worse, the *Gilcruix* was approaching this savage cape in the midst of the southern winter, when the uncompromising stretch of water was at its most malignant. Masefield had already had a taste of heavy weather following that exhilarating burst off River Plate. Once the vessel had become overpowered, Masefield had been ordered aloft to wrestle with the mizzen royal sail. This was the uppermost of all the square sails in the ship and was recognised as the domain of the apprentices. This was his first true tussle with the elements and is worth recounting:

And there was the mizzen royal. There was the sail I had come to furl. And a wonder of a sight it was. It was blowing and bellying in the wind and leaping around like a drunken colt and flying over the yard, thrashing and flogging. It was roaring like a bull with its slatting and thrashing. The royal mast was bending to the strain of it. To my eyes it was buckling like a piece of whalebone.

I lay out on the yard and the sail hit me in the face and knocked my cap away. It beat me and banged me and blew from my hands. The wind pinned me against the yard and seemed to be blowing all my clothes to shreds. I felt like a king, like an emperor. I shouted aloud with joy of the 'rastle' with the sail.

Masefield's description of the royal mast 'bending' is no exaggeration. These upper spars all had an alarming degree of flex in them once it really started to blow, and Frank Baines, who served in the tall ship *Lawhill* (a ship not nearly as heavily sparred as *Gilcruix*), attests to the upper masts flexing to such an extent that the rigging he was climbing went completely slack to the point that he was spun around as he clung on until he was facing outwards *away* from the mast, only to be spun back facing toward the mast as the great spar flexed back and pulled the rigging taut again. This gives you some idea of the kind of risk involved with climbing the rigging and explains why so many men fell to their deaths.

As the *Gilcruix* descended into the southern latitudes, temperatures began to plunge, although the weather was surprisingly clement. In the crystal clear conditions, the rigging was bejewelled with frost, and the sheets and sails became stiff with ice. If this ice was left too long, it built up to such a level that the stability of the ship could be compromised, so sailors had to go aloft and whack it off periodically: a nasty, chilly job. The apprentices were fortunate in being able to rig up a small stove in the half deck, which must have been a great consolation after several hours spent freezing on deck. Arrival off the Horn was marked out by an eerie calm:

Off Cape Horn there are two kinds of weather, neither of them a pleasant kind. If you get the fine kind, it's dead calm, without even enough wind to lift the wind vane. The sea lies oily and horrible, heaving in slow, solemn swells, the colour of soup. The sky closes down upon the sea all round you, the same colour as the water. The sun never shines over those seas, though sometimes there is a red flush, in the east or west to hint that somewhere, very far away, there is daylight brightening the face of things.

If you are a ship in the Cape Horn calm you forge ahead under all sail, a quarter of a mile an hour. The swell heaves you up and drops you, in long, slow, gradual movements, in a rhythm beautiful to mark. You roll too in a sort of horrible crescendo, half a dozen rolls and a lull. You can never tell when she will begin to roll. She will begin quite suddenly for no apparent reason. She will go over and over with a rattling clatter of blocks and chains.

It is cold, this fine variety, for little snow squalls are always blowing by, to cover the decks with soft, dry snow, and to melt upon the sails. If you go aloft you must be careful what you touch. If you touch a wire shroud or a chain sheet, the skin comes from your skin as though a hot iron had scarred it. If you but scratch your hand, in that fierce cold, the scratch will suppurate. I broke the skin of my hand once with a jagged scrap of wire in the main rigging. The scratch festered so that I could not move my hand for a week.

We had rigged up a bogey stove ... It did not burn well this stove, but we contrived to cook by it. We were only allowed coke for fuel, but we always managed to contrive to steal coal enough either from the cook or from the coal hole. It was our great delight to sit upon our chests in the dogwatch, looking at the bogey, listening to the creaking chimney, watching the smoke pouring out of the chinks. In the night watches, when the sleepers lay quiet in their bunks behind the red baize curtains, one or two of us who kept the deck would creep below to put on coal. That was the golden time, the time of the night watch, to sit there in the darkness among the sleepers hearing the coals click.

Yet this was a false tranquility, an uneasy truce with Cape Horn, which could not last. All the while, the sailors awaited heavy weather, and when it came, it came with an absolute vengeance. The Antarctic winter exploded upon the *Gilcruix*, hurling all of its fury upon the ship, and the men suffered terribly. Weathering Cape Horn when you come from the Atlantic side is an art in itself. The westerly winds mean that you are essentially going to have to batter your way through against the elements. Square-rigged ships were never notable for their ability at sailing into the wind, even in their last evolutions, and the trick was to tack back and forth awaiting a favourable slant to get you round. This meant exposing yourself for days, even weeks at a time to some of the meanest weather known to man. The tall-ship record for weathering Cape Horn east to west is five days, achieved by the clipper *Flying Cloud* through endless hard driving and extreme good fortune. The slowest passage runs into hundreds of days. The *British Isles,* a contemporary of the *Gilcruix,* once took 84 days to weather the Horn. In heavy weather, these big iron ships lacked the buoyancy of their wooden predecessors and their decks were constantly flooded with icy water, which often came aboard with a force that swept men off their feet and even overboard. The *Gilcruix* lacked a central 'Liverpool House' a full-width raised deckhouse amidships, which some later vessels had, and this meant a sea could pour inboard forward of her poop and then sweep the length of the deck. If you weren't smart enough to jump for the rigging, you were simply hurled pell-mell along the deck, either overboard or smashed against some unforgiving piece of deck equipment. This was precisely what happened to Eric Newby aboard the *Moshulu:*

> *As I went another body bumped me and I received a blow in the eye from a seaboot. Then I was alone, rushing onwards and turning over and over. My head was filled with bright lights like a bypass at night and the air was full of the sounds of a large orchestra playing out of tune. In spite of this, there was time to think 'I'm done for'. At the same time, the lines of the sea poem: 'ten men hauling the lee fore brace ... seven when she rose at last', came back to me with peculiar aptness. But only for an instant because now I was turning full somersaults, hitting myself violently again and again, that might have been the top of the hatch. Then I was over it, full of water and very frightened, thinking 'is this what it's like to drown?' No more obstructions now, but still going very fast and still underwater, perhaps no longer in the ship, washed overboard, alone in the Southern Ocean. Quite suddenly there was a parting of water, a terrific crash as my head hit something solid, and I felt myself aground.*

The *Moshulu,* which Newby served aboard, was a larger ship than the *Gilcruix,* and her deck was more enclosed, so inundations of this nature must have been common as the ship laboured among the great greybeards of Cape Horn. Up above, the wind howled a great roaring moan in the rigging, utterly baleful in the lonely sky.

It was down here in this wasteland that Masefield first heard the haunting shanty 'Hanging Johnny', described by him thus:

> *It has the most melancholy tune that is one of the saddest things that I have ever heard. I heard it for the first time off the Horn in a snowstorm. We were hoisting topsails after heavy weather. There was a heavy grey sea running and the decks were awash. The skies were sodden and oily, shutting in the sea about a quarter of a mile away. Some birds were flying about us screaming.*
>
> *(Chantyman)They call me Hanging Johnny.*
> *(Sailors) Away-i-oh.*
> *(Chantyman) They call me Hanging Johnny.*
> *(Sailors) So hang boys, hang.*
>
> *I thought at the time that it was the whole scene set to music. I cannot repeat those words without seeing the line of yellow oilskins, the wet deck, the frozen ropes and the great grey seas running up into the sky.*

Off the Horn, Masefield's diary comes to an end, almost unquestionably because he was simply too frozen, exhausted and wretched to continue with it. We can get some idea of his sufferings from the recollections of the author Basil Lubbock who made a trip around the Horn west to east in the four-masted barque *Ross-shire* in 1899. He encountered a similarly epic storm to Masefield, and recalls the unimaginable scale of these great waves:

> *When on top of one of these great Cape Horners, looking forward was like looking from the top of a mountain; the first smaller mountains, then hills, until what looked like a valley, seemed miles away in the distance.*
>
> *I am very certain that it was a good deal nearer two miles than one mile from crest to crest of these enormous seas and I don't believe that any vessel under 500 tons could have lived in them for five minutes.*
>
> *The main deck is often out of sight now for some minutes, even the hatches being covered, and as the ship rolls it becomes a roaring, hissing, boiling cauldron.*

The difference for Lubbock was that his ship was running – or hove to – *before* this tumult. The *Gilcruix* was battling into this maelstrom and, in all, was 32 days extricating herself from it. This being the southern winter, her situation was made even worse when she became ensnared among icebergs, and some fairly serious damage was done following a collision with a small berg. Masefield never elaborated upon this period of hell and only commented on:

> *thirty two days of such storm and cold I hope never to see again. The Horn is a hard place in the winter, seas forty feet high and two miles long, and ice everywhere. On deck, in the rigging and tumbling in the sea.*

The closest we have to a full description of the conditions from Masefield is probably his poem *Dauber,* the tale of a sensitive young artist who goes to sea in order to learn more about the ships he loves to paint, and finds himself utterly rejected. He finally wins acceptance from his shipmates after an epic battle with the elements off the Horn. This piece is clearly written by one intimate with this desolate stretch of ocean:

> *The snow whirled all about – dense, multitudinous cold –*
> *Mixed with the wind's one devilish shriek, which whiffled out men's tears,*
> > *deafened, took hold,*
> *Flattening the flying drift against the cheek.*
> *The yards buckled and bent, man could not speak.*
> *The ship lay on her broadside; the wind's sound*
> *Had devilish malice at having got her downed*
> *How long the gale had blown he could not tell,*
> *Only the world had changed, his life had died.*
> *A moment now was everlasting hell.*
> *Nature an onslaught from the weather side,*
> *A withering rush of death, a frost that cried,*
> *Shrieked till he withered at the heart; a hail*
> *Plastered his oilskins with icy mail.*

Evidently this kind of treatment was enough to turn the mind of even the hardiest sailors, let alone a callow youth just turned 16. There is little doubt that at times Masefield must have thought the ship would perish, and at other times he probably wished she would, particularly as some of his writings suggest that the half deck's beloved bogey stove was washed out and unusable as they battled to turn the corner. Eventually, miraculously, the big ship won through and limped up the Pacific to Iquique. The passage had occupied some 13 weeks and without the delay off the Horn, would have been a fine one. Perhaps, had it not been for the ordeal off the Horn, Masefield would have stuck to the sea. As it stood, he was in a fragile state of mind as they approached their destination. The distant shores they had battled so hard to gain were sighted on a bright August morning, as Masefield recalled:

The water alongside us was no longer blue, but a dark green, which was not like the seas we had sailed. As it grew lighter, the mist which had lain along the land was blown away. We saw the land we had come so far to see, the land we had struggled for, the land we had talked of. It lay in a line to leeward, a grey, irregular mass, with the sun shining over it. Over us was a sky of deep, kindly blue, patrolled with soft, white clouds, little white Pacific clouds, delicately rounded like the clouds of the trade winds.

As they neared land, the crew made out the great snow-capped mountains, and the city of Iquique. The Chilean port was a ramshackle place, nestling in the tiny strip of land between the great Pacific and the mighty Andes. Not only is it a notoriously dangerous anchorage for ships, it's also a very stark, lonely, harsh place. The landscape is beautiful but the town had grown up rapidly around shipping and trade and, as such, was full of all the filthy drinking dens and brothels that sailors were so fond of. In other words, it was no place for a boy in a delicate frame of mind. What happened next is not entirely clear, and Masefield never chose to talk of it at any length. All that is certain is that, after the ship was some time in Iquique discharging her cargo, Masefield was himself discharged on the grounds of being a DBS or Distressed British

Sailor. He later simply stated that he had 'had a bad time and almost died'. The reason for this is often given as 'sunstroke'. Was this the case? It seems like a very extreme measure if it was, for as a DBS he was entitled to be transported home by mail steamer, at the expense of the White Star Line. This seems a very extravagant measure for someone suffering from sunstroke. The more likely reality was that he suffered something of a breakdown while in Iquique and the captain, being a merciful man, gave him the opportunity to leave the ship and get home in a more comfortable fashion.

The closest hint we get to his mental state was an incidental part of a tale Masefield wrote over a decade later about a man murdered in a barroom brawl. The incident occurred after Masefield had been give a day's leave and had headed up into the foothills of the Andes:

> *High up in the hills I came to a silver mine with a little inn or wine shop at the top of it. There was a bench near the door of the tavern, so I sat down to rest; and I remember looking at the russet coloured earth from the shaft and wondering whether silver mining was hard work or not. I had had enough of hard work to last me through my time. There was a view over the sea from where I sat. I could see the anchorage and the ships and a few rocks with surf about them, and a train puffing into the depot. A barquentine was being towed out by a little dirty tug; and very far away, shining in the sun, an island rose from the sea, whitish like a swimmer's shoulder. It was a beautiful sight that anchorage, with the ships lying there so lovely, all their troubles at an end. But I knew that aboard each ship, there were young men going to the devil and mature men wasted, and old men wrecked and I wondered at the misery and sin which went to make each ship so perfect an image of beauty.*

Hardly positive thoughts for a young man of 16, but they do perfectly illustrate his internal struggle with ships and the sea; the beauty and the loathsomeness of it all. The tale goes on to recount a rather shocking murder that had evidently just occurred inside the tavern. Not the kind of thing a brooding Masefield needed to witness at that moment. The true reasons for his sick leave will never be known, but after a short while convalescing in a Valparaiso hospital, he returned home via the Panama Isthmus and the Atlantic. It was far from a wasted trip, and many of the thrilling sights and people found their way into his later books. The fictional Santa Barbara, which makes an appearance in several of his novels, is a sort of distillation of everything he saw out in South America.

He returned home to the utter derision of his Aunt Kate, who taunted him on his failure – a failure that certainly haunted him the rest of his life in one way or another. His sister Ethel recalled that he was in a pretty poor state on his return to Ledbury that autumn, and spent much time muttering the words to the shanty 'Hanging Johnny', which had struck a chord in the desolate wasteland of the Horn. In the spring, his Aunt announced that she had secured him a place on another windjammer, the big four-masted barque *Bidston Hill,* loading case oil in New York and bound for the East. John was dispatched to New York to serve, once again, as an apprentice. Masefield's thoughts on this matter were very clear, as he later recalled:

The sea seemed to have me in her grip. I was to pass a life beating other men's ships to port. This was to be 'life' for me. The docks and sailor town and all the damning and the heaving.

It was likely he reported aboard the *Bidston Hill,* but a few days of the usual toil was enough for him, 'I deserted my ship in New York. I cut myself adrift from her and from my home. I was going to be a writer come what might.'

And that was that: a couple of years of landlocked adventures in the US were followed by a working passage home as a bar steward aboard a transatlantic passenger vessel. Aside from a burst of seafaring serving on a hospital launch during World War One, Masefield was finished with the sea. Yet when he picked up his pen in earnest around 1900 at the age of 22, he returned immediately to the oceans and the ships he had so loved and loathed. To Masefield the writer, the sea was everything. His one voyage as a true sailor, and his experiences on the *Conway,* seeped through much of his best poetry and prose. His first published poems were overflowing with the romance and mystical beauty of the oceans and the elegant windjammers that plied them in ever diminishing numbers. And this brings us back to the start of this tale, and the young poet, so embarrassed of his lack of 'real' sea knowledge. True, next to Conrad, who had worked on the sea for many years and even commanded a clipper ship, he was a novice, yet his one epic voyage had taught him all he ever needed to know about the sea. He was not benumbed to its charm and horror by years of grind. He saw and fully understood with great clarity how sailors come to love and hate it in equal measure. He also understood how sometimes you need to turn your back on the sea to love it and, in many cases, to live. Many of his *Conway* contemporaries died tragically young. Despite this, he wasn't above occasional regrets:

> *There is solid comfort in a roaring storm ashore here, but on a calm day, when it is raining, when it is muddy underfoot, when the world is the colour of a drowned rat, one calls to mind more boisterous days, the days of effort and adventure; and wasn't I a fool, I say, to come ashore and live a life like this. And I was surely daft, I keep saying, to think the sea as bad as I always thought it. And if I were in a ship now, I say, I wouldn't be doing what I'm trying to do. I wouldn't be hunched at this desk, I say, I'd be up on a bridge – up on a bridge with a helmsman, feeling her do her fifteen knots.*

Yet, there was another factor in his young life that contributed to, and in some ways marred, his writing. Masefield's youth was all about failure, isolation and loneliness. In many of his books there is such a longing for a happy ending that it tarnishes the story itself. Perhaps this is why his children's fiction *The Midnight Folk* and *The Box of Delights* are still cherished while works such as *Sard Harker* and the *Bird of Dawning* are largely overlooked. Both these books are packed with beautiful descriptions and narrative, but are spoilt by the perfection of the hero and the ludicrously neat conclusions. Graham Greene once wrote that *Sard Harker*, 'would have been the greatest adventure story in the English language if it hadn't got that ridiculous ending.'

Fortunately Masefield's life *did* have the happy ending he craved. He married, settled in Oxfordshire and was poet laureate for 37 years. Perhaps the greatest contributor to this good fortune was Masefield's ability to love and appreciate the sea but accept that it was necessary for him to turn his back on it. Naturally, the best insight into this complex relationship comes from the man himself, pithily summing up his feelings after meeting up with an old shipmate from the *Gilcruix*, who had remained at sea and commented how 'old' Masefield had become by sticking to the land. Reflecting later on the conversation, he pondered that epic voyage:

> *That was youth, that was the flower of youth, the glory of it, the adventure accomplished. It had been much to me, it is much to me. It had been much to my friend; it was nothing to him now. I was getting old, yet the thing [the voyage] comes back to me, it is my youth, I am young in it. It is my friend who is old; it is he who has lost his youth, it has gone from him, it is dead, he has lived his vision.*

Herman Melville

Literary leviathan

Six months at sea! Yes reader, as I live six months out of sight of land cruising after the sperm whale beneath the scorching sun of the line and tossed on the billows of the wide rolling Pacific. The sky above, the sea around and nothing else!

Melville's *Ty-Pee*

If ever there was a man who suffered for his art it was Herman Melville. The reason so much of his seafaring prose evokes scenes so vividly is that much of what he described he lived through. When Melville writes of 'six months at sea' he speaks from his own knowledge of what it was like to spend months on end drifting across the Pacific in search of sperm whales, having signed up for a five-year trip aboard the whaler *Acushnet* in 1840. Yet he did far more than simply cruise for whales: misadventures included everything from several weeks of captivity among a cannibal tribe in the Marquesas to taking part in a full-blown mutiny in Tahiti. Little wonder that Melville later reflected on his departure from his home as, 'the point when I began to live.'

Perhaps the reason that Melville's nautical writing has such an earthy and accessible feel to the reader is because during his entire seafaring career, which stretched from 1839 through to 1844, he served as an ordinary or able seaman.

These are two of the lowest ranking roles aboard a ship and gave his writings a clear empathy with the underdog. They also meant he was able to evoke with great eloquence the bawdiness, tedium, humour and camaraderie found in a ship's fo'cs'le. Yet, although Melville came to be a champion of the ordinary man, in his youth few would have dreamed that he would have moved in such circles long enough to empathise with the lower classes. Herman was born in 1819 into a family of both wealth and gentility. His father, Alan and his mother, Maria could trace their lineage back to the early settlers of North America, and their families had ancestors who had served with distinction in the War of Independence and had the medals to prove it. Such pedigree was important to Americans looking to forge some kind of heritage of their own and it commanded respect. Even in his most servile roles aboard a ship, Melville was always aware of where he came from and the pedigree of his family.

His early upbringing in New York would have seemed happy to the youngster, yet there was always a crisis lurking below the surface. Alan Melville was a charismatic man who ran a business importing fine luxury goods from overseas. In the course of his business he travelled abroad frequently, and often held his children spellbound with tales of far-flung places on his return. By 1829 however it was evident that he had overreached himself financially and, as the creditors closed in, the family were forced to move from their New York City home and resettle in Albany in upstate New York. Alan was hellbent on winning back the Melville fortune and continued to borrow heavily from members of his influential and wealthy family. Unfortunately, his efforts were in vain and the extreme stress of the situation led to his untimely death at the age of 50. He left his widow penniless and with the burden of eight children to feed. This fall from grace and descent into poverty had a profound effect on young Herman and played a great part in shaping the angry young man who turned his back on society and headed off to sea in search of adventure.

Prior to this, Melville had tried to make a fist of being a landsman, but seemed thwarted at every turn. He was an educated man and this should, in theory, have given him a step up the ladder, yet attempts at working as a teacher and a traineeship as an engineer both ended fruitlessly. In 1839, at the age of 20, Melville determined to go to sea. It is unclear what first drew him down to the water, for although there was some history of nautical adventuring among the Melvilles and his mother's family, the Gansevoorts, there was no direct family member for Melville to latch on to. What is unquestionably true is that he was an adventurous young man and his father's tales of foreign lands probably inspired him. His experiences during his first voyage were part fictionalised in his later novel *Redburn*, and it is probable that the book's eponymous hero speaks for Melville when he states: 'Sad disappointments in several plans; the necessity of doing something for myself united to a naturally roving disposition had conspired within me to send me to sea.'

Melville signed on for his first position aboard the *St Lawrence*, ship-rigged and 119ft long. She was engaged in the transatlantic trade between New York and Liverpool. At the time, this run was almost entirely in the hands of US ship owners and their vessels had gained a reputation for hard driving and fine seamanship that ensured smart passages and maximum work from a crew. Shipping lines such as the Black Ball and Black Cross companies were providing regular and relatively swift passages across the Atlantic long before steamships swept them aside. Although the *St Lawrence* traded regularly between New York and Liverpool, she was not owned by any of the famous shipping lines and was likely considered a slower vessel than the regular packet ships. Her captain, Oliver Brown, was in charge of 17 crew including Melville, who would have been regarded as a 'greenhorn' by the rest of the crew. Melville was fortunate to sail from New York in the month of June, for this ensured a relatively gentle crossing. A midwinter traverse of this desolate, ice-strewn stretch of water would have been a far more unpleasant undertaking. Nevertheless, Melville would have faced a very testing time on this first voyage, for a tall ship can seem a very bewildering place to the novice, presenting an absolute maze of ropes, and all manner of alien phrases as this passage from *Redburn* illustrates:

People who have never gone to sea for the first time as sailors, cannot imagine how puzzling and confounding it is. It must be like going into a barbarous country, where they speak a strange dialect, dress in strange clothes, and live in strange houses. For sailors have their own names,

even for things that are familiar ashore; and if you call a thing by its
shore name, you are laughed at for an ignoramus and a landlubber.

It is also highly likely that Melville was both seasick and homesick. In
Redburn, he uses the departure of the *St Lawrence* (renamed *Highlander* in
the novel) as a chance to ponder on better times in New York, when he and
his family had been used to easy privilege. Certainly, the early stages of this
voyage would have been a humbling experience, for Melville was really the
lowest of the low aboard the *St Lawrence*.

He was also being forced to mix with men he would have always been told
were far inferior to him socially, and their rather coarse manners probably
grated with this sensitive, well to do young man. Most of all, however, he
was probably simply terrified of the towering masts and yards that he was
expected to climb, as he recalls in *Redburn*:

My heart was like lead, and I felt bad enough, Heaven knows; but
then, there was plenty of work to be done, which kept my thoughts from
becoming too much for me ... When I looked up at the high, giddy masts,
and thought how often I must be going up and down them, I thought sure
enough that some luckless day or other, I would certainly fall overboard
and be drowned. And then, I thought of lying down at the bottom of the
sea, stark alone, with the great waves rolling over me, and no one in the
wide world knowing that I was there. And I thought how much better and
sweeter it must be, to be buried under the pleasant hedge that bounded
the sunny south side of our village grave-yard, where every Sunday I had
used to walk after church in the afternoon; and I almost wished I was
there now; yes, dead and buried in that churchyard. All the time my eyes
were filled with tears, and I kept holding my breath, to choke down the
sobs, for indeed I could not help feeling as I did, and no doubt any boy
in the world would have felt just as I did then.

In writing of Melville's experiences aboard the *St Lawrence*, it would be very
handy to simply take *Redburn* as gospel. Certainly Melville presented this as

autobiographical, but much written in the book must be taken with a pinch of salt, for there are several notable incidents within the text – such as the loss of a man overboard – which simply did not happen. Nevertheless, much of the emotion, such as that expressed in the previous paragraph, is clearly real enough and written with genuine feeling. The same is true of Melville's other more famous reminisces, *Ty-Pee* and *Omoo* which, although based on his own memories, are often shamelessly embellished. Yet, by careful study, it is possible to tease the truth out of Melville's tales. It is also important to enjoy them as they should be enjoyed; salty yarns spun by a master storyteller.

Melville was evidently a smart seaman, for on this first voyage, he does not seem to have fallen afoul of the mate too seriously. American ships of this era were gaining a fearful reputation for ill treatment of men and the fulcrum of this was generally the mate. A 'bucko' mate would get work done aboard by a constant regime of 'hazing' the men into submission, often with the use of force. In this violent world it was frequently the weakest that were singled out. On this voyage you would expect it to be Melville. Fortunately, apart from a few snide words from the crew regarding his privileged background, Melville's first trip seems to have been free from any such unpleasantness.

In this atmosphere, doubtless aided by the clement weather, Melville was able to enjoy himself and the heady freedom and poetry in motion that is a sailing ship at sea. It is clear that the sea and all of its wilful charm seduced the youngster, as this passage from *Redburn* illustrates:

> At last we hoisted the stun'-sails up to the top-sail yards, and as soon as the vessel felt them, she gave a sort of bound like a horse, and the breeze blowing more and more, she went plunging along, shaking off the foam from her bows, like foam from a bridle-bit. Every mast and timber seemed to have a pulse in it that was beating with Me and joy; and I felt a wild exulting in my own heart, and felt as if I would be glad to bound along so round the world.
>
> Then was I first conscious of a wonderful thing in me, that responded to all the wild commotion of the outer world; and went reeling on and

on with the planets in their orbits, and was lost in one delirious throb at
the center of the All. A wild bubbling and bursting was at my heart, as
if a hidden spring had just gushed out there; and my blood ran tingling
along my frame, like mountain brooks in spring freshets.

Yes I yes! give me this glorious ocean life, this salt-sea life, this briny,
foamy life, when the sea neighs and snorts, and you breathe the very
breath that the great whales respire! Let me roll around the globe, let
me rock upon the sea; let me race and pant out my life, with an eternal
breeze astern, and an endless sea before!

The *St Lawrence* was 28 days crossing the Atlantic, which is probably
about par for the course in this leisurely age. Even the smartest packet ship
struggled to make the trip in under 20 days at this time and it wasn't until the
advent of the clippers a decade later that passage times were dramatically
reduced. The *St Lawrence* proceeded to Liverpool where her cargo of cotton
bales was to be unloaded. Melville's first impression of Liverpool was
distinctly underwhelming, as he noted:

Looking shoreward, I beheld lofty ranges of dingy ware-houses, which
seemed very deficient in the elements of the marvelous; and bore a most
unexpected resemblance to the ware-houses along South-street in New
York. There was nothing strange; nothing extraordinary about them.
There they stood; a row of calm and collected ware-houses; very good
and substantial edifices, doubtless, and admirably adapted to the ends
had in view by the builders; but plain, matter-of-fact ware-houses,
nevertheless, and that was all that could be said of them.

To be sure, I did not expect that every house in Liverpool must be a
Leaning Tower of Pisa, or a Strasbourg Cathedral; but yet, these edifices
I must confess, were a sad and bitter disappointment to me.

Given that most of New York's warehouses and buildings at this time
would doubtless have aped the British style, it is not so surprising that the
buildings looked near identical, but his disappointment is understandable.

After this came a six-week wait for a new freight to be secured. This was a comfortable time for the sailors of the *St Lawrence* who were able to relax ashore in a boarding house at the expense of the ship owner. This was a very unusual state of affairs and came about due to safety regulations in Liverpool forbidding the lighting of fires aboard vessels in port. This would have been a real trial for visiting sailors, as cooking and heating aboard were rendered impossible. Fortunately for American sailors, the US consul had dictated that they must be lodged and fed ashore for the duration of the stay, so Melville resided in a humble guest house in the centre of Liverpool. This must have been a considerable expense to the owners of the *St Lawrence* and it is easy to perceive why many crewmembers were encouraged to desert ship. Indeed, many of the men were siphoned off into the establishments of the many 'land sharks' and 'crimps' who haunted the back alleys of Liverpool and whose only aim was to drug a sailor and bundle him aboard a new ship, bound to god knows where, in exchange for a modest commission from the skipper of the recruiting ship. The next thing the 'Shanghaied' sailor knew he would be waking up at sea with a sore head bound on a voyage to distant lands.

Melville was far too savvy to fall into such a trap, however, and devoted much of his time to exploring the mighty city of Liverpool and taking in the squalid deprivation and heady opulence of this great trading city in equal measure. While the ship was idle, the crew was required to do little other than the bare minimum aboard, even loading, when a cargo of steel bars finally arrived, was in the hands of the Liverpool stevedores. Thus Melville padded the narrow streets and walked in the footsteps of his father, who had visited the city in very different circumstances.

After six weeks' leisure, the *St Lawrence* was once again loaded and ready to go. She carried with her 32 passengers, who were probably Irish emigrants looking to escape the grinding poverty of their own blight-stricken land. Off Ireland, Melville relates a comic scene whereby many of the passengers became overexcited as they believed the new world was in sight and, by measure, equally disillusioned when it was revealed that this was actually their homeland.

The return trip was an arduous 48-day slog back across the Atlantic, as the *St Lawrence* battled with light headwinds. The westerly passage across the Atlantic is generally slower than the run eastward and it must have come as a blessed relief to all aboard when she finally arrived in New York with passengers and crew alive and well. It was a common occurrence for a substantial portion of the emigrants to expire on this tough passage, but with only 32 passengers, life aboard the *St Lawrence* was comfortable enough. The voyage was at an end, and Melville had proven himself a competent seaman. He must have hoped to head home and spin a few yarns about the trip, but there was no respite for the youngster, who returned to discover that his mother was in even more severe financial straits and had been forced to sell furniture in order to cover the mortgage repayments.

Melville was therefore unable to bask in the glory of his great adventure and instead went straight back to work teaching in a school with the aim of providing his mother with some extra funds. Unfortunately, the school seems to have been most erratic in paying its teachers. No doubt it was suffering due to the economic depression that afflicted the US during this period and it wasn't long before the frustrated young teacher was once more dreaming of the sea and adventure. Reading Richard Henry Dana's *Two Years Before the Mast* had also fired Melville's imagination. The book narrated a trip from Boston around Cape Horn to San Francisco and back. Dana was a Harvard graduate who had shipped aboard the brig *Pilgrim* as ordinary seaman for health reasons. His subsequent book was a big hit and contains some deeply evocative descriptions. His narration of the rounding of Cape Horn makes one shiver just to read it and, as Melville himself later noted, 'must have been written with an icicle'.

Melville began to cast around for a ship, and news of a boom in the price of sperm whale oil pushed him in the direction of the whaling fleet. He headed to Fairhaven, Massachusetts where he signed on as an ordinary seaman aboard the whaler *Acushnet*, commanded by Captain Valentine Pease Jr. The *Acushnet* was a new ship, 104ft in length, somewhat squat and stumpy in design, but also setting a good spread of canvas. Her hull was painted black with a white line down each side punctuated by painted gun ports, which at the time were used to discourage pirates, or in the *Acushnet's* case South Sea islanders, by giving the impression that the vessel was a man-of-war. The ship was bound around Cape Horn in search of the sperm whale, noted as the most fearsome of all the leviathans that waft their way peacefully across our oceans. The voyage would endure until the hold of the *Acushnet* was full of barrels of sperm oil. This could take up to four or five years. Initially she was probably fully provisioned to be able to sail for a full year afloat without touching land, although it was customary for captains to pause at natural provisioning points such as Rio in order to top up these supplies.

Given that the sperm whale was believed to be one of the most dangerous creatures of the deep, there had to be extenuating reasons to seek out the great leviathan, and they were that his head was full of spermaceti, or sperm oil. This clear, yellowish liquid – technically a form of wax – was in high demand during the mid-1800s, both as a lubricant for machinery and also as an illuminant, as it burns with a bright, odourless flame. Demand for sperm oil reached a peak during the 1850s, when a gallon of the stuff could fetch $1.50 on the open market. The *Acushnet* would aim to fill her holds with around 2,000 barrels of this oil. Given that the average sperm whale holds between 25 and 40 barrels worth of the precious oil within its head, you get some idea of the magnitude of the task awaiting the crew, who were expected to lower the whaling boats rain or shine to capture these mighty creatures.

For these efforts, each member of the crew could expect a proportion of the profits of the trip. This was known as a 'lay', and the size of your lay depended on your experience. Melville, as a novice, could expect one of the lowest lays and had to satisfy himself with 1/175 of the total profit from the voyage. On arriving home, all aboard were at the mercy of the very volatile sperm oil market, which ultimately decided how much they made from the trip. Melville arrived when the *Acushnet* was almost ready to sail, and observed the last of the supplies being loaded aboard prior to departure. It was the depths of winter, and icy cold, which must have set young Melville dreaming of the exotic lands to come. On 3 January 1840, the whaler slipped her cable and nosed down the icy Acushnet River bound around Cape Horn and beyond to the South Seas in pursuit of the whale.

His voyage aboard the *Acushnet* was later published in *Ty-Pee*, Melville's first and, for the duration of his lifetime, most successful novel. He was always at pains to state that the book was based solely on fact and, if this is the case, then Captain Pease does not come off well at all. Re-named Captain Vangs, Pease is described thus:

> *The usage on board of the ship was tyrannical; the sick had been inhumanly neglected; the provisions had been doled out in scanty allowance; and her cruises were unreasonably protracted. The captain was the author of the abuses; it was in vain to think that he would either remedy them, or alter his conduct, which was arbitrary and violent in the extreme. His prompt reply to all complaints and remonstrances was – the butt-end of a handspike, so convincingly administered as effectually to silence the aggrieved party.*

Just how bad Pease was is hard to ascertain. What is true was that the crew of the *Acushnet*, having signed the ship's articles, were by and large at the mercy of the captain, who could be as cruel or as kind as he wished. It is unquestionably true that seamen were often treated disgracefully aboard ships and, as late as 1851, the American clipper *Challenge* limped in to San Francisco with 11 sailors dead from the mistreatment that had allegedly been doled out on the trip around the Horn. In this instance, the captain and mate were both acquitted of any wrongdoing. Nevertheless, whaling vessels tended to be more harmonious, due to the extreme length of their voyages. Between launching for whales, the crew could generally take it easy. On the other hand, Pease had already been taken to task by some of his crew during a previous whaling voyage, with some of the ship's complement complaining of substandard supplies and poor treatment.

Melville had all this to come as the *Acushnet* meandered slowly down the Atlantic toward Cape Horn. There was plenty of opportunity to take stock of his surroundings. He was part of a crew of 26, made up of the captain, three mates, two junior officers, a cook, two carpenters, a blacksmith and 16 seamen or 'foremast hands'. All of these foremast hands were housed in the fo'c'sle, a low, dark hovel situated right in the bows of the boat, which must have been intolerably stuffy and a veritable pit of filth and frustration after several weeks at sea. Melville describes a typical whalers fo'c'sle thus in his later book *Omoo*:

> *The general aspect of the forecastle was dungeon-like and dingy in the extreme. In the first place, it was not five feet from deck to deck and even this space was encroached upon by two outlandish cross-timbers bracing the vessel, and by the sailors' chests, over which you must needs crawl in getting about. At meal-times, and especially when we indulged in after-dinner chat, we sat about the chests like a parcel of tailors.*
>
> *In the middle of all were two square, wooden columns, denominated in marine architecture 'Bowsprit Bitts.' They were about a foot apart, and between them, by a rusty chain, swung the forecastle lamp, burning day and night, and forever casting two long black shadows. Lower down, between the bitts, was a locker, or sailors' pantry, kept in abominable disorder, and sometimes requiring a vigorous cleaning and fumigation.*

With the sailors thus crammed together in such a deplorable manner, the *Acushnet* wafted her way into warmer climes. Doubtless the crew would have been set to work at practising lowering the boats and rehearsing their roles for a real live chase of the leviathan. A whaler generally carried four whaleboats slung on davits, or cranes, along her side. These boats were double ended and around 25-30ft in length and were powered along by five oarsmen, who manned extremely long oars up to 18ft in length. To aid with the stealthy pursuit of the whale, matting was placed under the rowlocks or 'thole pins', which ensured that the whaleboats could glide along in almost total silence. As the greenhorns found their place, they would have observed the respect and obsessive care with which their seniors handled all of the whaling gear; harpoons were honed and pared down to razor sharpness, while the long whale lines, which were attached to the harpoons, were coiled down into tubs with total precision. One snarl up while this line was paying out when a whale dived could drag the whole crew down to Davy Jones' locker.

The crew were divided in to two watches, port and starboard, under the command of the first and second mate respectively. Each watch would be four hours in length and two men were stationed aloft throughout the day keeping up a permanent search for whales. On sighting a whale, the following exchange, as told in *Moby Dick*, was typical:

> 'There she blows! there! there! there! she blows! she blows!'
> 'Where-away?'
> 'On the lee-beam, about two miles off! a school of them!'
> Instantly all was commotion. The Sperm Whale blows as a clock ticks, with the same undeviating and reliable uniformity. And thereby whalemen distinguish this fish from other tribes of his genus.
> 'There go flukes!' was now the cry; and the whales disappeared.

There is no record of the first lowering in anger aboard the *Acushnet*, but it definitely occurred before the ship touched at Rio, for at this point over 100 barrels of sperm oil were shipped to a vessel heading back to the US. No doubt Melville was utterly focussed on his own role as oarsman when it occurred. The most important thing for him was staying in time with the rest of the crew, urged on as they were by the mate, who would entreat them to pull for all they were worth. Woe betide the man who got out of time and 'caught a crab', as this could be the end of the chase.

Quite how Melville felt as the boats were lowered for that first chase is not fully recorded, but this passage from *Moby Dick* gives a fair indication:

> Not the raw recruit, marching from the bosom of his wife into the fever heat of his first battle; not the dead man's ghost encountering the first unknown phantom in the other world; – neither of these can feel stranger and stronger emotions than that man does, who for the first time finds himself pulling into the charmed, churned circle of the hunted sperm whale.

The time to strike a whale is just after it has surfaced, as it will not have been able to take in enough air to dive too deep once it has been 'darted' (harpooned) by its assailants. It was the role of the foremost oarsman, known as the 'boatsteerer' to hurl the first harpoon into the unsuspecting creature once within close range. Once darted, the chase entered its most dangerous phase, for the whale often hurled itself in the air, thrashing its flukes around in rage and pain, before descending into the deep. Meanwhile, onboard, the hundreds of metres of line attached to the harpoon fizzed out of the customised tub, where the line had previously been painstakingly coiled. Whale, harpoon and line all plunged down to the depths, while another oarsman poured water on the line to cool it down. While all of this was going on, the boatsteerer raced aft and swapped ends with the mate, in order to steer the vessel as it was towed along at great speed by the frantic whale. Sometimes a whaleboat could be towed out of sight of the mother ship by an enraged whale, and many a crew simply disappeared. It was also common in this initial frenzy for the whaleboat to be smashed by its prey if the crew were not smart enough at backing away.

Once in tow, the crew awaited the resurfacing of their adversary and, as the whale weakened, would pull in on their line until once more within range. At this point, the mate would finish the unfortunate beast off with an onslaught of repeated blows from his lance until the huge creature surrendered to death. Things did not always go this well, and the risk of the whaleboat being dragged under, swamped or sunk by the thrashing whale was extremely real. Nevertheless, if successful, this most dramatic and dangerous part of whaling, the chase, was over but the hard work had only just begun.

With the whale dead, the crew could inspect their prey. Sperm whales are generally around 50–60ft in length and can live up to 80 years. On close inspection it was often discovered that an elderly whale would already have several rusted harpoons sticking out of its skin from previous unsuccessful attacks. If a crew was fortunate, the mother ship would be close at hand and could sail over and collect its prey but, all too often an exhausting row, towing the dead whale, was required. Whales are naturally buoyant, but in some cases, all the hard work was undone and the whale would inexplicably sink without a trace. Melville records this occurrence in *Moby Dick* and the dismay and frustration must have been palpable.

Once alongside, the great carcass was lashed to the ship, tail forward and work had to continue at a fast pace, for all the time the waters between ship and whale were a frenzy of sharks, snapping away at the whale's tasty blubber. Above this frenzy, a number of unfortunate men were lowered on a 'cutting stage': simply a short plinth attached to the side by two ropes, and from this vulnerable position the men dangled while they cut a deep incision in the whales blubber in order to insert a 'blubber hook', which was lowered from the rigging on a very substantial block and tackle. At this point, the unfortunate boatsteerer was ordered to jump on top of the whale and insert the hook. Although he was attached to the ship by a thin rope, the danger of this operation can be appreciated to some extent even as you sit comfortably reading this book. It certainly does not bear thinking about how the man felt who lowered himself onto the slimy corpse as it pitched around in the seas. One slip could mean being crushed between boat and whale or gobbled up by the voracious sharks.

With the hook attached, a strip of blubber about six feet wide was cut around it, and the crew manned the windlass in order to haul up the hook, which bit deep into the whale and, under immense strain, ripped the flesh away from the carcass as the mighty creature rolled over and over, unpeeling in much the same manner as an orange. Once the tackle had run out of bight to haul up, a new hook was inserted lower down in this same strip of blubber and so the process continued. Meantime, the head of the whale, containing all that precious spermaceti, was carefully amputated from the body and once the great strips of blubber were peeled away from the carcass it was cast loose and drifted off to be chewed over by the insatiable sharks. The head was then secured alongside and carefully dissected. In most cases it would be too big to haul up on deck, so the extraction of the oil would have to be carried out with the great head hauled up almost level with the deck. With the ship heeling over drunkenly under the weight of what was left of the whale, a hole would be cut in the head and buckets would be lowered into it from whence gallons of the precious sperm oil were extracted.

By now the men at the capstan, of which Melville would certainly have been one, would be utterly exhausted from hours of backbreaking work. Their hands would be blistered from gripping the capstan bars and their thighs and calves would be screaming from the exertion. Yet the labour was far from over, for it was now time to wring out every single ounce of oil from the blubber and head of the whale. Between fore and mainmast were situated the 'try works', essentially a great stone furnace built into the ship in order to treat the blubber and remove the last drop of oil from the unfortunate creature. With the blubber aboard, the great fires of the try works were lit, and blubber and 'junk' (part of the head made up of large, oil filled membranes) were loaded into huge copper pots and heated until the oil was rendered. First the 'junk' was treated, then the blubber was minced and heated through, the residue being thrown back onto the fires to burn and crackle. All the while the men toiled, soaked in oil and blood, working shifts of six hours on, six off. As night fell, the great furnace would glow eerie and red, reflecting in the dark, lonely ocean and shooting sparks into the empty sky. The scene is described vividly in *Moby Dick*:

> *By midnight the works were in full operation. We were clear from the carcase; sail had been made; the wind was freshening; the wild ocean darkness was intense. But that darkness was licked up by the fierce flames, which at intervals forked forth from the sooty flues, and illuminated every lofty rope in the rigging, as with the famed Greek fire. The burning ship drove on, as if remorselessly commissioned to some vengeful deed. So the pitch and sulphur-freighted brigs of the bold Hydriote, Canaris, issuing from their midnight harbors, with broad sheets of flame for sails, bore down upon the Turkish frigates, and folded them in conflagrations.*

Finally, the casks of oil were made ready to be stowed and, following a full scrub down, the labours of the men were at an end. Yet the ever-vigilant lookouts remained at the topmast, and it was only a matter of time before the cry of, 'Thar she blows!' would be heard again. In fact, the more of this sort of work, the better as far as the whaler was concerned, for once a ship's hold was full, she could return home.

After calling in to Rio to drop off some of this hard-earned sperm oil, the *Acushnet* pressed on toward the dark waters of Cape Horn. The little whaler had to round this fearful headland in order to reach the rich whaling grounds of the Pacific, and there was much to fear from the dreaded Cape, for the *Acushnet* was headed 'westabout' the Horn, meaning she would have to beat against the prevailing easterly gales that howled around this bleak outcrop. Ships could be stuck down for weeks at a time in this snow-strewn, godforsaken spot as they attempted to reach the Pacific, and more than one ship had been known to turn tail and run eastabout almost around the world in order to make the Pacific via Australia. This exact circumstance happened to the *Bounty* in 1787 when bound to Tahiti, and the demoralising effect of the battering off the Horn certainly contributed to the subsequent mutiny.

Fortunately, the *Acushnet* was new, well-found and evidently a handy vessel. Most importantly she encountered very clement weather and took a mere 12 days to enter into the welcoming waters of the Pacific. Melville could now count himself a true sailor, for he had crossed the line and rounded the Horn. From now on, every mile gained to the north took them into more pleasant weather and the warm, rolling billows of the Pacific. The *Acushnet* was heading for the 'offshore grounds', a rich whaling area off the coast of South America. The crew of the *Acushnet* could expect to spend the best part of the next three years rolling around on this great blue nothingness, wandering seemingly without direction save for the endless quest for the whale. The awful ennui and loneliness of such a life is hard for people to conceive these days, but many men led this existence for years on end. Aside from the few hours of terror and adrenaline that occurred each time the boats were lowered, there were only two other occurrences to break the terrible boredom of life aboard: the first was that the captain would be compelled to touch at some lonely port for water and supplies – at which point many men took the opportunity to break the tedium by deserting – or the chance meeting of a fellow whale ship. Whalers were, understandably, very sociable vessels and it was rare that two vessels meeting in this lonely expanse would not heave to and lower their boats in order to have what was known as a 'gam'. This was a great opportunity to swap stories, possibly get news from home and generally enjoy other people's company. It was probably in the course of one of these gams that Melville heard related the tale of the whaler *Essex*, which in 1820 was hunting sperm whales when a particularly large specimen turned on the ship and repeatedly rammed the vessel until it sank. The survivors had no choice but to remain in their whale boats, and endured a gruelling voyage, in the course of which some members of the crew drew lots to decide who should be eaten, and only a handful of survivors made the mainland. The story of the whale attacking the *Essex* was to form the tumultuous climax of *Moby Dick*, while other yarns of mutiny and unrest, which would have been spun at these gatherings were also interwoven into the plot of Melville's masterpiece.

Apart from the odd gam, the only other diversion for many months was a stopover in Santa, Peru, where the men were given shore leave, the *Acushnet* was given a thorough clean, and running repairs were carried out. Melville wrote to his mother from here stating that all was well and that the crew were an excellent bunch. This was odd, for it would only be a matter of months before he deserted the ship. It is possible, however, that he was simply putting a brave face on things for his mother's benefit. From Santa, the *Acushnet* continued to plod her way through the whaling grounds; by now her sails would have been well patched, threadbare and stained with the smoke of the tryworks; her once white decks would be marked with grease and oil, and her paint would be peeling. As for the men, all would now be struggling with the mind-numbing prospect of at least two more years of this drifting. Some passed the time working on scrimshaw, a method of carving whalebone and marking it with ink, which often produces the most delicate work. Others would busy themselves with model making, reading, arguing or lolling around the deck. All would have been desperately sexually frustrated and fairly sick of each other's company.

There were, however, rewards, for the *Acushnet* was crisscrossing lazily along one of the most perfect cruising grounds a sailor could dream of, and when there were no whales in sight, life aboard was extremely relaxing, as Melville recalled in *Ty Pee*:

What a delightful, lazy, languid time we had whilst we were thus gliding along! There was nothing to be done; a circumstance that happily suited our disinclination to do anything. We abandoned the fore-peak altogether, and spreading an awning over the forecastle, slept, ate, and lounged under it the live-long day. Every one seemed to be under the influence of some narcotic. Even the officers aft, whose duty required them never to be seated while keeping a deck watch, vainly endeavoured to keep on their pins; and were obliged invariably to compromise the matter by leaning up against the bulwarks, and gazing abstractedly over the side. Reading was out of the question; take a book in your hand, and you were asleep in an instant.

Nevertheless, Melville must have been bored by the lack of intellectual stimulus and was firm friends with Richard Greene, who shared with Melville a wider interest in the world and was well educated. Greene later recalled how the pair 'had whiled away many a watch in yarn and song' doubtless dreaming of adventure. It is therefore not surprising that it would be with Greene that Melville eventually hatched the plan to desert the ship. This desertion would not take place until June 1842, when, after touching briefly in Tumbez, Peru and the Galapagos Islands in search of a turtle, the *Acushnet* set a course for the Marquesas and the island of Nuku Hiva. After four and a half months at sea, the *Acushnet* finally raised the towering pinnacles and verdant slopes of this savage land.

'No description can do justice to its beauty,' Melville later wrote of Nuku Hiva Bay, which is a bit of a cop out, but suffice to say that it is everything you picture if you try to conjure up a perfect South Sea bay; lush slopes tumbling steeply down to the waters edge fringed with powdery white sand and iridescent blue sea. It was like something out of a dream and the sailors must have rubbed their eyes in disbelief at what they saw. As the *Acushnet* approached the bay, she was surrounded by native canoes and boarded by a white man who described himself as a pilot; this despite the fact he was clearly drunk. Captain Pease no doubt ignored the entreaties of this washed up old beachcomber as he endeavoured to pilot his vessel into the sheltered bay, where several French warships lay. The *Acushnet* had arrived just in time to witness the first overtures of the French in a series of greedy expansionist plans that would eventually lay the island to waste. Yet the crew of the *Acushnet* cared little for this. Fed on tales from some of the more experienced crew of native savagery and debauchery they were rubbing their hands together at the prospect of an exciting stay in this idyllic setting.

They were not to be disappointed. As the *Acushnet* stole through the glassy waters of Nuku Hiva Bay, Melville perceived what he first thought was a large school of fish in the water, but as they drew closer it was evident that this was actually a mass of Nuku Hivan girls, swimming off to greet the mariners. Melville describes the scene thus:

We were still some distance from the beach, and under slow headway, when we sailed right into the midst of these swimming nymphs, and they boarded us at every quarter; many seizing hold of the chain-plates and springing into the chains; others, at the peril of being run over by the vessel in her course, catching at the bob-stays, and wreathing their slender forms about the ropes, hung suspended in the air. All of them at length succeeded in getting up the ship's side, where they clung dripping with the brine and glowing from the bath, their jet-black tresses streaming over their shoulders, and half enveloping their otherwise naked forms. There they hung, sparkling with savage vivacity, laughing gaily at one another, and chattering away with infinite glee. Nor were they idle the while, for each one performed the simple offices of the toilette for the other. Their luxuriant locks, wound up and twisted into the smallest possible compass, were freed from the briny element; the whole person carefully dried, and from a little round shell that passed from hand to hand, anointed with a fragrant oil: their adornments were completed by passing a few loose folds of white tappa, in a modest cincture, around the waist. Thus arrayed they no longer hesitated, but flung themselves lightly over the bulwarks, and were quickly frolicking about the decks. Many of them went forward, perching upon the headrails or running out upon the bowsprit, while others seated themselves upon the taffrail, or reclined at full length upon the boats. What a sight for us bachelor sailors! How avoid so dire a temptation? For who could think of tumbling these artless creatures overboard, when they had swum miles to welcome us?

Their appearance perfectly amazed me; their extreme youth, the light clear brown of their complexions, their delicate features, and inexpressibly graceful figures, their softly moulded limbs, and free unstudied action, seemed as strange as beautiful.

The Dolly *[Melville substituted the name* Acushnet *for* Dolly *in Ty-Pee] was fairly captured; and never I will say was vessel carried before by such a dashing and irresistible party of boarders! The ship taken, we could not do otherwise than yield ourselves prisoners, and for the whole period that she remained in the bay, the* Dolly *as well as her crew, were completely in the hands of the mermaids. Our ship was now given up to every species of riot and debauchery.*

There is a clear inference, backed up by other contemporary accounts from visiting ships that the crew of the whaler essentially indulged in a very lengthy orgy. In *Ty-Pee*, Melville stays aloof from this scene of debauchery, but it is very difficult to judge whether he actually did in real life. It is doubtful he would have had religious or moral scruples, but it is possible that Melville, as an educated man, would have considered how many whaling ships touched at this spot throughout the course of a year and stood aloof simply out of fear of sexual transmitted diseases. Indeed, this may have been one of his reasons for choosing to desert the ship, which he and his companion Richard Greene did shortly afterwards when the crew was granted shore leave.

Venereal diseases are one thing, but it is also likely that Melville and Greene were simply utterly seduced by the beauty of this place, and the promise of adventure after all those weeks and months at sea. Whalemen deserting their ship was simply a fact of life during such protracted cruises and was far from surprising given the intimidating lengths of time spent afloat. Yet the decision to quit the ship in Nuku-Hiva was a brave one, for the people of the island definitely still enjoyed the taste of human flesh, although it was far more likely they would eat the flesh of an enemy tribe rather than a white man. Nevertheless, this was not a gamble particularly worth taking, and Greene and Melville must have been pretty hacked off to abandon their ship in search of adventure. True, after a promising start, the *Acushnet* had hit a dry spell and the crew had been further discouraged by rumours of a crash in the price of sperm oil back home, yet you still have to admire the pluck of the two adventurers as they headed into the unknown.

This is a book about seafaring, so I will not dwell in detail on the adventures of Melville and Greene in the interior of Nuku-Hiva. Nevertheless, I will briefly explain what happened in order to give this tale some continuity. After being granted shore leave by Pease, the pair loaded up their pockets with as much food as they dared and waited for a suitable moment to slip away from their crewmates on the beach. The aim was to head for the valley of the Happar tribe, who were known to be friendly towards white men. By the same token, it was imperative that they avoided the valley of the Ty-Pees, who were famed for their ruthlessness. Inevitably, after much battling with the undergrowth, the pair got hopelessly lost and stumbled into the valley of Ty-pee. Here, they received a warm welcome, but got the distinct impression that they were prisoners. After a couple of days friendly captivity, Greene was able to escape after word got around that a white man's boat was down at the beach. Unfortunately, Melville had injured his leg during the gruelling walk to the valley and was unable to follow. Although Greene promised to return with help, none ever came, and Melville was trapped for another three weeks. During this period he recovered somewhat, took a lover by the name of Fayaway and spent time observing the Ty-pee, generally concluding that they were a pleasant bunch with a comfortable lifestyle. He was able to effect his own escape when another whaler, the *Lucy Ann* touched at Nuku Hiva. Desperate for crew, her captain, Henry Ventom, got word that a sailor was hiding in the Ty-Pee valley. A boat was landed in the bay of Ty-Pee and Melville, aided by Fayaway, was able to escape.

These are the bare facts, related in far greater detail in Melville's first ever novel, *Ty-Pee*. Ever since its publication, people have been arguing about how much of the story is actually true, with many dismissing it as nonsense as soon as it was published. Melville swore blind it was factual, and was backed up by Richard Greene – lost since he departed the valley of Ty-Pee and presumed dead – but re-emerged when Melville's tall tale found fame. At any rate, whatever the ins and outs of the tale, there is no doubt that the essential premise is true. The upshot of the adventure was that Melville found himself aboard the British whaler *Lucy Ann*. It is also fair to say that once he discovered the circumstances of the cruise, he would definitely have felt that it was a case of out of the frying pan into the fire, for all was not well aboard the little ship.

The vessel was a decrepit little barque, 87ft in length and built in 1819. Melville described her as he was rowed toward her following his rescue:

> *A small, slatternly-looking craft, her hull and spars a dingy black, rigging all slack and bleached nearly white, and everything denoting an ill state of affairs aboard. The four boats hanging from her sides proclaimed her a whaler. Leaning carelessly over the bulwarks were the sailors, wild, haggard-looking fellows in Scotch caps and faded blue frocks; some of them with cheeks of a mottled bronze, to which sickness soon changes the rich berry-brown of a seaman's complexion in the tropics.*

She was owned in Australia and although she was rather shabby Melville spoke very highly of her sailing qualities. Her main problem was that there appeared to be a lamentable lack of discipline aboard her, for the crew had clearly lost all faith in Captain Ventom. The result was that the entire duration of Melville's cruise aboard this ill-starred vessel seemed to consist of a never-ending battle between crew and afterguard, while many aboard were ailing with sickness.

Melville was not to know this when he signed up for a place aboard the *Lucy Ann*. Initially, Captain Ventom had doubts about shipping Melville, who was still struggling with his leg injury, but the vessel was so short handed, that he had little choice in the matter and Melville committed to a single cruise and would therefore be able to leave as soon as the *Lucy Ann* touched at her next port.

All of this seemed highly favourable to Melville, and things looked even rosier once it became clear that he would be entitled to a 1/120 'lay' of any sperm oil secured during the voyage. This was far more favourable than the 1/175 he had been due to receive aboard the *Acushnet*, but Melville was not aboard the troubled vessel long before he was sorely disillusioned. The story of the voyage prior to his arrival had been a weary tale of rebellion, dissatisfaction and mutiny ever since the vessel had departed Sydney in 1842. Five months into her whaling cruise she had pulled into Nuku-Hiva and eight of her complement, including the second mate, promptly deserted, stealing one of her whaleboats as a means of escape. Although two men and the whaleboat were recaptured, the rest of the crew appeared far from happy and Ventom had to enlist the help of a French naval vessel, which was lying in Nuku-Hiva, in order to subdue his men. The upshot was that a further eight men were arrested and imprisoned. Ultimately, six were returned to resume the cruise while the most troublesome pair remained in Nuku-Hiva awaiting transport to Valparaiso to be tried.

The following day the *Lucy Ann* headed out to sea, but Captain Ventom soon found that the men were still in an ugly frame of mind, and many refused duty – a real problem on a vessel already desperately shorthanded. Ventom managed to subdue his men sufficiently to set them back to work, but still needed extra crew and a month later he was back in Nuku-Hiva searching for someone – *anyone* – to man his ship. The stopover almost had the reverse effect, for three sailors jumped ship but were later recovered. At this point, Ventom's luck took a turn for the better, and he managed to enlist three more hands, including one lame seaman by the name of Melville. It was into this atmosphere of seething resentment that Melville signed up and, given this history of trouble, it is hardly surprising that more was just around the corner.

The events of this ill-starred voyage are narrated in Melville's *Omoo*, but it is never clear why the crew harboured such a vehement dislike for the skipper and mate. In *Omoo*, Melville characterises the mate, James German, as a hail and hearty West Country man, very competent, but rather too fond of the bottle. Captain Ventom gets more withering treatment:

The captain was a young cockney, who, a few years before, had emigrated to Australia, and, by some favouritism or other, had procured the command of the vessel, though in no wise competent. He was essentially a landsman, and though a man of education, no more meant for the sea than a hairdresser. Hence everybody made fun of him. They called him 'The Cabin Boy,' 'Paper Jack,' and half a dozen other undignified names. In truth, the men made no secret of the derision in which they held him; and as for the slender gentleman himself, he knew it all very well, and bore himself with becoming meekness. Holding as little intercourse with them as possible, he left everything to the chief mate, who, as the story went, had been given his captain in charge.

This, at least to some extent, explains the general bad conduct of the crew, for a captain without respect is a captain only in name. Nevertheless, there is no reference to ill treatment or even bad food aboard the vessel. So perhaps the part of the explanation was simply that Ventom had shipped a thoroughly awful crew, and topping it up with deserters from other ships and the type of drifters who washed up on the beaches of the South Seas was never likely to improve the situation – particularly as many of these men (like Melville) were unwell or incapacitated before they even arrived on board.

On departing Nuku-Hiva, the *Lucy Ann* added to her motley crew with more deserters from another island and then headed out on another cruise in search of whales. The trip was short lived, for Ventom himself was now taken ill and John German found himself fully in charge of the seemingly doomed little vessel. German wisely shaped a course for Tahiti and after a couple of weeks at sea, with not one whale caught or even chased, the vessel arrived off Papeete. However, to the utter consternation of the crew, the *Lucy Ann* did not enter the harbour. Instead, the headsails were backed and the barque was left hove to outside while German himself rowed in to get medical assistance. Doubtless this was a measure taken to prevent further desertion, but with five members of the crew plus the captain ailing, this served to infuriate all hands. It cannot have pleased Melville greatly either, for the terms of his signing on would have allowed him to quit the luckless boat as soon as she touched land. In the circumstances, it is entirely understandable that he would have been desperate to do so. What happened next whipped the already restive crew into a fury. The doctor who was brought aboard ordered the seriously ill Ventom ashore, while the British Consul was brought with him to explain to the men that the ship was now temporarily in command of German while their skipper recuperated. This news promptly led to a stand off, with several men refusing duty on the grounds of signing on to serve Ventom, not German, while others, Melville included, argued that they were too sick to continue with the cruise. In the end, a compromise was reached, and two men were taken ashore for treatment. The rest – and this included Melville – were declared by a doctor as fit for the cruise and the vessel departed. She did not get far.

Shortly after departing Tahiti, trouble once again broke out. This time Benbow Byrne, a boatsteerer who had been promoted to officer ordered one of the crew to help him shorten sail. The response was simple but offensive: 'Ask my arse'. The upshot of this was fisticuffs, and pretty soon the whole vessel was once again in uproar. This was the last straw for German and in despair he determined to head back to Papeete, anchoring there the following morning to the relief of all except the horrified citizens of that port, none more so than the British consul, who must have been beside himself with frustration.

The result of the *Lucy Anne*'s return was that ten of the leading troublemakers were once again arrested and confined aboard a French frigate anchored in the bay. By now though, the British consul's façade of authority was starting to crack, and was further undermined when the French frigate departed, after unceremoniously ejecting the mutineers. Prior to this, the fear had been transportation to Valparaiso, where the troublemakers could have been tried and potentially executed. The departure of the French warship and the ejection of the prisoners showed that this was all a bluff. The mutiny was rapidly descending into a farce, all the more so when the men were placed in a local prison or 'calaboose Brereton' (British prison) as it was known locally, which consisted of an open building with very limited security and extremely friendly local warders, led by the Tahitian 'Captain

Bob' who hated the British consul and consequently gave the prisoners almost unlimited liberty. It was at this point that Melville opted to join the troublemakers, no doubt reasoning that the well-fed men in the calaboose were better off than those aboard the *Lucy Ann*. He probably also sensed that freedom was at hand.

Meanwhile, Captain Ventom was convalescing and was soon prepared to head to sea once more. It was abundantly clear that the II men in the calaboose would not serve him, so more drifters and deserters were recruited and, to the relief of everyone, the *Lucy Ann* departed. It was not long after this that Melville himself also left Tahiti. The prisoners from the *Lucy Ann* were such only in name, and were allowed to roam far and wide during the day, only reporting back as night fell. It was therefore with no great difficulty that Melville and three other sailors slipped away from the calaboose and made their way to the neighbouring island of Eimeo. Their disappearance barely raised a murmur and it is highly likely that the humiliated British consul was mighty glad to see his embarrassing problem simply disappear.

Melville was once more adrift; a beachcomber wandering through these enchanted islands at his leisure. He was accompanied by an Englishman, John Troy, who had initially served as steward aboard the *Lucy Ann* but had been demoted after being suspected of theft. In *Omoo* he is given the name of Dr Long Ghost and cuts the figure of a kind of lanky, languorous, droll lothario. The text of the book is generously laced with sexual innuendo relating to Long Ghost and you get the strong impression that he was the kind of fellow your parents would always tell you to steer clear of because he was a bad influence. Again, their land-based adventures do not belong in this nautical tome, but the pair occupied themselves by working briefly for a pair of farmers, one British, one American. Clearly the lazy sailors were almost worse than useless farmhands and utterly unwilling to work, as the manner of their departure illustrates:

One morning, before breakfast, we were set to weeding in a potato-patch; and the planters being engaged at the house, we were left to ourselves. Now, though the pulling of weeds was considered by our employers an easy occupation (for which reason they had assigned it to us), and although as a garden recreation it may be pleasant enough, for those who like it – still, long persisted in, the business becomes excessively irksome.

Nevertheless, we toiled away for some time, until the doctor, who, from his height, was obliged to stoop at a very acute angle, suddenly sprang upright; and with one hand propping his spinal column, exclaimed, 'Oh, that one's joints were but provided with holes to drop a little oil through!'

Vain as the aspiration was for this proposed improvement upon our species, I cordially responded thereto; for every vertebra in my spine was articulating in sympathy.

Presently, the sun rose over the mountains, inducing that deadly morning languor so fatal to early exertion in a warm climate. We could stand it no longer; but, shouldering our hoes, moved on to the house, resolved to impose no more upon the good-nature of the planters by continuing one moment longer in an occupation so extremely uncongenial.

Thus the pair quit their employment and, after a brief attempt at becoming courtiers in the house of the Queen Pomare, the exiled ruler of Tahiti, they separated. Melville again turned to the sea and signed aboard the whaler *Charles and Henry* of Nantucket. The ever languid Troy decided at the last moment that the trip would simply be too much, and remained lolling on the beach, while Melville headed out into the rolling billows of the Pacific to battle the great whale once more.

Melville's third stab at whaling was far less of an eventful affair than the previous two attempts. The *Charles and Henry* was nearly two years into her cruise and was having a pretty lean time of it. Her captain, John Coleman was, by all accounts, a very competent master, a 'fighting master' in whaler's parlance, as he still took an active part in hunting the whales once found, just as Melville's Ahab did in *Moby Dick*. Yet on this cruise, all his efforts had so far been in vain and he had just 350 barrels of sperm oil to show for two years at sea. Melville served for six months during which time *Charles and Henry* added a further 150 barrels of sperm oil. Melville later claimed that he served as a harpooner in a whaler and, if this was the case, it would no doubt have been aboard this ship, for Melville was now a seasoned hand. In this role he would have occupied the boatsteerer's oar in the whaling boat, and it would have been he who first 'darted' the mighty sperm whale before swapping ends with the mate and steering the boat as it was towed helter skelter by the enraged creature. Whether this was the case or not, it was not long before he again sought his discharge, taking the first opportunity when the ship touched at Maui, Hawaii. This was the last of Melville's whaling activities and whether it was the lean times in the *Charles and Henry,* the discord in the *Lucy Ann* or the hard treatment in the *Acushnet* that decided him on turning his back on this perilous trade we will never know, but lovers of nautical fiction can be grateful that he went to such extreme lengths to gather the source material for later masterpieces.

Yet this was not the end of Melville's seafaring career; you must remember that he was still trapped on the opposite side of the world and that getting home was far from easy. After a brief stay in Hawaii, where he worked in a bowling alley setting up skittles and also briefly as a clerk, Melville saw his chance at getting home when the American naval vessel *United States* arrived off Honolulu. It was known that she was homeward bound and recruiting and Melville signed up for 'three years aboard or the cruise' in August 1843. He had been adrift for over two years and must have been itching to get home. His exploits aboard are recorded in great detail in his later book *White Jacket,* which he opens with the following sentence:

'All hands up anchor! Man the capstan!'
  'High die! my lads, we're homeward bound!'
  Homeward bound! – harmonious sound! Were you ever homeward bound? – No? – Quick! take the wings of the morning, or the sails of a ship, and fly to the uttermost parts of the earth. There, tarry a year or two; and then let the gruffest of boatswains, his lungs all goose-skin, shout forth those magical words, and you'll swear 'the harp of Orpheus were not more enchanting.'

The sigh of relief is almost audible; yet Melville still had a long way to travel before he was home and he now found himself in a new and strange environment ill suited to his free-spirited itinerant ways. As an ordinary seaman serving aboard a US naval vessel, he could expect strict discipline, and none of the carefree loafing and laxness of his whaling days: desertion or mutiny would carry the sentence of flogging and death respectively.

There were many other contrasts too; the *United States* was a fast frigate 178ft long. She would have looked very smart alongside the slovenly whaler, with her gleaming white decks and acres of highly polished brass. But all of that smartness came at a price; soul destroying, mind numbing toil. The biggest contrast with the whaling vessels was the immense size of her crew. She carried 480 men all told and this must have made for a very cramped and unpleasant trip. Her captain was one James Armstrong, who was renamed Captain Claret in *White Jacket*, as Melville felt he was rather too fond of a tipple. In actual fact, Melville would have had precious little to do with the captain and he was given the role of 'maintopman'. This meant that during his watch he was continuously stationed in the maintop and was therefore easily at hand if there was any sail to be taken in or loosed. Melville stated in *White Jacket* that it was his personal responsibility to loose the main royal sail, which is one of the uppermost sails on the ship. He was accompanied by several other maintopmen, commanded by an Englishman, Jack Chase, who supervised his men with aplomb and seems to have been the object of hero worship from Melville, for Chase was a different class of seaman: erudite, debonair and extremely well read. Thus, hours in the top seem to have been whiled away discussing literature and composing witty observations, which must have been a pleasant change.

If all was well in the maintop, little else aboard the *United States* served to please Melville. This was no place for a nonconformist and it didn't help that his first order on stepping aboard was to strip so that he could be fully inspected for any ailments or bodily defects. Thankfully he passed the test and was then immediately forced to observe the brutal flogging of several men who had committed various minor offences. It was all going to be a bit much for a young idealist who had already railed against the stupidity of missionaries in the South Seas and had struggled with the harsh treatment aboard the *Acushnet*. Nevertheless, Melville was bound to the ship by the Articles of War and had little choice but to bite his tongue. His later book, *White Jacket* is damning of the US Navy, and finds fault with almost everything therein: floggings are excessive (he devotes three chapters to this), the hierarchical system is flawed, the officers are ignorant, the midshipmen are brats, sexual deviancy among the crew is heavily hinted at, and the list goes on. Melville was also horrified with the general attitude of the officers when rumour got around that war might break out between the US and Mexico. While the men were downhearted, Melville noted with a sneer that the officers were clearly excited:

> But why this contrast between the forecastle and the quarter-deck, between the man-of-war's-man and his officer? Because, though war would equally jeopardize the lives of both, yet, while it held out to the sailor no promise of promotion, and what is called glory, these things fired the breast of his officers.
>
> It is no pleasing task, nor a thankful one, to dive into the souls of some men; but there are occasions when, to bring up the mud from the bottom, reveals to us on what soundings we are, on what coast we adjoin.
>
> How were these officers to gain glory? How but by a distinguished slaughtering of their fellow-men. How were they to be promoted? How but over the buried heads of killed comrades and mess-mates.

Clearly these are not the words of a man who truly belonged in a man-of-war. Nevertheless, the passage progressed peacefully enough and Melville was to enjoy yet another visit to Nuku-Hiva prior to quitting the South Seas. On this occasion there is little doubt that he would have regaled his mess mates with tales of his exploits in this beautiful island and, consciously or subconsciously, he was already piecing together the plot for, *Ty-pee*, written on his return.

The passage home was largely a fair weather one, but there was still the dreaded Cape Horn to be rounded, and the *United States* received the usual harsh treatment at the hands of this rugged meeting of land and water. After enduring an eerie calm, the vessel was pinned over in a ferocious gale and Melville, in his role as maintopman, left a beautiful and vivid description of the fight aloft and the feeling of being lost within the fury of the storm:

> By assisting each other, we contrived to throw ourselves prostrate along the yard, and embrace it with our arms and legs. In this position, the stun'-sail-booms greatly assisted in securing our hold. Strange as it may appear, I do not suppose that, at this moment, the slightest sensation of fear was felt by one man on that yard. We clung to it with might and main; but this was instinct. The truth is, that, in circumstances like these, the sense of fear is annihilated in the unutterable sights that fill all the eye, and the sounds that fill all the ear. You become identified with the tempest; your insignificance is lost in the riot of the stormy universe around.

After a lengthy stay in Rio, the United States made her way back to Charleston Navy Yard, arriving in October 1844. No doubt Melville must have been shell shocked to be home after such an epic adventure. He had been away for four years and it must have been disillusioning to find that all those dreary everyday problems of debt and unemployment were still there, lurking in wait. He did have much to be thankful for, even if he did not know it just yet, for he had gathered all the source material required for his first six novels, Ty-pee, Omoo, Mardi, Redburn (a narration of his 1839 transatlantic voyage), White Jacket and Moby Dick. During this period he had experienced things that were far beyond the imagination of ordinary people leading humdrum lives and it was apparently this that made Melville take up his pen and begin to write Ty-pee. Even without his splendid prose, the book was so crammed with adventure that it was bound to be a hit and its success sent Melville down a new path, far away from the sea. His first book was his most successful during his lifetime while Moby Dick, that 'great blasphemous book' as Melville described his epic of madness, monomania and malice, was only regarded as a classic after the author's death, which came in 1891.

Melville's seafaring days were not quite over, however, for 16 years after he was discharged from the *United States*, he once again paced the deck of a mighty tall ship bound around Cape Horn. This time, however, he was a paying passenger and the vessel was the clipper ship *Meteor*, commanded by Melville's younger brother, Thomas, who was keeping up the family tradition of seafaring with admirable aplomb. She made the trip from New York to San Francisco in 120 days and was actually three days longer than the stumpy old *Acushnet* off the pitch of Cape Horn. Clearly Melville had not fully lost his love for the sea, which not only brought him great adventure, but also provided lovers of literature with some of the finest tales of adventure and misadventure afloat you could ever imagine. His writings are far more comic than many give them credit for and are accompanied with a flair for description that brings nautical scenes to life in a manner few others have managed. I will leave this chapter with a short passage describing a calm off Cape Horn that encapsulates his skills in a few well-formed sentences:

> *And now coming up with the latitude of the Cape, we stood southward to give it a wide berth, and while so doing were becalmed; ay, becalmed off Cape Horn, which is worse, far worse, than being becalmed on the Line. Here we lay forty-eight hours, during which the cold was intense. I wondered at the liquid sea, which refused to freeze in such a temperature. The clear, cold sky overhead looked like a steel-blue cymbal, that might ring, could you smite it.*

Makes you shiver just to read it.

Arthur Ransome

In search of utopia

Houses are but badly built boats, so firmly aground that you cannot think of moving them. They are definitely inferior things, belonging to the vegetable not the animal world, rooted and stationary, incapable of gay transition. The desire to build a house is the tired wish of a man content thenceforward with a single anchorage. The desire to build a boat is the desire of youth, unwilling yet to accept the idea of a final resting place.

Racundra's First Cruise

This was the opening gambit in Arthur Ransome's career as a nautical writer and this single paragraph gives you a great insight into Ransome the sailor and writer. He managed to convey the joy of sailing effortlessly, genuinely and with a unique charm. For all that, if you had told Ransome at the age of 30 that he was going to become one of the bestselling nautical writers of all time, he would have been utterly bemused. Yet by the time of his death at the age of 83, this is exactly what he was. The mass following that his cosy, slightly otherworldly children's tales of sailing have gained is extraordinary, and the affection many adults retain for them is staggering. Working between the two grim pillars of the World Wars, Arthur Ransome succeeded in creating an idyllic England of ginger beer, jolly adventures and chaps who start their sentences with, 'I say...' Alongside PG Wodehouse, Ransome managed to conjure up a kind of English utopia, inviting his reader to forget about the pointless savagery and cruelty of World War One, and ignore the storm clouds again gathering on the continent by escaping to a different, less complicated England where the sun always shone (even in the Lake District). To immerse yourself in one of Ransome's incomparable tales is akin to sitting down in your favourite armchair in front of a roaring fire – preferably in some kind of low-beamed Lakeland cottage – and tucking into hot buttered toast, laden with Oxford Marmalade. His stories are pure balm; the soothing hand on a fevered brow, utterly irresponsible escapism from the rigours of daily life.

Of course, his tales are also rattling good seafaring stories, bubbling over with the life-affirming joy of being afloat. This is doubtless why his *Swallows and Amazons* series remains so fiendishly popular with children of all ages, even beyond the context of the two World Wars. Indeed, so much has been written about *Swallows and Amazons* that I really don't think I can add much more. Instead, I would like to explore *how* Ransome became the bestselling nautical author of the 20th century. To find out, we have to head back to 1920, when Ransome stepped aboard his first command, the *Slug*, a 18-foot open sailing boat with sails looking suspiciously like old bed sheets, and planned a highly foolish trip from Reval (now Tallinn) to his home, some 40 miles along the Estonian coast. To understand why Arthur Ransome was in this unlikely spot in the first place also requires a bit of explaining, so at this point we must leave him standing on the shores of the Baltic, clutching *Slug's* battered gunwale and dipping his toes into that crystal clear water, and go right back to the start.

Arthur Ransome was born in Leeds in 1884 to Edith and Cyril Ransome, a very respectable middle-class couple. He was the eldest of four children and right from the start he approached life with a puppyish enthusiasm that drove his father, a professor of history at what was to become Leeds University, quite round the bend. He never seemed to settle on anything, charging from one project to another without ever completing the job in hand. His father died of tuberculosis when Arthur was 13, but not before he had introduced Arthur to the three things that would dominate his adult life: fishing, the Lake District and the nagging feeling that his father was in some way disappointed in him. Around the time of his father's death, Arthur won a scholarship to Rugby School where he failed abysmally. He then went to Leeds University, where he was pressured into studying science at which he also failed abysmally, yet cheerfully. Mid-way through his degree, he decided he was going to be a writer, and headed to the capital, determined to immerse himself within London's bohemian set, which he did with a modicum of success. For the next few years he proceeded to write, for the most part badly, and marry unhappily. Things were not looking too positive, but Ransome was, if nothing else, a livewire of enthusiasm and each fresh failure was greeted with gung-ho optimism, almost as if it was an opportunity. He continued to holiday in the Lake District, which was unquestionably his great love in life, but until 1920 his sailing experience was limited to the odd excursion across Lake Coniston in the *Jamrach* and the *Swallow*, two dinghies owned by his firm friends, the Collingwood family.

This still leaves us a good few leagues short of Estonia, and how he got there owes a lot to three things: his wife, his lover and fishing. Ransome had married unwisely. His enthusiasm and his youth made him prone to rashly falling in love with any young lady that gave him the time of day, and even some who didn't. He met Ivy Walker at a social gathering in 1908 and shortly after had jocularly suggested they should get married. To his surprise, Ivy took him up on the idea and Ransome was too polite, feckless and smitten to wriggle out of it. After their wedding, the pair struggled to get along for several years, through what Ransome later described as, 'a bad, incredible dream'. Ivy was – to put it mildly – highly strung. An indication of the strain she put on Ransome is illustrated by a short walking trip he took with Ivy and a mutual male friend. At the end of the trip, Ivy hysterically told Ransome that she was having an affair with the mutual friend. Arthur replied that they, 'had better see about a divorce then' and Ivy promptly admitted it was all a fiction. Despite these dramas, the pair did have a child, Tabitha, but by 1913 the situation was too much for Arthur. He took the unusual step of simply disappearing to Russia on the rather flimsy pretext of going to Sweden for a holiday. Why he chose Russia is unclear, except that it was the most far-flung outpost of Europe and his wife was unlikely to track him down. He rapidly gained a real affection for the country, learning Russian and gleefully integrating into the cosmopolitan life of St Petersburg. Ransome was still lying low here when war broke out in 1914 and he remained there as a reporter. He had never wanted to be a journalist, but was keen to serve his country in some way and had been advised that his eyesight was far too weak to serve in the armed forces. At 30, he was also getting a bit old to fight and he reasoned that as a reporter fluent in Russian he could be of use.

As a Russian correspondent in St Petersburg (renamed Petrograd during the war, as St Petersburg was deemed too German-sounding), Arthur was given a grandstand view of Russia's descent into revolution, witnessing first hand the jubilation as the Tsar was overthrown in 1917. He felt the great wave of optimism that swept through the country and was there to witness all the growing pains of the new Soviet Republic. In the process, he became one of the foremost reporters on the subject, working closely with the Bolsheviks, whom he came to admire. He played chess with Lenin, sparred verbally with many of the Bolshevik elite, and fell in love with Trotsky's secretary, Evgenia Shelepina, a woman who was to be his faithful companion for the rest of his life. I am aware that this still leaves us some miles short of sailing on the Baltic, and, furthermore that it is still unclear where the fishing comes into any of this, but bear with me. Anyhow, by the end of the war, Ransome had become close enough and sympathetic enough to the Bolshevik cause that he was suspected by the British of being a Bolshevik himself. This seems laughable with hindsight, but it is true that Ransome had been caught up in the political optimism that had swept through Russia during this period, and his writing reflected that. He was also strongly opposed to the British policy at the tail end of the war, which involved sending troops into Russia to support the White Army, with the aim of crushing the Bolshevik movement. Ransome's inside knowledge of Russia meant he felt this was untenable and he was sufficiently vocal in this view to upset the authorities back home. At this point, he headed back to the UK for a holiday, and received a nasty jolt when, on arriving at King's Cross Station, he was promptly apprehended by an officer and taken to Scotland Yard for questioning by Sir Basil Thomson, head of Special Branch. 'Spycatcher' Thomson was a serious man and, still operating under the special wartime jurisdiction granted to him during this state of emergency. Under this jurisdiction, he had been given sweeping powers to interrogate and prosecute anyone he deemed a threat to national security. To make matters worse, he had a reputation for hating Bolsheviks and he always seemed to get his man. Basically, things weren't looking too positive for the young idealist as the interview commenced. What happened next is recalled by Ransome as follows:

> *Sir Basil, looking extremely grim, looked hard at me. After a moment's silence, he said, 'Now, I want to know just what your politics are.'*
>
> *'Fishing,' I replied.*
>
> *He stared. 'Just what do you mean by that?*
>
> *I told him the exact truth, that in England I had never had any political views whatever, that in Russia I believed this very fact had let me get a clearer view of the revolution than I could otherwise have got, that I now had one clear political opinion which was that intervention was a disastrous mistake and that I hoped it would come to an end and so release me to turn to my ordinary interests.*
>
> *'Fishing?' He said.*
>
> *'We are very near the beginning of the season.'*

Thomson was charmed, seeing Ransome for what he really was: likeable and a little bit politically naive but most of all, harmless and well meaning.

More acute readers may have noted that none of this has much to do with sailing, but I am getting to that. Thomson's assessment of Ransome meant that he was free to return to Russia at the end of his holiday, and there were pressing reasons to do so. It looked as though, after all, the White Army would defeat the Red Army and, with Evgenia in Moscow serving as Trotsky's secretary, the future looked far from rosy for her. Ransome determined that he must find her and bring her to safety. This was easier said than done, for he would have to get through the lines of both the White Army and the Red Army to reach Moscow, then re-cross them in order to escape with his lover. In order to do this, he landed in Estonia and passed through the front line of the White Army with no trouble, having all the relevant papers. The next step was the tricky one; after being dropped in the no man's land between the Whites and the Reds by a guide, I leave it to Ransome to describe the rest of the story:

> *I filled a pipe, lit it and, with typewriter in one hand and bag in the other, walked over the hummock behind which we had stopped and set out across the open country towards the line that might or might not be the trenches of the Russians. I puffed pretty hard on my pipe, burning my tongue, but producing lots of smoke. Nobody, I reasoned, was going to shoot at a man walking slowly across and obviously enjoying his tobacco. Certainly no Russian, whose curiosity was sure to be greater than any wish to let off a rifle.*
>
> *Suddenly I caught a glint of light on rifle barrel. I puffed harder than ever. With my hands full I could not wave a greeting and knew that any stoppage to put down my baggage might cause a regrettable misunderstanding. So I walked on and presently saw half a dozen men with their elbows on the parapet and their rifles pointing in a direction I deplored.*

After being seized by the officers, Ransome was told that orders were to shoot any spies crossing the front. Despite this unpromising start, Ransome managed to persuade them to make him a cup of tea and explained that he was going to see Lenin and they might as well let him past as, once he was shot, they couldn't undo it and Lenin might well be annoyed. Thus, he won his way through to Russia, found Evgenia and, after further exploits, the pair re-crossed the Red and White trenches and returned to Reval. This was 1919 and the couple remained here or in neighbouring Latvia until 1922, while Arthur tried to obtain a divorce from his abandoned and increasingly angry wife. On arriving in Reval, Arthur had entered a state of physical and mental collapse and was laid low for several weeks. As he convalesced in his hotel bed, he wrote this solemn affidavit to himself:

> *Dear Arthur,*
>
> *I hereby promise you on my word of honour that I will undertake no political commissions from the Bolsheviks or any other political party and*

further that I will engage in no conspiratorial work whatsoever without expressly informing you that I consider this promise no longer binding.

In the meantime, he continued to work as a reporter on the Russian situation, fished a little and became hooked on the idea of going sailing. Finally, we are where we want to be, on the shores of the Baltic, Arthur clutching the gunwale of *Slug* preparatory to his maiden voyage in her. Ransome had been hankering to get in a boat for some time, and the picturesque old port of Reval has a most inviting view out onto the Baltic Sea, as Arthur explained in his memoirs:

> *Reval, our metropolis and shopping centre, was built as a fortress on a rock, and from that rock one looks out over a wide bay, with the green wooded island of Nargon on one side of it, a long promontory on the other, and far out beyond the bay a horizon of open sea.*
>
> *I do not believe that any man can look out from that rock and ever be wholly happy until he has got a boat of his own. I could not, and on each of my visits to Reval, I walked round the harbour looking for something that would float and had a mast and sail.*

Arthur had also been inspired to some extent by EF Knight's memoir of his own cruise in the Baltic, entitled *Falcon on the Baltic*, and was keen to acquire a vessel of his own. This *Falcon* had been a converted ship's lifeboat, and for some time Arthur pestered various ship's captains to bring him a lifeboat from the UK that he could convert for himself. Although many humoured him, none actually came up with the goods, and brought one back. An increasingly desperate Ransome eventually spotted a mariner daubing a rather battered looking vessel with green paint. Arthur enquired as to the price and, shortly thereafter he was the proud owner of a very old open boat some 18ft in length, soon to be named *Slug* on account of her sailing abilities.

The *Slug* was a most unpromising vessel and Ransome arranged for her to be inspected by a seafaring friend who was in port at the time. He eyed her dubiously and said that she would be fine for sailing in the bay. Once Arthur had explained that he wanted to sail her to his home in

Lahepe Bay, some 40 miles away, the sailor raised his eyebrows and said, with great understatement, 'pick your weather'. The next day, with Evgenia accompanying him 'full of unjustified faith in me as a mariner' (as Arthur put it) they set off. His memoirs recall the voyage vividly:

> Next day there was almost a dead calm. We were in a hurry to try the new boat. The owner had brought down to the beach an ancient, patched gaff mainsail and a staysail. Several boulders from the beach had vanished and were now in the boat. 'Big sail' said the owner. 'You want plenty stone for ballast.' We climbed in and were pushed off. There were a pair of abominable heavy sweeps [oars] with which I pulled offshore, determining never to use them again. I hoisted the sails. There was a breath of wind and slowly, slowly, so slowly we there and then christened her Slug, she moved out into the middle of the bay and we were looking at the rock of Reval from the sea as I had so often promised that we should.
>
> We were in the middle of the bay when the wind died to nothing. Slug lay with drooping sails on glassy water. It was very hot. I jumped overboard to get cool and to look at my lovely command. I lay in the water admiring her and did not notice a light ripple that crept across the bay. The sails filled and Slug began to move. She moved slowly, but I should have liked her to move slower. Evgenia shouted at me to come back to the ship. I swam after her as hard as I could, caught hold of her gunwale, which now seemed a long way above me, and found that I could not get into her. I tried again and again, and began to think that I should have to hang there until she found her way into shallow water. But the wind was getting up and Slug was heading as if for Finland. I pulled myself hand over hand along her gunwale to her bow. She had a short iron bowsprit, and with the help of this unsympathetic bit of iron, I scrambled back aboard to be received, very properly, with curses. Afterwards, in shallow water, I tried many times to climb aboard in that way. I could not do it. I suppose the knowledge that there was no other way was the only thing that made it possible. Once I was aboard, the wind dropped again and we slowly drifted to the eastern side of the

*bay, landed, took the anchor up the beach, made a fire and camped. It is
astonishing that this experience did not deprive me of my crew.*

This gives you a fair indication of what Ransome the sailor was like; good
humoured, hardy, and just a little bit foolish. The *Slug* headed on for Lahepe
via the island of Nargon. Quite incredibly, Ransome was happy to indulge
in a night sail with nothing but a prismatic compass to guide him. He had no
chart. I will leave him to conclude this foolish episode:

*There were no lights ashore. It must have been about two in the morning
and wise folk on land were asleep. Suddenly, close by, we heard a loud
barking. Next moment, I thought our keel must grind ashore. I dropped
the anchor over and found the bottom with it in two fathoms. I brought
the sails down. Tired right out, too tired to talk, we fell instantly asleep.*

*We were woken by more barking, so loud and near that I thought we
must have drifted ashore while we slept. The dawn had come. I looked
sleepily over the gunwale into the eyes of a large seal who, with shining
head and dripping whiskers, might have been an elderly business man
bathing at Margate. He blew through his whiskers, barked again, dived,
and was gone. What I had thought for a moment were other seals were
the tops of rocks. I still do not understand how we had come to where we
were without hitting any of them.*

Thus ended Ransome's first meaningful cruise and both he and Evgenia
were remarkably fortunate to escape unscathed. *Slug* was retained at Lahepe
Bay, but was not a huge success, sinking at her mooring on several occasions
and also having her rather questionable mainsail stolen. Nevertheless,
she was a start and, following this, as Ransome noted, the couple were
never without a boat of some sort for the rest of their lives. The following
season, Arthur had a new command, the *Kittiwake*, a tiny 16-foot cutter with
an equally tiny cabin. In the choice of *Kittiwake*, Ransome betrayed his
inexperience as a boat owner. There are pictures of this little vessel under sail
and, quite frankly, she looks ridiculous. She is so tiny that her cabin makes

her look ludicrously foreshortened and stubby, while her sail area seems disproportionately huge. Meanwhile, clinging to her mast, a crewmember teeters ponderously. How they got back to the cockpit without flipping the little boat right over is a mystery. In his desire to get a yacht with a cabin, Ransome had bought rashly, and a quick test sail in the little vessel did not inspire confidence, for she was dangerously unstable. How Arthur and Evgenia, both over 6ft, ever managed to squeeze themselves into her narrow bunks is never touched upon. Nevertheless, she was a command, and the little cutter was fitted out with new mattresses, a primus stove and some much-needed extra ballast. One of the problems with *Slug* had been that, in order to get to shore, the couple had been forced to swim or wade. A more practical solution was required, but dinghies were at a premium in post-war Estonia, and Ransome was eventually forced to commission an undertaker to build one. The result was, less than astonishingly, coffin-like and even more unstable than *Kittiwake* herself. Ransome used to claim that she would capsize if he so much as shifted his pipe from one side of his mouth to the other. With two such tenuous craft, it is unsurprising that sailing trips were limited to day excursions from Baltic Port, near Reval, where the couple were based for most of that summer. But *Kittiwake* did make Arthur realise that if he was serious about going sailing he needed a proper boat. That boat was to be *Racundra,* the yacht that launched his career as a nautical writer and set him on the path that led inexorably to *Swallows and Amazons.*

It was during the summer of 1920 that Arthur and Evgenia met and 'fell in love' with the boatbuilder Otto Eggers. Eggers was a German living in Estonia and prior to the war he had established a reputation for building excellent and seaworthy craft. During the war he had lost his boatyard and, as a German, there was little hope of him ever getting it back. He could, however, still design yachts and after several hours of earnest discussion about the perfect boat agreed to draw up the plans for Arthur and Evgenia. The problem was now the simple one of finding a boatbuilder who had sufficient experience of putting together and commissioning yachts. This was not an easy task in post-war Estonia, and Ransome eventually plumped for a boatbuilder in Riga, Latvia, who had initially built Arthur a less coffin-like dinghy and professed to some experience with building yachts. In the autumn of 1921, Arthur took the plunge and signed a contract to have the *Racundra* built, on the understanding that she would be ready for the next season's sailing, which in the Baltic generally began around late May. In the meantime, Ransome waited with all the puppyish eagerness of his younger days for his dream boat to become a reality.

The specifications that *Racundra* was built to are described by Arthur as follows:

She was to be a cruising boat that one man could manage comfortably if needs be, but on which three could live comfortably. She was to have writing table and book-case, a place for a typewriter, broad bunks where a man might lay him down and rest without bruising knee and elbow with each unconsidered movement. She should not be fast, but she should be fit to keep the sea when other little boats were scuttling for shelter. In fact, she was to be the boat that every man would wish who likes to move from port to port – a little ship in which, in temperate climates, a man might live from years end to years end.

That Arthur did not live in a temperate climate is brought home quite nicely by the fact that he was able to go to the boatbuilder's shed, situated on a small island just outside Riga, by skating across the thick ice that had formed in the mouth of the River Dvina. His pleasure at seeing the little yacht take shape was meted by his desperate frustration at what seemed to be an endless succession of delays. *Racundra* was meant to be ready by late April, just as the River Dvina was starting to crack and thaw and great floes of ice began to drift lazily seaward. She was not ready nearly in time and henceforth, Ransome referred to the boatbuilder simply as 'the Swine'. Delay followed delay, and Arthur could see the whole summer of cruising ebbing away. Perhaps only he can fully convey the extent of his frustration:

I pass over briefly as briefly as I may the wretched story of the building and the hundred journeys over the ice to the little shed in which Racundra *slowly* turned from dream into reality. She was to be finished in April, was promised to me on May 1, May 15, May 20th and short intervals thenceforward. She was launched, a mere hull, on July 28. I went for the hundred and first time to the yard and found Racundra in the water. The Lettish workmen by trickery got the builder and me close together. They planted us suddenly on a wooden bench which they had decked with bean-flowers stolen from the neighbouring garden and lifted us, full of mutual hatred, shoulder high. The ship was launched. Yes, but the summer was over, and there had been whole weeks when the Racundra had not progressed at all while the builder and his men did other work. He promised me then that she should be ready to put to sea on August 3rd. She was not. On August 5th I went and took the boat away unfinished. Not a sail was setting properly. The centreboard was half up, half down and hopelessly stuck. But under power and sails, somehow or other, I got the ship under way and took her round to the lake, had her out on the yacht club slip, removed the centreboard, had another one built, relaunched her, and just over a fortnight later turned the carpenters out of her and put to sea.

Many a boatbuilder will give a wry smile at this description of the many delays entailed in putting together a yacht, 'fools build and wise men buy', Ransome reflected. Nevertheless, unfinished as she was, the *Racundra* was a sturdy, well-built vessel, double ended with a stupendous beam. Ransome loved her from day one and described her with great affection in the postscript to *Racundra's First Cruise*:

Racundra is nine metres overall – something under thirty feet long. She is three and a half metres in beam – nearly twelve feet. She draws three feet six inches when the centreboard is lowered. Her enormous beam is balanced by her shallowness, and though for a yacht it seems excessive, thoroughly justified in her comfort and stiffness.

She is very heavily built and carries no inside ballast. Her centreboard is of oak. She has a three and a half ton iron keel so broad she will rest comfortably on it when taking the mud, and deep enough to enable us *to do without the centreboard altogether except when squeezing her up against the wind. Give her a point or two free and a good wind and her drift, though more than that of a deep keel yacht, is much less than that of the coasting schooners common in the Baltic. With the centreboard down she is extremely handy.*

But the chief glory of Racundra is her cabin. The local yachtsmen, accustomed to the slim figures of racing boats, jeered Racundra's beam and weight, but one and all, when they came aboard her, ducked through the companionway and stood up again in the spacious cabin agreed there was something to be said for such a boat. And as for their wives, they said frankly that such a cabin made a boat worth having, and their own boat, which had seemed comfortable enough hitherto, turned into mere uncomfortable rabbit hutches. Racundra's cabin is a place where a man can live and work as comfortably and twice as pleasantly as any man ashore. I lived in it for two months on end, and, if this were a temperate climate, and the harbour not a solid block of ice in winter, so that all yachts are hauled out and kept in a shed for half the year, I should be living in it still. Not only can one stand up in Racundra's cabin, one can walk about in there, and that without interfering with anyone who may be sitting at the writing table, which is a yard square. In the middle of the cabin is a folding table, four feet by three, supported by the centreboard case; and so broad is the floor that you can sit at that table and never find the case in the way of your toes.

So he goes on and on, with evident pride and affection for his little yacht. There is little doubt that she was about as commodious a vessel as you could cram in to 30ft. You will have noted several references to a writing table, and, if you were wondering how Ransome was funding the largesse of buying a brand new yacht, here is a clue. He was still a reporter for the *Daily News* and also the *Manchester Guardian,* but he still harboured dreams of becoming a full time novelist, viewing being a journalist as 'rather like a substitute on a cricket field, only on because of injury and liable to be removed at any moment.' His writing, although stymied by war and revolution, had continued to some extent and the publication of *Old Peter's Russian Tales*, a translation of a number of Russian folk stories such as *The Fool of the World and the Flying Ship*, was rapidly becoming Ransome's best selling and most coherent work to date. That book had been published in 1918, however. It was now 1922 and, aside from two small pamphlets entitled *Six weeks in Russia* and *The crisis in Russia*, both dealing with the state of the country post revolution, and a few odd bits of writing here and there, Ransome had precious little to show for the post-war years. Thus, *Racundra* proved to be a step in the right direction, for financial necessity meant he would need to turn back to writing books to supplement his income. Reflecting in later years, Ransome concluded that the commissioning of *Racundra* was one of the few wise things he did in his life, for it got him away from politics and journalism and took him back to his true vocation.

Preparations for the long-awaited cruise continued apace and, on 17 August, about the time many yachtsmen in these waters were starting to think about winding up their sailing activities and finding a snug berth to lay up their boat, Ransome was just about ready, writing to his mother thus:

After all kinds of tribulations which I will not recount in detail I have got the Racundra *in the water, taken her away from The Swine, and with a couple of workmen have got her almost ready for sea. Ship's papers are ready and I hope to move down to the mouth of the river, starting for Reval (about 250 miles away) with the first S.W wind. I have slept onboard since getting her. The workmen turning up at six and working until dark, and today, really all of the important things are done. I had to make a new centreboard, the old one being stuck and hopelessly warped, and took her up on the slip, after which I made sail and brought her back to the little harbour all by my wild self, the two workmen hammering away till I got halfway and they put up their astonished heads. She is very easy to manage, and so slow on her helm that I have plenty of time to run about and do things while she takes care of herself. But SLOW. My word. Something terrific. Our motion has a stately leisuredness about it that is reminiscent of the middle ages.*

This slowness was not altogether *Racundra's* fault. She was ketch rigged, but carried such a moderate sail plan that it must have been hard to truly get her going in light winds, particularly given her heavy build. This may have been a hangover from the *Kittiwake* experience, as that boat was poorly ballasted, over canvassed and tender to the point of being dangerous. *Racundra* was one of the new breed of yachts that carried an auxiliary engine, although this was not initially a great success, Ransome noting sardonically that it was a five-horsepower motor, but seemed to need forty horsepower to start it.

Thus, on 20 August, the *Racundra* finally left Riga with Ransome the proud master and commander of his new vessel, the redoubtable Evgenia relegated to cook, and a third crewmember, Carl Sehmel. This wizened old mariner had served aboard the celebrated clipper ship, *Thermopylae* and also aboard the famous *Sunbeam* which, under the ownership of Liberal MP Thomas Brassey, became the first privately-owned yacht to circumnavigate the globe. Sehmel was always referred to simply as 'the Ancient' for the duration of the voyage and proved invaluable to Arthur and Evgenia as they learned the ropes. He also played an important role in getting the little yacht shipshape following her rather hurried departure. Sehmel was later immortalised in Ransome's *Peter Duck*, the third in the *Swallows and Amazons* series. Here, the experienced sailor is portrayed as a native of Norfolk, but in other details is the same stolid, wise and steady seaman he was on this voyage. The interplay between him and the eager, excitable Captain Flint is a very clear link between *Peter Duck* and *Racundra's First Cruise*.

Thus the crew was complete and a course was set northwards, although not before customs had been cleared. This was quite an undertaking in itself, involving all manner of bribes, including vodka and a ham sandwich. The rough plan was to sail up to their old haunt of Reval, some 400km (250 miles) to the north, and then head on to the Finnish port of Helsingfors (Helsinki to us) another 160km (100 miles) or so miles northward again. Ransome was the chief navigator and, as a novice, he faced a fairly tough challenge. Granted, the Baltic has a negligible amount of tide, but the coast is dotted with an absolute myriad of tiny islands and rocks, all of which would have to be negotiated with skill, accuracy and confidence. Given that two years previously Ransome had been pottering around in *Slug* with no chart at all, he had already come a long way. In addition to this, there was the added challenge of heading out so late in the season; the Baltic is not a particularly forgiving place even in the middle of summer, but by late August, things are starting to get serious, and it is no place for the inexperienced. Thus, Ransome must have been pretty apprehensive as he swung out of Riga and headed north for Runo Island, the first stop. Despite a heavy swell on that first day out, the novice skipper wasn't nervous for long, and once the afternoon drifted by and the evening glow faded from the sky, Ransome found himself at the tiller of his own yacht and he was beguiled by the experience of command:

> *At ten o'clock, the others turned in. For the first time, not on paper or in dreams, I had the little ship alone in my hands in a night of velvet dark below and stars above, pushing steadily along into unknown waters. I was extremely happy.*

This set the pattern for the trip. Ransome really was exceedingly happy and this translated into his good-humoured writing. The trip was not exactly crammed with incident, but it was carefully and joyously observed, seen with the kind of child-like wonder that many of us lost long ago. The first landfall, the island of Runo, was typical:

> *I suppose most readers of this book [*Racundra's First Cruise*] have already lost the ecstatic joy of sighting land at sea. Yet no, I do not believe that even for the oldest mariner that joy can ever fade. It is always new, always a miracle, never in the common ruck of absolutely predictable events. Islands especially stir the blood, and Runo, that lonely place, only fifty miles out from Riga and nearly as far from the Estonian coast, with its Swedish seal-hunters using words that in Sweden have become archaic, living in the twentieth century a life of medieval communism, a place where the steamer calls but once a year, coming up out of the*

sea before me, sought and found by my little ship, gave me moments of unforgettable delight.

So *Racundra* and her crew were able to sail back in time to a less complicated world untainted by war, and Ransome continued to wax lyrical about the abandoned shore and whispering pine trees, until jolted from his reverie by the old lighthouse keeper of Runo, who accosted him by asking how things were between Britain and Ireland. Ransome was resentful of this rude intrusion of modern politics which he felt had no place on his cruise. On they went, Ransome's belief in his navigation gaining strength with every new landfall. They threaded the narrow channel of the Moon Sound without incident and it wasn't until they were at Baltic Port, near Reval, that *Racundra* took a real battering from the elements and some of the Swine's suspect workmanship was exposed. *Racundra*'s master had hoped to make it to safety before night drew in, but as they pushed the little boat to windward in deteriorating weather and rough seas, the jaws of her main gaff started to part. In the fading light it was soon obvious that they would have to drop the mainsail. This made her dreadfully unhandy and incapable of beating into the mounting gale. There was no option but to stand off the land and await morning in order to effect repairs. Thus they ran back out to open water and prepared for a night bobbing around in increasingly unpleasant weather. As was so often the case with Ransome, the experience ended up being a cheerful one:

> *As we careered in the dark over waves which always seem bigger at night, I had the definite impression that* Racundra *was enjoying it in her fashion. I found myself, who does not sing in happier moments, yelling 'Spanish ladies' and 'summer is icumen in' and 'John Peel' at the top of my voice. The Cook struggled up the companion way with a sandwich. She asked, with real inquiry, 'Are we going to be drowned before morning?'*
>
> *I leaned forward from the steering well and shouted, 'Why?'*
>
> *'Because I have two thermos flasks full of coffee. If we are, we may as well drink them both. If not, I'll keep one till tomorrow.'*
>
> *We kept one.*

This is the first meaningful contribution of the 'Cook' in his story. If you get the impression that Ransome had a rather derogatory view of the love of his life to simply refer to her thus throughout the book, there were pressing reasons. Ransome was still very much married to his wife Ivy, despite his desperate pleas for divorce she remained intransigent on the matter. This meant that for the sake of Edwardian delicacy, he was obliged to refer to his lover as the 'Cook' throughout *Racundra's First Cruise*. In fairness, Evgenia also definitely *was* the cook and certainly seems to have displayed a level of stoicism rarely witnessed either in her time or ours. It was clear that she took to the sea like a duck to water (if you'll excuse the phrase) and was just as comfortable helming as battling with the cooking.

It is also perhaps fortunate that none of the crew, most particularly Evgenia, was prone to seasickness. Anyhow, the cruise continued with a welcome stop at Reval, where they were reunited with Otto Eggers, who was able to remedy a number of *Racundra's* defects and to fit some battens in her sails, which greatly improved her ability upwind.

From here, the cruise continued up to Helsingfors in Finland. Perhaps due to the strenuous nature of Evgenia's role, she opted to remain with friends in Riga during this part of the voyage, and was replaced by a mysterious chum known as 'Mr Wirgo' who seemed to spend the entirety of the trip in his bunk. Who cooked in the meantime is not elaborated upon. The only drama on this leg was in trying to pick up a pilot to take them through the tricky entrance into Helsingfors. The pilot spotted the *Racundra* approaching the coast through the dusk, but assumed she was a smuggler and let her be. It therefore took strenuous efforts and the blasting of the foghorn to persuade him that they needed his assistance.

The return leg was pretty much a repeat of the outward trip, although they took in a few more island stopovers on their way back. The weather grew increasingly inclement and they were stormbound in Werder, just to the north of Riga, before bowling into their home port on 26th September. Ransome wrote triumphantly to his mother upon arriving home:

The Equinox flung us home with a flick of his mighty tail after giving us a lively time for a fortnight or so. In the way of writing I did pretty well, and came home with eighty photographs and over 30,000 words. My greatest joy is the navigation, which went through in all four of the out of sight of land passages without a hitch. The sheer excitement of being out of sight of land for 24 hours and then seeing the land appear and finding that you have hit it exactly as you have intended is something not to be equalled in any other way.

The trip had been a success and all had enjoyed it, even the long-suffering cook. Although yachts had sailed the Estonian, Finnish and Latvian coastline before, Ransome must have been one of the first Englishmen to do it and, as such, it remains an impressive effort. Even to this day it remains a beautiful but rather obscure cruising ground. All that was left to do was to write up the trip, and Ransome set to work in earnest almost as soon as he returned to land. By the time he visited friends and relatives in England in December, the book was pretty much complete and he was further encouraged by positive noises made by his old Lake District friends and mentors, the Collingwoods, who expressed their enjoyment of the manuscript. He was also buoyed by the news that his wife had finally consented to a divorce. It began to look like he would be able to escape his self-imposed exile and he and Evgenia could begin to plan a life together in England. Although Ransome loved the Baltic states and Russia itself, by 1922 he was beginning to seriously miss home.

These hopeful thoughts must have been with him as he made the final amendments to *Racundra's First Cruise* in January 1923. Yet, although the outlook was rosy, he became increasingly dissatisfied with the content of his latest book, noting to his mother that, 'In parts I do not care for it and find it rather dull ... Nobody will read it, of course, but I shall be glad to have a few copies to give to one or two folk.'

Ransome was an optimist when it came to most aspects of his life, but he often plunged into bouts of severe self-doubt when it came to his writing. This was to become progressively painful as he worked on his *Swallows and Amazons* pieces, and his dissatisfaction with *Racundra's First Cruise* was an early instance of this. In fairness, the story is not crammed with high drama, but what it lacks in that respect, it makes up for with Ransome's own gentle wit and the interaction between the crew and *Racundra* herself, who often takes centre stage. This was the book where Arthur found his voice as an author of nautical literature, and there are plenty of signposts in *Racundra's First Cruise* that point firmly toward the inimitable style to be found in the *Swallows and Amazons* series. Perhaps not least because its almost aggressively non-political content pointed toward the pastoral utopia he would create in his later books for children. If Arthur had wished, he could have peppered the book with digs relating to politics, for they were never far away in this war-ravaged region. It is telling that in one of their stopovers they commented on the damage wrought by the Germans, only to be to be informed that these had been 'Churchill's Germans, paid by the British'. This was an allusion to Britain's anti-Bolshevik meddling in Russia at the end of World War One, a subject close to Ransome's heart. Yet he wisely resisted the temptation to politicise *Racundra's First Cruise*, and it gives the book a wonderfully dreamy, escapist feel.

Arthur relented in his dismissive views toward the book once it was published. In July 1923 it was handsomely packaged, and his usual enthusiasm returned when he received a copy of it, writing to his mother that, 'Unwin has made really quite a nice book of it and I am full of joy over my new baby, my first non-political book since the war.'

The book was a relative success, and the publishers were more than happy to accept a proposal for a sequel. Thus, the sailing season of 1923 was devoted to gathering material for a new book, and the original crew, augmented by a grass snake that Evgenia insisted on having aboard and slept with entwined around her neck, gathered in Riga. Arthur harboured dreams of sailing *Racundra* through the Baltic and the North Sea to England, and this was certainly an achievable trip for both yacht and crew. Sadly, work intervened and a commission from the *Manchester Guardian* ensured that there was no way he had enough time for such an extended voyage. *Racundra* and her crew satisfied themselves with further exploration of the Finnish and Estonian coast. Later in the cruise they were joined by an extra crewmember, Ernest Boyce, who was head of the Russian branch of MI6. The revised plan was to get to St Petersburg, but even this was scuppered by bad weather, and Ransome did not feel there was enough excitement in the trip to justify a sequel to *Racundra's First Cruise*. Perhaps the dramatic highlight was an encounter with a waterspout:

> *Away to the westwards was a dark strip of cloud, with clear greenish sky beneath it. Suddenly we noticed what looked like a straight indiarubber tube connecting the dark cloud with the sea and moving rapidly between cloud and sea, towards us, as it seemed. It was of course very hard to judge its distance, but we thought it must be something over half a mile in height. I closed the companionway hatch but the Ancient said there was small use in doing that, 'for if one of them water spouts touches a ship it'll break it like a matchbox'.*

To illustrate the impact of these adventures on later stories, contrast the incident above with this fictitious encounter with a waterspout in *Peter Duck*:

> *The waterspout was changing shape with every moment. It was like a tremendous indiarubber tube connecting sky and sea ...*
>
> *'Close all hatches!' Captain Flint suddenly saw how very near the waterspout was going to pass. 'If that thing hits us, it isn't the hatches'll save us' said Peter Duck quietly. 'Smashed to match-board we'll be, with that weight of water on top of us.'*

By September, *Racundra* was once again laid up for the winter, this time in Reval, as bad weather had made the last part of the trip back to Riga impossible. Arthur and Evgenia did not realise it, but the next time they sailed the *Racundra*, it would be as man and wife, for in April 1924 the divorce from Ivy Walker became absolute. It is clear, even on this dramatic day, what the plans were for the summer, for he wrote to Evgenia from England with wild enthusiasm:

> *My dearly beloved old madam, All Clear at last. I signed documents yesterday. Today at one, we exchanged documents with the other side. I am tired completely out but feel a sort of undercurrent of hope and the feeling*

that now we can make a fresh start. TELL SEHMEL TO VARNISH
THE FISHING BOAT AND PUT IT IN THE WATER! MAKE
HIM GET IT READY AT ONCE SO THAT IT HAS TIME TO DRY.

Any fresh start that Arthur proposed clearly involved sailing. On the morning of 10 May, the couple were married at the British Consulate in Reval and from the consulate the newlyweds rushed off to the shipyard carrying an enormous tin barrel of paint for *Racundra's* topsides. On 15 May, they were back on the water, cruising to Riga. From Riga, the Ransomes determined to have a honeymoon cruise, heading inland up the Bolderaa River (now known as the Lieupe River) to the town of Mitau, many miles inland. By now, Ransome had perfected the art of coercing the recalcitrant little engine into action and this was just as well, for he would need it on the tortuous, marshy and often deeply confusing waterways of the Latvian interior. The cruise did not get off to a good start, for even as the newlyweds were being waved off by the Ancient, who had opted to remain at home for this romantic voyage, *Racundra's* engine conked out and it was some time before they were back on their way. Ransome's log of the trip alludes to endless fishing and an almost ceaseless quest for milk for their porridge every morning, entailing any number of picturesque encounters with rustic local folk along the way. All the while the little yacht threaded the maze of marsh, reeds, and river, often coming across ruined factories, a harsh reminder of the devastation that had swept through this region only a few years before. Yet on the whole, the river trip was most picturesque, and a romantic way to spend a honeymoon, as this log entry suggests:

We chose a gap in the reeds and pulled the dinghy ashore on a flat, gravelly area all set up for camping with the remains of a fireplace and a log seat. The Cook set to work on supper while I put up the tent on the edge of the pine forest. We had no light. Our torch batteries had failed, and we had found none in the shops. No matter. It was a clear night, the moon was rising and we had a good camp fire. We ate chicken and drank champagne.

Despite idyllic evenings like this, days of relentless rain made for trying times as well. It was during one of these depressing episodes that the previously stoical Evgenia cracked:

> *The cook says there is no point living in* Racundra. *She says that only children are glad to live in a ship. That there is nothing to see, nothing to write about, that she is sick of wind and rain and living in a small cabin; that I grow worse with age, and that proper authors live at home and write books out of their heads.*

On September 4, the final catastrophe came, which (temporarily at least) split the honeymooners asunder, as Ransome's log notes:

> *The cruise has ended or is on the point of death. I am alone in* Racundra. *Or rather not quite alone. I am alone with a mouse, which has sent the whole six foot three of the cook, hitherto undaunted by anything but calms, in headlong flight to Riga. The discovery was made this morning. I woke at five and heard what I thought was an unmistakeable mouse, but, believing it rather good luck, besides a miracle, I said nothing about it and went fishing. When I came back I mentioned it and got into rather a row for even pretending such a thing. I went fishing again and in about an hour heard the foghorn going from* Racundra *so hurried back. The cook keeps things for darning under her mattress. A pair of half darned stockings had been found there, gnawed all to pieces. The Cook was convinced and was for starting for Riga at once. This determination was presently petrified and steel bound when she found a crowd of its footprints, little three toed paddy marks, in the sour cream. We started just as we were with the dinghy full of fishing rods and tackles.*
> *At half past six we were just coming near Dubbeln where for a hundred yards or so the railway skirts the river. I shouted to a man to know when the next train went for Riga. We had twenty minutes. The cook was dressed for Riga in ten. In fifteen we were close to the station, which is on the very bank of the river. I rounded up, dropped the anchor*

and rowed like the boatrace for the embankment. The Cook hared it up and crossed the line just in front of the engine and was gone and I paddled back to Racundra, *got my anchor again, chose a decentish berth, anchored again for the night, stowed the sails, ate two three quarter pound perch of my own catching and a large bar of chocolate, opened a bottle of beer, which still stands beside me, and settled down a little breathless, to recount these alarums and excursions. The cruise is all but over. The Cook has gone, and I am the hero left to face the raging lion in a mouse's skin.*

Presently, the shamefaced Evgenia returned with two mousetraps and the cruise did resume, if only in order to get the *Racundra* back safely to Riga in order to lay her up. If it sounds like Arthur's second marriage was already on the rocks, this was not the case. Evgenia had always possessed a sharp temper, but the many years of happy marriage ahead of them is proof that this flight from the mouse was simply a temporary hitch. Yet the marriage was to sound the death knell for the partnership between the Ransomes and *Racundra*. This inland cruise was to be their last. That winter, the pair headed to England where Ransome's beloved mother met Evgenia for the first time and made her most welcome. Shortly after this, the couple bought a beautiful cottage, Low Ludderburn, situated high in the South Lakes, and commanding fine views over both Ambleside and also south to Morecambe Bay, where a tiny strip of sea was visible. It was everything Arthur had ever dreamed of. If he had once written that, *'The desire to build a house is the tired wish of a man content thenceforward with a single anchorage'*, then he was evidently happily resigned to this fate. After all, he was now 40 and had been living a more or less itinerant life since he was 29. The one fly in the ointment was that he had little choice but to sell *Racundra*, for his divorce, coupled with the purchase of a new house, had to be paid for in some manner. *Racundra* had to go.

The gallant little vessel was advertised for sale in *Yachting Monthly* and her eventual purchaser was one K Adlard Coles, also an aspiring author, who later became a successful publisher (in fact, it is his name that appears on the spine of this book). He planned to sail *Racundra* to England and write about the trip, just as Ransome had hoped to do. Ransome sold her with the caveat that she should be renamed, and Coles' subsequent book was later published as *Close Hauled*. The to-ing and fro-ing of correspondence between Ransome and Coles is quite entertaining and reveals Ransome as amusing and tolerant where a misunderstanding over money (Coles underpaid Ransome by £30) would have left some feeling bitter. Not so, and he was keen to help Coles along his way:

> The Ancient will rig and get Racundra *ready for sea in a very few days AFTER your arrival. It is quite useless to tell him to do anything before that as he simply won't do it.*
>
> *He will ship with you for the passage for England if he likes you, not otherwise. He is called Captain Sehmel by me. Other people address him less respectfully and get less out of him. He is an extremely charming old man and makes himself very useful.*

In the end, Sehmel did not ship with Coles, but it doesn't seem as though there was anything personal in it and Coles recalls that he was clearly very upset to see the *Racundra* sail out of his life, standing at the pier in Reval waving her off with a handkerchief until she was all but out of sight. In the meantime, Ransome settled down to life ashore almost full time, apart from the odd sailing trip on Coniston aboard *Swallow*, a small lug-rigged dinghy he shared with the Barbara and Ernest Altounyan and their five children, Taqui, Susan, Titty, Roger and Bridget. Barbara was one of the Collingwood clan, and Arthur had become friends with Ernest many years before while he had been in Coniston pursuing Barbara (and after being rebuffed by Barbara Arthur fruitlessly pursued another of the Collingwood girls, Dora). During this period the two had enjoyed a number of sailing trips on Coniston. Subsequently, Arthur had been in frantic contact with Ernest while trying to work out how to sail *Slug* all those years ago.

The Ransomes and Altounyans enjoyed many pleasant summer days sailing both the *Swallow* and the *Mavis* (this boat became the *Amazon* in *Swallows and Amazons*). Ransome was still working freelance for the *Manchester Guardian*, but he was mulling over new writing projects and, sitting in his workroom, high in the fells, he came up with a new children's story centred around the sailing adventures of the *Swallow* and the Altounyan family. Ransome himself made an appearance as 'Captain Flint' or 'Uncle Jim', a bald, irascible old man who the children believe to be a 'retired pirate' and harass accordingly. In a very short time he had the bare bones for the plot of *Swallows and Amazons* and in 1930, when Arthur was 46, the book was published to very good reviews. Ransome had finally found his niche. It wasn't until the publication of the third book in the series, *Peter Duck*, that success was totally assured, but after that the books became a phenomenon – the *Harry Potter* of their day, one might say, and he continued to mine this rich seam, catering for his audience of 'brats' as he termed them, until 1945. At this point a crisis of confidence in his own work – not helped by Evgenia's rapier criticism – brought him to a grinding halt. He never wrote another work of fiction, although he tinkered with his autobiography for many years to come.

Following Arthur's success came boats, and plenty of them. His first sizeable replacement for *Racundra* was the *Nancy Blackett*, a handy little cutter which he kept at Pin Mill, Suffolk. She was destined to appear as the *Goblin* in *We didn't mean to go to Sea*. Next came the *Selina King*, a very beautiful canoe-sterned cutter, built especially for the Ransomes. His next yacht was to be *Peter Duck*, built with old age and easy handling in mind and described by Ransome as a 'nautical bath chair'. He was never terribly fond of this vessel and she was followed by another small sloop, the *Lottie Blossom*, which he kept in Chichester harbour.

What is perhaps surprising was that Arthur never returned to his first love, *Racundra*. During the period in which Ransome's fame was growing, the old boat was knocking around the South Coast. After being brought over to England by Adlard Coles, she had been re–rigged with a much larger Bermudan sail plan. What this took away from her in terms of ease of handling, it added greatly to her performance. Coles had struggled on the trip home to the UK, simply because the *Racundra* needed a pretty stiff breeze to get her going at all. The engine was as despised by Coles as it had been by Ransome, and was renamed by him the 'smelly monster'. Shortly after arriving back in the UK, Coles put *Racundra* – temporarily named *Anette II* – up for sale for £350 and even had the nerve to try to sell her back to Ransome, which was pretty cheeky considering he hadn't even paid for her in full the first time around. Some years later, Ransome himself saw her in Chichester harbour and, although Evgenia couldn't bear to look at her, Ransome had a poke around and found that, 'She was still the same old boat. Someone had built a ridiculous dog house on her cabin top, but otherwise she looked as smart as ever.'

For many years she was owned by the MP JM Baldock and then she disappeared. In 1976, she was rediscovered by the well-known cruising yachtsman Rod Pickering, lying in a dilapidated state in Tangier Harbour. Pickering purchased her and set about restoring her. His plan was to sail her to the UK via the Cape Verde Islands and the West Indies. Sadly, he only made it as far as Caracas, where in 1982 she hit a reef and foundered off the Venezuelan coast. The crew survived but it was the end of the old boat. Nevertheless, it is perhaps fitting that the vessel that inspired so many scenes from Ransome's *Peter Duck*, which was based in the Caribbean, should find her way there and end up resting her bones on some exotic shore.

By the time *Racundra* plunged to her watery grave, Ransome was already long in his own. He died in 1965 at the respectable age of 80. Evgenia battled on until 1973, dying at the age of 81. She stayed at least partly true to her old Bolshevik leanings by steadfastly refusing any suggestion she should get a servant to help her around the house. It is easy to underestimate Ransome's nautical writing: after all, it was specifically aimed at children. Yet reading his descriptions of life afloat, both in dinghies and yachts, is like taking all the best things out of every sailing trip you have ever undertaken and compressing them into one memory. You need those kind of sepia-tinted dreams as you scrape antifoul and barnacles from the underside of your yacht, or hunch against a chilly easterly breeze laced with drizzle in order to catch the 4am tide. At that moment, it's important to remember how magical Ransome made it all sound.

In almost all areas of his life, Ransome was an optimist. He had witnessed much of the difficulties and hard knocks that life can throw up, but he had a way of seeing the sunny side, the romance in even the most trying situation, and translating that into writing. Given this talent, the first-hand observer of the Russian revolution had run the danger of being perceived as a Bolshevik traitor, swept up in the emotion of such a remarkable event, but it is invaluable in a writer of nautical fiction. Some see Ransome's *Swallows and Amazons* as absurd escapism to a place that never existed; yet between the two wars, in a country wracked by depression, people needed to dream of a world with the hard edges removed. Perhaps the secret of the enduring success of the books is that we still do.

Tobias Smollett
Grudging grandfather of the nautical novel

There has to be a first time for everything, and when you are looking at the nautical novel, you'd have to say that Tobias Smollett's *Roderick Random*, published in 1748, set out the blueprint from which so many other writers created their own seafaring stories. Smollett was able to evoke life afloat in a manner that none had been capable of before. Guided through the musty lower decks and wooden walls of an eighteenth-century naval vessel by Smollett's skilful pen, you can almost hear the groaning of the great wooden walls, get a whiff of tar, oakum and bilgewater and witness first hand the terror of a storm and the simple-hearted generosity of Jack Tar in his native domain. Prior to Smollett, a sea voyage was generally a rather incidental irritation to the plotline of a book; in his hands it came alive and was peopled with sailors of great character, comedy and cruelty, while the sea became a living thing, and a capricious mistress at that.

So what brought about this sea change? The answer is very simple: Smollett had first-hand experience of the foibles and quirks of the sea, having studied life afloat in great detail during his years serving as a surgeon's mate in the Royal Navy. Armed with this knowledge and experience, he was in an enviable position to paint a realistic picture, and he did so with great panache, pulling no punches in his portrayal of all its bawdy, brutal unwholesomeness. So who was Smollett? His name still resonates with some literati, but to most of us he is a forgotten figure. He was a Scotsman, born just outside Glasgow in 1721. His family was part of the established gentry of the area but Tobias was the youngest son of a youngest son and, as such, had little to look forward to by way of an inheritance. It was probably this fact that prompted him to train as a surgeon, learning his trade in Glasgow. Surgeons these days are considered to sit somewhere near the pinnacle of their profession, but in Smollett's time things were rather different. Surgeons were looked down on by physicians, who considered themselves far too important to deal with any of the unsavoury blood and guts side of medicine and rarely actually even touched a patient. It was also only physicians that were allowed to use the title of 'Doctor' in those days, surgeons satisfying themselves with being a simple 'Mr'.

This snobbery was of only minor interest to young Smollett, for he harboured far greater ambitions. It was his dream to become a playwright, which back in the eighteenth century was akin to dreaming of going to Hollywood and becoming a scriptwriter. Smollett had reason to be confident of success, however, for in the spare hours that his medical apprenticeship allowed him, he wrote a play called *The Regicide*, centred on an imagined assassination of King James I. By the time it was completed he was certain that he had struck theatrical gold with this rollercoaster of a play in ten sizzling scenes. He simply needed to get it placed in a theatre in order to make his fortune, and it may well have been this very ambition that prompted Smollett to hotfoot it to London in 1739, his masterpiece tucked into his back pocket, success all but assured.

He was soon to be bitterly disillusioned. All efforts to tout *The Regicide* to London's many theatres ended in failure. There was a very simple reason for this: his play was, on the whole, utter drivel, and the only person unable to see this was, apparently, the author. He was also infuriated by the disingenuousness of theatre managers who, instead of telling him outright that the play was garbage, tended to humour him in true English style. Thus Smollett was left simmering with frustration and indignation, convinced that he was the victim of racism due to his Scottish nationality. Some years later, when he was famous, he himself would sponsor the showing of his 'masterpiece' prompting this piece of drollery from a contemporary writer:

Whoever read the Regicide, but swore
The author wrote as man ne'er wrote before?
Others for plots and underplots may call,
Here's the right answer – have no plot at all

While Smollett was doing the rounds of the numerous theatres and generally getting into a terrible stew over his lack of recognition, his slender funds were rapidly dwindling and it wasn't long before he was in an exceedingly parlous position. There is little doubt that this played a part in persuading him to sign up to serve as surgeon's mate aboard the HMS *Chichester*, an 80-gun full-rigged ship, 155ft in length. If he stepped aboard this vessel an embittered and frustrated young playwright, he would have benefitted greatly from a glimpse into the future, for his experiences were to form the backbone of his first and most successful novel, *Roderick Random*, a story that follows the fortunes of a young Scottish gentleman and aspiring playwright as he tries to make his way in the world. It was a tale which was to establish him as one of the great writers of his time. Of course, he couldn't see into the future, however, as he stepped aboard the HMS *Chichester*. She lay, fitting out on the Thames, and what he saw proceeded to make him very irritable. He noted the hideous conditions aboard, being particularly disgusted by the stench of 'rancid cheese' that engulfed his nostrils when he stepped below.

The seafaring adventures of *Roderick Random* commence with the young hero being pressganged by a group of rogues. Now, whether this was the actual fate of Smollett will never be known, but what is beyond doubt is that many young men who strayed too close to the Thames found themselves beaten up and forced or 'pressed' into serving in the Georgian Navy at this time. The reason for this was simple: Britain had declared war with Spain, and every able-bodied man that could be found was needed to serve for king and country. It was October 1740 and Britain had been at war with Spain since 1739. The conflict nowadays is remembered more for its name, 'The War of Jenkin's Ear', than anything else. Back then, however, it was a very serious affair as Spain, the ailing superpower, came into conflict with the increasingly rapacious and bold British merchants over trade and territories in the Caribbean, along with South and North America. Under the existing trade agreement, Spain allowed British merchants very limited rights to trade with their colonies, monitored by Spanish *Guarda Costas* – coastguards. Given the demand for British goods in these same colonies, this set up the ideal backdrop for smuggling and it wasn't long before there was a thriving black market, which infuriated the Spanish authorities. In turn, the British were outraged by the brutal treatment meted out to the smugglers by the *Guarda Costas* and things came to a head – somewhat literally – when, following the boarding of the British trader *Rebecca*, a particularly sadistic member of the *Guarda Costa* seems to have chopped off the ear of the captain, Robert Jenkins. Captain Jenkins took the somewhat unusual step of pickling his severed ear and parading it in front of MPs in the House of Commons. There followed a period of intense agitation, which ultimately led to Robert Walpole, the peace-loving Prime Minister of the time, reluctantly declaring war with Spain. As the bells rang out across London in celebration of the start of a much longed for war, Walpole wryly noted: 'They may ring their bells now; they will be wringing their hands before long.'

This brings us back to Smollett, treading tentatively across the decks of HMS *Chichester*, and sniffing the putrid air of the 'tween decks with visible disgust. The *Chichester* was part of a great fleet that was being assembled with the intention of heading across to the Caribbean and teaching the Spaniards a lesson. This was no mean feat, for although the eighteenth century was to witness the rise of Britain as a naval superpower, in 1739 the navy was a somewhat shambolic institution. Walpole, as mentioned, was not terribly interested in war, and many of the great ships of the line were in a poor state of repair. There were other problems too; quite frankly, there simply weren't enough men available to adequately staff the navy during wartime. This was to prove a persistent problem throughout the next century. The problem was that in peacetime, the Royal Navy only needed a kind of skeleton staff of around 10,000 mariners to run their ships. In wartime, the figure could rise to as much as 80,000. It is therefore hardly surprising that there was a deficit of sailors, and this was particularly true in 1739, as the navy endeavoured to fit out a fleet of 25 fighting ships, plus innumerable bomb ketches, store ships, fireships, and hospital ships. The only solution to this chronic shortage of personnel was impressment, whereby men were forcibly dragged aboard naval vessels, imprisoned, and signed up for lengthy periods of service against their will. The whole unpleasant procedure is described in *Roderick Random* thus:

> As I crossed Tower Wharf, a squat tawny fellow with a hanger by his side, and a cudgel in his hand came up to me, calling, 'Yo ho! brother, you must come along with me.' As I did not like his appearance, instead of answering his salutation, I quickened my pace, in hope of ridding myself of his company; upon which he whistled aloud, and immediately another sailor appeared before me, who laid hold of me by the collar, and began to drag me along. Not being in a humour to relish such treatment, I disengaged myself of the assailant, and, with one blow of my cudgel, laid him motionless on the ground; and perceiving myself surrounded in a trice by ten or a dozen more, exerted myself with such dexterity and success, that some of my opponents were fain to attack me with drawn cutlasses; and after an obstinate engagement, in which I received a large wound on my head, and another on my left cheek, I was disarmed, taken prisoner, and carried on board a pressing tender, where, after being pinioned like a malefactor, I was thrust down into the hold among a parcel of miserable wretches, the sight of whom well nigh distracted me. As the commanding officer had not humanity enough to order my wounds to be dressed, and I could not use my own hands, I desired one of my fellow captives who was unfettered, to take a handkerchief out of my pocket, and tie it round my head, to stop the bleeding. He pulled out my handkerchief, 'tis true, but instead of applying it to the use for which I designed it, went to the grating of the hatchway, and, with astonishing composure, sold it before my face to a bumboat woman then on board, for a quart of gin, with which he treated his companions, regardless of my circumstances and entreaties.

Whether this truly was Smollett's introduction to the navy, or whether he entered the service of his own volition will never be known. Whether or not he was impressed *into* service, it is abundantly clear that he was deeply unimpressed *with* the service and this unpropitious beginning set the template both for his early fictional and later factual accounts of his time in the navy. It is important to mention at this juncture that Smollett could often be quite a tricky character: a red-headed, somewhat fiery Scot, he could be very thin-skinned when criticised, and revenge was often wrought with the pen, which in his hands became a lethal weapon, delivering some memorably vicious pieces of satire. In the navy, he found the perfect target for his savage disdain, and no one emerges from his reminisces on the subject with much credit.

Smollett – either voluntarily or involuntarily – was now installed as surgeon's second mate aboard the *Chichester*, a rather ancient, three-decked vessel dating back to 1695. She mounted around 80 guns and carried a quite staggering crew of 600. How all these men managed to pack into the *Chichester*'s modest 155 feet is not clear but, with so many people living in such a confined space, there was certainly plenty of call for the surgeon. Although the vessel had not yet left London, the surgeon's 'cock pit' as his working place was known in the navy, was already crammed with sick men. Scurvy, cholera, small-pox and distemper were all common problems in the service at this time – these were the days before a daily ration of lime juice was introduced to good effect – and it didn't help that ships were often manned with men fresh from the gutter. Smollett gives a clear indication of the impossible working conditions in this makeshift sick bay in *Roderick Random*:

I could not comprehend how it was possible for the attendants to come near those who hung on the inside towards the sides of the ship, in order to assist them, as they seemed barricaded by those who lay on the outside, and entirely out of the reach of all visitation; much less could I conceive how my friend Thompson [the surgeon's second mate] would be able to administer clysters, that were ordered for some, in that situation; when I saw him thrust his wig in his pocket, and strip himself to his waistcoat in a moment, then creep on all fours under the hammocks of the sick, and, forcing up his bare pate between two, keep them asunder with one shoulder, until he had done his duty. Eager to learn the service, I desired he would give me leave to perform the next operation of that kind; and he consenting, I undressed myself after his example, and crawling along, the ship happened to roll: this motion alarming me, I laid hold of the first thing that came within my grasp with such violence, that I overturned it, and soon found, by the smell that issued upon me, that I had unlocked a box of the most delicious perfume. It was well for me that my nose was none of the most delicate, else I know not how I might have been affected by this vapour, which diffused itself all over the ship, to the utter discomposure of everybody who tarried on the same dock! neither was the consequence of this disgrace confined to my sense of smelling only; for I felt my misfortune more ways than one. That I might not, however, appear altogether disconcerted in this my first essay, I got up, and, pushing my head with great force between two hammocks, towards the middle, where the greatest resistance was, I made an opening indeed, but, not understanding the knack of dexterously turning my shoulder to maintain my advantage, had the mortification to find myself stuck up, as it were, in a pillory, and the weight of three or four people bearing on each side of my neck, so that I was in danger of strangulation. While I remained in this defenceless posture, one of the sick men, rendered peevish by his distemper, was so enraged at the smell I had occasioned and the rude shock he had received from me in my elevation, that, with many bitter reproaches, he seized me by the nose, which he tweaked so unmercifully, that I roared with anguish.

There is little doubt that conditions were far from pleasant, and you have probably already gathered that Smollett viewed the navy with a gimlet eye and pulled no punches in describing it in all its grubby glory. *Roderick Random* went on to describe the filth, cruelty and ineptitude of the navy with undisguised glee. Captain Oakum is a brutal and brainless disciplinarian, who parades sick men on deck until they drop dead, and doles out numerous lashings with the cat o' nine tails for almost any reason at all. Smollett's navy is unclean, unfair and utterly unpleasant. His rather relentless highlighting of bad practice has unquestionably had a profound effect on the layman's view that life aboard a naval vessel was all about 'rum, sodomy and the lash' as Winston Churchill so picturesquely put it many years later. This has led some revisionists to rather condemn Smollett for exaggerating. Yet they are overlooking the fact that he was writing, if not fiction, an embellished and exaggerated version of his own experiences for comic effect, in order to sell his book. Another factor that doubtless contributed to Smollett's rather jaded view of the navy was that he took part in one of the most disastrous campaigns in its history. This was the Seige of Cartagena, a disaster that ensured that the War of Jenkin's Ear was a total pig's ear.

The plan was a simple one: HMS *Chichester* was part of a great fleet Britain had assembled, which was to sally forth across the Atlantic. Arriving in Port Royal, Jamaica, the fleet would be bolstered by further troops and ships from the Caribbean fleet and, under the joint command of Admiral Vernon, who ran the naval side of things, and General Cathcart, who would deal with the troops, the fleet would proceed to seize the main Spanish trading posts in the Caribbean. The major targets were identified as Havana in Cuba, Portobello in what is now Panama and Cartagena in modern day Colombia. British confidence was buoyed by an earlier success in 1739, which had seen Vernon, then vice admiral, with a force of six ships, briefly take Portobello from the Spaniards. Celebrations of this achievement were wild and disproportionate; commemorative medals of Vernon were produced and a famous road in London still bears the name of this brief and rather pointless victory. The huge fleet gathering in London was being despatched to finish the job off.

Things did not go well from the start: there were long delays in the preparations. The truth was that it was incredibly difficult to find enough sailors and troops to support such an epic mission, and there were further hold-ups while the fleet awaited a favourable wind. In total, three months were lost and Smollett finally took leave of the English coastline with a heavy heart. It was not long before they were in even more trouble, as he recalls thus:

It was not without great mortification I saw myself on the point of being transported to such a distant and unhealthy climate, destitute of every

convenience that could render such a voyage supportable, and under
the dominion of an arbitrary tyrant, whose command was almost
intolerable; however, as these complaints were common to a great many
on board, I resolved to submit patiently to my fate, and contrive to make
myself as easy as the nature of the case would allow. We got out of the
channel with a prosperous breeze, which died away, leaving us becalmed
about fifty leagues to the westward of the Lizard: but this state of inaction
did not last long; for next night our maintop-sail was split by the wind,
which, in the morning, increased to a hurricane. I was awakened by a
most horrible din, occasioned by the play of the gun carriages upon the
decks above, the cracking of cabins, the howling of the wind through the
shrouds, the confused noise of the ship's crew, the pipes of the boatswain
and his mates, the trumpets of the lieutenants, and the clanking of the
chain pumps. I went above; but if my sense of hearing was startled
before, how must my sight have been appalled in beholding the effects
of the storm! The sea was swelled into billows mountain-high, on the top
of which our ship sometimes hung as if it were about to be precipitated to
the abyss below! Sometimes we sank between two waves that rose on each
side higher than our topmast-head, and threatened by dashing together
to overwhelm us in a moment! Of all our fleet, consisting of a hundred
and fifty sail, scarce twelve appeared, and these driving under their bare
poles, at the mercy of the tempest. At length the mast of one of them gave
way, and tumbled overboard with a hideous crash! Nor was the prospect
in our own ship much more agreeable; a number of officers and sailors
ran backward and forward with distraction in their looks, halloaing to
one another, and undetermined what they should attend to first. Some
clung to the yards, endeavouring to unbend the sails that were split into
a thousand pieces flapping in the wind; others tried to furl those which
were yet whole, while the masts, at every pitch, bent and quivered like
twigs, as if they would have shivered into innumerable splinters! While
I considered this scene with equal terror and astonishment, one of the
main braces broke, by the shock whereof two sailors were flung from the
yard's arm into the sea, where they perished.

After this alarming start, things settled down and the fleet made stately progress across the Atlantic. In his role of surgeon's second mate, Smollett would have been far from idle, for, as the great ship drifted into warmer latitudes and the temperature rose, so too did the number of men on the sick list, which was only kept under control by the steady flow of people dying. For every day of the *Chichester*'s 54-day transatlantic crossing, a man died and was unceremoniously dumped over the side. Smollett's daily routine was an endless round of tending to the sick and dying; bleeding, dressing wounds and emptying the putrid chamber pots. In *Roderick Random*, this routine is broken by a disastrous breakdown in the relationship between the physician, Doctor Mackshane, and the surgeons, Thompson, Random, and the somewhat verbose Welshman, Morgan. This eventually results in Morgan and Random being disciplined and imprisoned, and Thompson throwing himself overboard in order to escape this humiliating treatment. Although it is doubtful there was any such a dramatic rift between the physician and his staff in real life, what is certainly true is that one man did indeed throw himself overboard and drowned, 'after undergoing the shameful discipline of the ship' as Smollett noted. All the while, Smollett was absorbing and assimilating every aspect of the seedy existence of life aboard ship, and his later writings were able to bring to life the camaraderie, bawdy humour and discomfort in a way few would match for realism and wit until Cooper, Marryat and Melville took up their pens many years later.

After many weeks of drifting, the fleet finally made its landfall, the islands of Martinique and Guadeloupe slowly materialising through the clouds. It must have felt like the promised land, although Smollett makes no mention of any feelings of wonder or joy. Perhaps it was because, at that time, the Caribbean's greatest claim to fame was not so much pristine beaches and azure waters as yellow fever, malaria, despair and death. As a surgeon, Smollett knew that his work had only just begun. From here, the fleet threaded through the Leeward Islands to the neutral island of Dominica, where provisions and much needed fresh water supplies were replenished. It was at this point that General Cathcart, leader of the military arm of the planned offensive, died. This was a significant loss, and one that was to have a huge bearing on the eventual outcome of the mission. He was replaced by the rather inexperienced General Wentworth, 'an officer of neither knowledge, weight nor self confidence to conduct an enterprise of such importance,' as Smollett noted. The fleet then headed to Port Royal, Jamaica to prepare for action, but not before it had encountered a detachment of five French warships off the island of St Christopher (now known as St Kitts). Although France and England were not at war, the decision was taken to send a squadron of six ships to investigate. Before long, shots were exchanged and soon a full-scale naval battle was in progress. Smollett described it with disgust:

> *The two squadrons, being very equally matched, fought all night with equal courage; and in the morning, the English commodore seeing French colours displayed, hailed his antagonist and pretended he had mistaken them for Spaniards; the battle was forthwith suspended, mutual compliments passed, and, having treated each other with great marks of politeness, they parted with the loss of about a hundred men killed on each side.*

If Smollett had ever harboured any patriotic fervour, it is clear that it was evaporating quickly, and worse was to come. In Port Royal, the British fleet was joined by the Caribbean fleet and further bolstered by a North American squadron. The result was a truly intimidating force consisting of 186 ships including 29 ships of the line, 22 frigates, two hospital ships, various fireships, and bomb ships armed with a total of some 2,000 cannon. These were supported by 80 troop transports and 50 merchant ships. There were at least 27,400 military personnel, of which the land force totalled 12,000. This seemed like a pretty invincible armada, and all were reasonably confident that victory was more of a formality than anything else. The decision was taken to head to the mainland port of Cartagena first and capture that, before turning to Portobello and Havana. Given the gargantuan size of this fleet, it is perhaps unsurprising that it took several weeks for the vessels to finally assemble off Cartagena, and all had suffered greatly in the meantime, as Smollett noted:

We had languished five weeks on the allowance of a purser's quart per day for each man in the Torrid Zone, where the sun was vertical, and the expense of bodily fluid so great, that a gallon of liquor could scarce supply the waste of twenty-four hours; especially as our provision consisted of putrid salt beef, to which the sailors gave the name of Irish horse; salt pork, of New England, which, though neither fish nor flesh, savoured of both; bread from the same country, every biscuit whereof, like a piece of clockwork, moved by its own internal impulse, occasioned by the myriads of insects that dwelt within it; and butter served out by the gill, that tasted like train oil thickened with salt. Instead of small beer, each man was allowed three half-quarterns of brandy or rum, which were distributed every morning, diluted with a certain quantity of his water, without either sugar or fruit to render it palatable, for which reason, this composition was by the sailors not ineptly styled Necessity.

This was one of the first incarnations of Admiral Vernon's soon to be famous 'grog'. Basically, the navy faced a real problem in the Caribbean when it came to 'refreshing' the crew by splicing the mainbrace. Back home in England, sailors could expect a daily ration of ale to keep them happy. In the Mediterranean, this was substituted with wine, while in the Caribbean, rum was generally used, with disastrous effect, the result being that crew were often utterly sozzled. Vernon's solution was to add water mixed with lime juice to the rum. The name 'grog' came about because the Admiral was nicknamed 'old grog' on account of his favouring a jacket made out of grogram cloth. Smollett was particularly scathing about grog, also describing it as 'a most unpalatable drench which no man could swallow without reluctance'. But to return to main body of Smollett's rantings:

Nor was this limitation of simple element [water] owing to a scarcity of it on board, for there was at this time water enough in the ship for a voyage of six months, at the rate of half-a-gallon per day to each man: but this fast must, I suppose, have been enjoined by way of penance on the ship's company for their sins; or rather with a view to mortify them into a contempt of life, that they might thereby become more resolute and regardless of danger. How simply then do those people argue, who ascribe the great mortality among us, to our bad provision and want of water; and affirm, that a great many valuable lives might have been saved, if the useless transports had been employed in fetching fresh stock, turtle, fruit, and other refreshments from Jamaica and other adjacent islands, for the use of the army and fleet! Seeing it is to be hoped, that those who died went to a better place, and those who survived were the more easily maintained. After all, a sufficient number remained to fall before the walls of St. Lazar, where they behaved like their own country mastiffs, which shut their eyes, run into the jaws of a bear, and have their heads crushed for their valour.

Given this delay and the evident damage to the health of the men, the need for haste was palpable, as the onset of the rainy season was just around the corner and all knew that once this set in, disease could decimate the British Forces within a matter of days. There were other problems too: the city of Cartagena was substantial and well fortified, with a population of around 10,000. It was notable for its wonderful enclosed harbour, considered one of the finest natural havens in the Caribbean. It was here that the stately Spanish galleons filled their holds with all the ill-gotten gains of El Dorado, before dipping through the tropics by the palm-green shores, loaded with cargoes of diamonds, emeralds, amethysts, and gold moidores. Given the value of the cargoes loaded at the port, it was only natural that it should be well defended. The only deep water access was through a narrow channel, known as the Boca Chica (small mouth in English) and naturally both sides of this channel were bristling with well armed batteries. Once inside, there was the further problem of besting the main armament of the city itself. Francis Drake had managed this with his usual aplomb in 1585, but an attempt to take the city by Admiral Vernon the previous year had ended in failure. Now Vernon was back with a much stronger force, but a number of notable weaknesses. For some reason, there was no overarching commander. Vernon was in charge of the navy, Wentworth in charge of the army and the two did not get on, each taking every opportunity to make the other look foolish. The results were distinctly mixed and I will leave it to Smollett to give you his characteristically withering assessment:

At length we arrived in a bay to the windward of Carthagena, where we came to an anchor, and lay at our ease ten days longer. Here, again, certain malicious people took occasion to blame the conduct of their superiors, by saying, that in so doing they not only unprofitably wasted time, which was very precious, considering the approach of the rainy season, but also allowed the Spaniards to recollect themselves from a terror occasioned by the approach of an English fleet, at least three times as numerous as ever appeared in that part of the world before. But if I might be allowed to give my opinion of the matter, I would ascribe this delay to the generosity of our chiefs, who scorned to take any advantage that fortune might give them even over an enemy. At last, however, we weighed, and anchored again somewhat nearer the harbour's mouth, where we made shift to land our marines, who encamped on the beach, in despite of the enemy's shot, which knocked a good many of them on the head. This piece of conduct, in choosing a camp under the walls of an enemy's fortification, which I believe never happened before, was practised, I presume, with a view of accustoming the soldiers to stand fire, who were not as yet much used to discipline, most of them having been taken from the plough-tail a few months before. This expedient, again, has furnished matter for censure against the ministry, for sending a few raw recruits on such an important enterprise, while so many veteran regiments lay inactive at home. But surely our governors had their reasons for so doing, which possibly may be disclosed with other secrets of the deep. Perhaps they were loth to risk their best troops on such desperate service, or the colonel and the field officers of the old corps, who, generally speaking, enjoyed their commissions as sinecures or pensions, for some domestic services rendered to the court, refused to embark in such a dangerous and precarious undertaking; for which refusal, no doubt, they are to be much commended.

Smollett was often singled out for his rather spiteful treatment of those he chose to satirise, but in the case of the leaders of the siege of Cartagena, his savagery seems entirely justified. Nevertheless, the British succeeded in taking the forts of the Boca Chica at the entrance channel of Cartagena. They now had access to the main harbour and it was at this point that things started to go badly wrong. The basic plan was sound enough; the fort of San Lazar stood just outside the main city on top of a hill and essentially commanded the city. Capture this, and you had the town at your mercy, so it was the obvious next step. All assumed that while Wentworth and his men were attacking this fortress, Vernon's ships would be employed in battering the main town in order to draw off troops and generally wreak havoc. This did not happen, Vernon making the bizarre excuse that there was insufficient depth off the harbour walls to be able to do this, even though it was plainly evident from the Spanish merchant vessels anchored under the walls that a ship could sail in close with no difficulty. At the same time he goaded the unfortunate Wentworth for his inactivity and perceived dithering until the inexperienced officer rashly proceeded without the much-needed covering fire from the fleet. The result was a humiliating defeat. It didn't help that the guides mistakenly led the troops to a section of the walls that could only be accessed by a very precipitous path, or that the scaling ladders deployed to storm the parapets were ten feet too short. The ultimate result was catastrophic. I will again leave it to Smollett to convey the absurdity of the situation and also wrap up the action:

> *Our chief, not relishing this kind of complaisance in the Spaniard's, was wise enough to retreat on board with the remains of his army, which, from eight thousand able men landed on the beach near Bocca Chica, was now reduced to fifteen hundred fit for service. The sick and wounded were squeezed into certain vessels, which thence obtained the name of hospital ships, though methinks they scarce deserved such a creditable title, seeing few of them could boast of their surgeon, nurse, or cook; and the space between decks was so confined that the miserable patients had not room to sit upright in their beds. Their wounds and stumps, being neglected,*

contracted filth and putrefaction, and millions of maggots were hatched
amidst the corruption of their sores. This inhuman disregard was imputed
to the scarcity of surgeons; though it is well known that every great ship in
the fleet could have spared one at least for this duty, an expedient which
would have been more than sufficient to remove this shocking inconvenience.
But perhaps our general was too much of a gentleman to ask a favour of
this kind from his fellow chief, who, on the other hand, would not derogate
so much from his own dignity, as to offer such assistance unasked; for, I
may venture to affirm, that by this time the Demon of Discord, with her
sooty wings, had breathed her influence upon our councils; and it might
be said of these great men (I hope they will pardon the comparison) as
of Cesar and Pompey, the one could not brook a superior, and the other
was impatient of an equal; so that, between the pride of one and insolence
of another, the enterprise miscarried, according to the proverb, 'Between
two stools the backside falls to the ground.' Not that I would be thought
to liken any public concern to that opprobrious part of the human body,
though I might with truth assert, if I durst use such a vulgar idiom, that
the nation did hang on arse at its disappointment on this occasion; neither
would I presume to compare the capacity of our heroic leaders to any such
wooden convenience as a joint-stool or a close-stool; but only to signify by
this simile, the mistake the people committed in trusting to the union of two
instruments that were never joined.

This was about the end of any meaningful action, but still Wentworth and
Vernon dallied, undecided on what to do. In the meantime the rains came in.
Day after day the heavens opened and lengthy, persistent deluges soughed
down on the fleet, the monotony only broken by intermissions of scorching
sunlight and heat which made the decks steam and the crew gasp like landed
fish. Most of the men who had not been killed in battle proceeded to die in
this festering steaming pit of disease and despair, as Smollett recalled:

Nothing was heard but groans, lamentations and the language of
despair, invoking death to deliver them from their miseries. What served

to encourage this despondence was the prospect of these poor wretches
who had strength and opportunity to look around them; for there they
beheld the naked bodies of their fellow soldiers and comrades floating up
and down the harbour, affording prey to the carrion crows and sharks,
which tore them in pieces without interruption, and contributing by their
stench to the mortality which prevailed.

After 67 days of almost unremitting ineffectiveness, the action was called off, and the British retreated to Port Royal to lick their wounds, which were significant: 18,000 dead, mostly from disease and 50 ships abandoned or lost. After the defeat, Admiral Vernon sent a letter to the leader of the forces in Cartagena stating: 'We have decided to retreat, but we will return to Cartagena after we take reinforcements in Jamaica', to which Blas de Lezo, leader of the Cartagena forces, responded ironically, 'In order to come to Cartagena, the English King must build a better and larger fleet, because yours now is only suitable to transport coal from Ireland to London'. The whole affair was a massive national embarrassment, exacerbated by the fact that Admiral Vernon had rather jumped the gun and, after the taking of the Boca Chica, had despatched a message to King George II stating that Cartagena had fallen. To this end, commemorative medals were issued, lauding Vernon as 'the scourge of the Spaniards' and there was much celebration, which fell rather flat once the truth came to light. In fact, King George II was so annoyed by the whole affair that he forbade his courtiers from speaking about the event thereafter.

Quite how involved in the action Smollett was is extremely difficult to ascertain; for one thing, the naval attack itself was rather limited due to the extreme lassitude of Admiral Vernon. What Smollett was able to gather from this catastrophic campaign was the material that would make up a large portion of his first, and most successful novel, *Roderick Random*. Not only is this a fine, salty account of life at sea, it is a viciously searing indictment of the entire operation. He was no less abrasive in his assessment of the officers of the navy. Here is his sneering depiction of Captain Harry Paulet, renamed by Smollett as Captain Whiffle:

... a tall, thin young man, dressed in this manner: a white hat, garnished with a red feather, adorned his head, from whence his hair flowed upon his shoulders, in ringlets tied behind with a ribbon. His coat, consisting of pink-coloured silk, lined with white, by the elegance of the cut retired backward, as it were, to discover a white satin waistcoat embroidered with gold, unbuttoned at the upper part to display a brooch set with garnets, that glittered in the breast of his shirt, which was of the finest cambric, edged with right Mechlin: the knees of his crimson velvet breeches scarce descended so low as to meet his silk stockings, which rose without spot or wrinkle on his meagre legs, from shoes of blue Meroquin, studded with diamond buckles that flamed forth rivals to the sun! A steel-hilted sword, inlaid with gold, and decked with a knot of ribbon which fell down in a rich tassel, equipped his side; and an amber-headed cane hung dangling from his wrist. But the most remarkable parts of his furniture were, a mask on his face, and white gloves on his hands, which did not seem to be put on with an intention to be pulled off occasionally, but were fixed with a curious ring on the little finger of each hand. In this garb, Captain Whiffle, for that was his name, took possession of the ship, surrounded with a crowd of attendants, all of whom, in their different degrees, seemed to be of their patron's disposition; and the air was so impregnated with perfumes, that one may venture to affirm the climate of Arabia Felix was not half so sweet-scented.

Such lampooning of the more ineffective members and practices clearly brought Smollett great pleasure and you can sense his glee as he humiliates Paulet. Yet it was to be some years before Smollett was able to sit down and write his first book. After the fleet arrived back in Jamaica, the surgeon's mate mysteriously disappears from the *Chichester*'s crew register, and very little is known of his movements for the next four years. It is believed that he settled in Jamaica for some time and this is corroborated by his subsequent marriage to Anne Lascelles, a Jamaican Creole heiress. It was not until 1746 that we know he was definitely back in London, new wife by his side. As an interesting aside, he moved into lodgings in Downing Street. No 10 was already occupied by prime minister Robert Walpole, the house being gifted to him by George II, but the rest of the street had not yet been acquired for the use of other ministers and Smollett was able to make himself comfortable and set up a surgeon's practice in this genteel suburb. It is possible that his travails in the Caribbean had left him rather unsuited to dealing with minor complaints such as gout and bunions and the kind of trifling ailments that his genteel clients presented him with. Certainly, he was not a success. Sir Walter Scott in his biography of Smollett states that he:

> ... failed to render himself agreeable to his female patients, certainly not from want of address or figure, for both were remarkably pleasing, but more probably by a hasty impatience of listening to petty complaints, and a want of sympathy with the lamentations of those who laboured under no real indisposition.

I am sure there are plenty of doctors out there today who could sympathise with this point of view. In the meantime the bored and irritable surgeon returned to trying to flog the wretched *Regicide* to the theatre managers of London, who were as unreceptive as they had been five years previously. Success, however, was just around the corner and in 1748, Smollett hit the big time with *Roderick Random*. The book was an immediate hit and Smollett found himself competing alongside Henry Fielding as the foremost writer of his time.

Although *Roderick Random* was not solely devoted to nautical adventure, it was to have a profound effect on the genre, not just because Smollett was able to bring the sea to life in a manner other authors could not, but also because it introduced into the canon of English literature that much loved character, the feckless old sea dog, stumping along on a wooden leg and, at least on land, cutting an utterly helpless figure. This character would pop up again and again in Smollett's novels, and later in the works of Charles Dickens and, most famously, in Robert Louis Stevenson's *Treasure Island*. In *Roderick Random* it is Tom Bowling, kindly uncle of Roderick, who supplies us with our archetype and he is succeeded by Commander Trunnion in his second novel, *Peregrine Pickle*, and Captain Crowe in his fourth novel, *Launcelot Greaves*. An example of Smollett's description of the old sea dog, marooned and helpless ashore can be seen in this picturesque piece of narrative from Commodore Trunnion, delayed on his way to a wedding:

> *Hark ye, brother, don't you see we make all possible speed? go back and tell those who sent you, that the wind has shifted since we weighed anchor, and that we are obliged to make very short trips in tacking, by reason of the narrowness of the channel; and that as we lie within six points of the wind they must make allowance for variation and leeway.*

As Sir Walter Scott later observed admiringly,

> *... the term of Smollett's service in the navy was chiefly remarkable from his having acquired, in that brief space, such intimate knowledge of our nautical world, as enabled him to describe sailors with such truth and spirit of delineation, that from that time whoever has undertaken the same task has seemed to copy more from Smollett than from nature.*

Understandably, Smollett was not eager to repeat his seafaring experiences aboard HMS *Chichester* and his life thereafter is singularly devoid of nautical exploits. After the success of *Roderick Random*, he was able to retire from the evident misery of being a surgeon and settled down to becoming a full-time writer, he even managed to get *Regicide* shown, although he had to pay for it out of his own pocket. His first book was to prove his most successful and many more received critical acclaim, but others have not survived the test of time. The Royal Navy continued to haunt Smollett and in 1857 he was actually imprisoned after describing Admiral Knowles, one of his contemporaries of the siege of Cartagena, as: 'An admiral without conduct, an engineer without knowledge, an officer without resolution, and a man without veracity.' Knowles had been one of the few officers to serve with distinction at Cartagena – there is even a possibility that Smollett served under him – but had subsequently landed himself in hot water over the bungled siege of Rochefort in France, and Smollett had written a suitably scalding rebuke of his conduct. This had led to him being sued by Knowles, subsequently fined £100 and sentenced to three months imprisonment. Given incidents such as these, along with overwork as a writer trying to pay off hefty debts, it is perhaps understandable that, over the years, Smollett's somewhat fiery, irritable nature and savage satirism were further enhanced by a sort of irascible curmudgeonliness. This was used to best effect in his astoundingly xenophobic *Travels through France and Italy*. It was while he was gathering material for this work in Italy that he was himself lampooned by a fellow writer, Laurence Sterne as 'Smellfungus', a kind of ultimate personification of the irritable, intolerant Brit abroad. Given this, it is ironic that he eventually died in Livorno, Italy, where he and his wife had settled in later years, partly for health reasons.

Although Smollett didn't write much about the sea, his influence was profound and he played an important part in shaping the way in which later novelists dealt with the subject. None could ever say that his was a particularly positive view of a sailor's life, and indeed, a contemporary of Smollett's observed that he seemed to have, 'dipped his pen in gall and bilge-water.' Nevertheless, he was able to bring sailors and the sea to life in a manner that none had done before. Prior to this, a sea passage was often summed up in a couple of bare sentences. Smollett was able to conjure up its hidden depths, its vagaries and also the joy and tedium of serving aboard a ship. If one could never exactly say that he was at one with the sea, his writing certainly showed that he was at one with the sailors; united with them against clueless captains and cruel mates, just as he had been on HMS *Chichester*. This understanding and love of the poor beaten-down tars, so ill used in both the merchant and Royal navies, 'at the mercy of every whim of a despotic leader,' allowed him to portray them on the page as none had done before and few have done since.

Robert Louis Stevenson
Home is the sailor – the final voyage

To write about Robert Louis Stevenson's seafaring adventures is to embark on a voyage full of contradictions. Here is a man who wrote one of the all-time classics of nautical literature, *Treasure Island*, yet at the time professed to know very little of the sea and ships. A man who wrote about swashbuckling action yet was himself so frail, weak and wracked with consumption that he spent much of his life laid up at death's door. This is a man who was a 'lighthouse' Stevenson, a member of the famous family of lighthouse builders who did more than any other to safeguard the lives of British sailors throughout the nineteenth century. This last attribute sounds like an excellent foundation for a seafaring adventurer, but it would be Robert Louis who broke the Stevenson family's proud tradition, turning his back on engineering to live the life of a louche bohemian, sponging off his father and gallivanting across Europe courting scandal at every turn.

With all this against him, it is easy to conclude that he was no sailor, for much of his life was spent miles from the rugged cliffs and towering seas upon which his forefathers had carved their reputations. Yet the final contradiction is that Stevenson would ultimately enjoy a seafaring adventure that almost matched that of his fictional characters in *Treasure Island* or *Kidnapped*. He left it late in life, but in 1888, Stevenson set out from San Francisco aboard the yacht *Casco*, bound for the South Sea Islands and the unknown. This was his only major sailing trip, yet it provided a fitting adventure for a man who wrote stories so rich in action and romance. This voyage and subsequent ramblings also provided him with fresh impetus to put together a number of stories such as *The Wrecker* and *The Ebb Tide*, not to mention *In the South Seas*, a diary of his journey. All are as awash with the languor, beauty and savagery of these islands as anything written before or since.

Before the yarn of this voyage can start, however, it is important to fully understand how Stevenson came to first set foot on the deck of the *Casco* as she headed through the Golden Gate. To comprehend that, we must get to know a little more about the man himself. Born in Edinburgh in 1850 to Margaret and Thomas Stevenson, Robert was an only child and a sickly one, inheriting a weak chest from his mother. He spent much of his youth convalescing from one illness or another. His parents had a tendency to mollycoddle this sensitive youth and despite his father's terrifying blood and thunder Scots-Calvinist veneer, both indulged their son dreadfully.

Growing up in Edinburgh was a misery for the youngster, who only later learned to love his hometown. Reminiscing on the place as a young author, he wrote of the 'gloom and depression of Edinburgh winter' and of something almost 'physically disgusting in the bleak ugliness of the easterly weather.' At home, the domineering figure of Thomas Stevenson was to loom large over Robert. As mentioned previously, Thomas had achieved fame as the foremost lighthouse builder in Britain, just as his father, also named Robert, had done before him. Between them, the pair had designed and overseen the construction of around 50 lighthouses up and down the country and had plenty of tales to tell of their adventures doing so. Writing of his grandfather's exploits, Louis recalled with admiration and a tinge of envy:

> *The seas into which his labours carried the new engineer were still scarce charted, the coasts still dark; his way on shore was often far beyond the convenience of any road, the isles in which he must sojourn partly savage. He must toss much in boats; he must adventure on horseback by the dubious bridle track through unfrequented wildernesses; he must sometimes plant his lighthouse in the very camp of wreckers; and he*

was continually enforced to the vicissitudes of outdoor life. The joy my grandfather took in this career was as strong as the love of a woman.

From the first, he was expected to go into lighthouse design and construction and sorely disappointed his father by rejecting it after a short attempt by the family to train him up. After a bit of dabbling with a law degree, Stevenson, reluctantly bankrolled by his family, determined to pursue a literary career. His parents did not approve in the least, and there is little doubt that the decision also bothered Stevenson. He was always well aware of how he had turned his back on the family tradition in order to 'sling ink', and reconciled himself to this in one of his poems:

Say not that weakly I declined
The labours of my sires, and fled the sea,
The towers we founded and the lamps we lit,
To play at home with paper like a child.
But rather say: In the afternoon of time
A strenuous family dusted from its hands
The sand of granite, and beholding far
Along the sounding coast its pyramids
And tall memorials catch the dying sun
Smiled well content, and to this childish task
Around the fire addressed its evening hours.

In all honesty, the decision to avoid the rigours of lighthouse building was a wise one, for Stevenson had developed from a frail youth into a physically feeble man, and his tall gangling frame was slender to the point of being puny. He was naturally dreamy and extremely sensitive, prone to fits of hysterics and bursting into tears at the drop of the hat. He was unashamedly bohemian and slightly camp, with flowing locks and an unwieldy frame almost permanently clad in a tatty velvet jacket. There were times in his youth when he strode the streets of Edinburgh pursued by a crowd of urchins jeering at his freakish appearance, yet, although Stevenson was frail and sensitive, he was far from shy, and took the untoward attention in his gangling stride. He was extrovert in other ways too and despite being a stout defender of feminist causes, Stevenson seems to have had a preponderance for prostitutes in his youth and was a man who greatly appreciated female company. At times he took this appreciation too far and more than once teetered on the edge of causing a family scandal, much to the horror of his parents. However, in 1878, his days as Jack-the-lad came very abruptly to an end, when he met the love of his life, an American lady ten years his senior named Fanny Osbourne. With her bolshy nature, bulldog jaw and pistol secreted within her petticoats, Stevenson had more than met his match with a redoubtable lady who was often incorrectly identified as his mother on first acquaintance. Given his love of the dramatic at the time, it was perhaps inevitable that this larger-than-life woman should already be married, and also have two children, but once extricated from this encouplement the pair remained more or less inseparable for the rest of Stevenson's life.

Romance aside, up until the day Stevenson departed aboard the *Casco*, his life seems to have been one long round of illness and recovery. No one knows exactly what was wrong with him, but he evidently suffered from some kind of chronic weakness of the lungs that often led to severe haemorrhages and horrific episodes where he coughed up great gobbets of blood. Not only was this very awkward at dinner parties, it also meant that he would spend most of his life travelling around Europe trying to find a suitable climate in which he could convalesce. Switzerland, France, Scotland, England, he tried them all and settled in none. Yet while his health failed, he succeeded in churning out classic literary works such as *Treasure Island, Dr Jekyll and Mr Hyde* and *Kidnapped* to name but a few.

Despite writing a good deal of literature with a nautical flavour, there is precious little evidence that Stevenson was much of a sailor. In fairness, there is little doubt that he knew the ropes, for in his youth he had engaged in a number of sailing expeditions connected with his father's lighthouse inspections accompanied by his friend, Walter Simpson, who taught him the basics. Nevertheless, up until the *Casco* arrived on the scene, the closest he had been to a full-blown waterborne adventure was a rather drizzly and dispiriting canoeing trip through the European inland waterways, an account of which was published as *An Inland Voyage*, his first ever book.

By 1885 even these modest adventures seemed to be behind him. He had settled in Bournemouth and lived very comfortably there for a number of years, to all intents and purpose an invalid. Outwardly he appeared settled and the course of his life set. His somewhat strained relationship with his father, who was often pained by his lifestyle choices, was on solid ground and the redoubtable man had even come to acknowledge there was at least some value in his writing career, his wife enjoyed Bournemouth, and he had a good circle of friends. The stage was set for a prosaic finale to his life.

Suddenly, everything changed; the writer packed his bags and uprooted his family, heading to America, leaving Bournemouth with barely a backward glance, and never saw England again. The excuse was, as ever, his health, which suffered in the damp British climate, but there is little doubt that the real reason for this hasty departure was that his father had died. Finally, he was free from the shackles of his domineering patriarch. There is no doubt his father loved him, but he also interfered terribly and could do so with impunity, having bankrolled his son his whole life. Now he was gone, Stevenson was free to do as he wished. Not only that, but his own literary successes were starting to pay dividends, allowing him even greater liberty. Taking his beloved mother with him, his first stop was the crystal clear fresh air of the mountains of Colorado, where his health flourished. Soon, however, Stevenson's restless soul was agitating for more adventure. There were murmurs of travelling further afield, and mutterings of the South Seas. Stevenson had long had a fascination with this part of the world, having read Melville's *Ty-Pee* in 1878, and even met the author himself while he was in the US. Melville's preoccupation with the South Seas may have fired his literary imagination, but you can trace his obsession with the area as far back as 1875, when he had written to a friend about how he was:

... sick with desire to go there; beautiful places, green forever; perfect climate; perfect shapes of men and women with red flowers in their hair; and nothing to do but study oratory and etiquette, sit in the sun and

pick up the fruits as they fall. Navigator's Island [Samoa] is the place;
absolute balm for the weary.

Thirteen years later and the dream looked like it might come to fruition.
Fanny was sent ahead to San Francisco to scout out a potential yacht for their
use, and by May 1888 she had secured the schooner *Casco* for a charter of
several months in duration. It was the beginning of Stevenson's final chapter
and he clearly sensed it, for he explained his reasoning behind the voyage in
his journal of the trip, *In the South Seas:*

> *For nearly ten years my health had been declining; and for some while*
> *before I set forth upon my voyage, I believed I was come to the afterpiece*
> *of life, and had only the nurse and undertaker to expect. It was suggested*
> *that I should try the South Seas; and I was not unwilling to visit like a*
> *ghost, and be carried like a bale, among scenes that had attracted me in*
> *youth and health. I chartered accordingly Dr. Merrit's schooner yacht,*
> *the* Casco, *seventy-four tons register; and sailed from San Francisco*
> *towards the end of June 1888.*

In selecting the *Casco* for the voyage, the Stevensons had chosen very well,
for she was a very beautiful 95-foot schooner built for Dr Samuel Merritt in
1878. Merritt, who had previously served as Mayor of Oakland, is worthy of
a chapter himself, for he had headed out to California in 1849 at the peak of
the gold rush. Being a shrewd man, he had purchased a ship in New York to
get him to California and loaded her with essentials before heading off on the
epic voyage around Cape Horn. On arrival in San Francisco, he had sold his
cargo at boomtown prices and made a killing. By the time Stevenson met him
he was a millionaire and the *Casco* appears to have been a retirement present
to himself; his justification for this extravagance being that he was getting too
fat and she would keep him trim. The schooner was the absolute apple of his
eye. She was built of teak, which made her very solid, but she was also a very
fast vessel, boasting tall spars and a big spread of sail. Like almost all yachts
of this era, she had no engine, which would make the intricate navigation

of the South Seas all the more testing. It was therefore a bonus that the *Casco* possessed a shallow draft and differed from many traditional designs because she was fitted with a centreboard, essentially a keel that could be raised and lowered. This was to prove invaluable in the maze of corals and shallows of the South Seas. Some months later, when the *Casco* was in Nuku Hiva, Captain Dewar, a Scotsman cruising in his own vessel, the *Nyanza*, visited her. He gives this rather scornful assessment of her:

> *I found her a vessel of the regular American type; great beam and little depth provide with a cockpit and a coach roof extending her whole length in order to give greater headroom below. Her accommodation was very limited, and she appeared to me more adapted for sailing around San Francisco Bay, than for a cruise across the ocean.*

This truly damning evaluation betrays many of the European prejudices toward the American school of design. Dewar's *Nyanza* was a traditional deep, narrow vessel; doubtless also very seaworthy, but it is perhaps telling that she was later wrecked in the China Seas after grounding on a shallow reef, bringing into question which boat was the more suitable for cruising. That said, a single glance at the *Casco*'s tall, raking masts would underline how heavily rigged the schooner was and there is little doubt she would have been a ticklish ship to handle. Technicalities of design aside, the *Casco* was far roomier than Dewar makes out. She was going to need to be, for in addition to Stevenson, the crew would consist of his wife, Fanny, her ne'er do well son from her first marriage, Lloyd Osbourne, Stevenson's mother, Margaret, their maid, Valentine, and a crew of six, led by the somewhat sardonic Captain Otis. Thus with 11 aboard all told, there would not be a great deal of room, but there were no recorded complaints from any aboard and it probably helped that the vessel was immaculate and sumptuously furnished throughout. Her interior is described thus by Margaret Stevenson:

> *From the deck you step down into the cockpit, which is our open-air drawing-room. It has seats all round, nicely cushioned, and we sit or lie*

there most of the day. The compass is there, and the wheel, so the man at the wheel always keeps us company. Here, also, is the companion, and at the bottom of the stair on the right-hand side is the captain's room.

Straight ahead is the main- or after-cabin, a nice bright place with a skylight and four port-holes. There are four sofas that can be turned into beds if need be, and there are lockers under them in which our clothes are stored away. Above and behind each sofa is a berth concealed by white lace curtains on brass rods, and in these berths we three women are laid away as on shelves each night to sleep.

There is a table fastened to the floor in the centre of the cabin, covered with crimson Utrecht velvet. The sofas are upholstered to match, and the carpet is crimson Brussels. There is one large, heavy swivel-chair, and opposite the entrance is a mirror let into the wall, with two small shelves under it. On each side of this mirror is a door. The one to the right leads, through a small dressing-room with a fixed basin, to Lloyd's cabin, and beyond that again is the forward cabin, or dining-room. The door to the left opens into another small dressing-room, and beyond this is Louis's sleeping-room. It is very roomy, with both a bed and a sofa in it, so that he will be very comfortable; and at night, when we are all in bed, all the port-holes and skylights and doors are left open for the sake of air.

The dining-room has a long table and chairs, two mirrors at the end, and between the doors a very ugly picture of fruits and cake. Louis would fain cover it up if we could spare a flag with which to do it. Two doors at the further end lead to the pantry and galley, and beyond these are the men's quarters.

Clearly, the boat was good enough, although it seems rather unfair that the gentlemen aboard got their own cabins, while the women slept on what appear to have been glorified bunks. It soon became evident, however, that the big question was whether the charterers were up to snuff: upon arriving in San Francisco to inspect the *Casco*, it became clear the Stevenson entourage was also subject to close scrutiny from Doctor Merritt. He had no great need for money, but he truly loved his yacht and had no wish to charter her to undesirables. The Stevenson party was not promising. In addition to the gawky, frail bohemian author, there was his mother, well into her seventies, and Fanny Stevenson, already greying and prone to bouts of hypochondria (just prior to departure, she claimed she had throat cancer). Hardly a promising bunch and, initially, Dr Merritt was sceptical as Margaret Stevenson noted:

> He had heard that Louis had a mother, and was not at all sure of allowing an old woman to sail on his beloved yacht, so he insisted on seeing me before he left. When I came in I found a very stout man, with a strong and humorous face, who sat still in his chair and took a good look at me. Then he held out his hand, with the remark, 'you're a healthy-looking woman! ' – so I am to be allowed on board, as he thinks I am good for a seven months' trip. But he added, 'The yacht is the apple of my eye, – you may think your husband loves you, but I can assure you that I love my yacht a great deal better, and I am just afraid that you will run away with her and never bring her back. Remember, if you do, I'll be after you with a revenue cutter, and when I catch you ... !'

Despite this reassuring interview, it is telling that Dr Merritt, having cast a cursory medical eye over the collection of skin and bones that was Stevenson, made Captain Otis stow aboard the *Casco* all that was required for a burial at sea. He was, however, convinced that the famous writer was a reasonably knowledgeable sailor. Thus, all was settled and the *Casco* was chartered for the princely sum of $500 per month plus all expenses incurred during the trip. Stevenson was able to justify this hefty outlay as he had signed a deal to have his letters from the Pacific serialised in the US and Britain.

The route settled on would take the vessel first to the Marquesas, then thread through the Paumotus to Tahiti, from thence to Hawaii and then, presumably, back to San Francisco. In doing this, Stevenson followed almost precisely the path that Herman Melville took through the Islands aboard various whaling vessels back in the 1840s. Whether this was deliberate or not is unclear. Certainly Stevenson would have consulted with Captain Otis who would have probably encouraged this route, as it is the most seamanlike way to take in these islands. A couple of decades later Jack London's *Snark* made the mistake of visiting Hawaii first (see London's chapter) and then endured a tortuous passage across to the Marquesas, battling unfavourable currents and contrary winds along the way, so perhaps plain common sense dictated the route. Still, all of this lay in the uncertain future as the *Casco* turned her back on San Francisco and was towed out to sea by the tug, *Pelican*. The Pacific does not always live up to its name and immediately the *Casco* was out in the open ocean, she was exposed to the huge boisterous ground swells that come rolling across this great stretch of water. The women on board were greatly alarmed, with Margaret noting that, 'Even the mountains of the coast, were shut out entirely. Our vessel seemed very small among those enormous waves, and I felt nervous when I saw how she heeled over; however, I was told it was all right.'

The *Casco* was actually in her element and made a number of fast runs in these rollicking conditions, for she was a flyer and the long, rolling swells married to a fresh beam wind would have ensured she skimmed the ocean like a bird on the wing. That said, her low freeboard would have meant she was a caution in a heavy sea, and she frequently put her rail under, scooping up gallons of water at a time. Stevenson was a natural sailor exhilarated by the freedom and speed of the flying yacht and the fresh, clean sea air, 'better than wine' as he wrote at the time. He clearly did not suffer from seasickness, unlike his wife, who was constantly ill during rough weather.

Out in the great expanse of the Pacific, all would have felt vulnerable. No doubt the fulcrum of the ship was Captain Otis, the bluff, flinty sailor who they were all relying on to get them to the Marquesas safely. Otis had long harboured a desire to cruise the South Seas, but he was far from delighted when he first surveyed his motley crew. He did, however, profess a liking for Stevenson's *Treasure Island* and was fast coming to admire its author. He gives a fascinating insight into Stevenson when he recounted their first meeting:

To say that I was favourably impressed with the great author would be stretching the truth – Imagine a man of medium height, so painfully thin that his clothes seemed a burden to him, his brown hair falling to his shoulders around a face of deathlike whiteness, but alight with the most fascinating brown eyes I had ever seen. It took me some time to discover Nature's purpose in giving the man such an unusual pair of eyes; but I finally determined that they were indicant of strength of character, accompanying absolute fearlessness. This discovery created so deep an impression on my mind that I forgot for a time the startling physical weakness of the man. But as soon as I was alone the thought returned to me with some force, that before sailing I had better make the necessary arrangements for his death at sea; in fact, as I looked him over in my mind, without the tonic of his sustaining eyes, I did not believe it would be possible for him to make the trip and return alive. But there was one thing that I liked about him from the first: he never referred to his calling in his conversation – never talked shop to strangers; one might have taken him for a lawyer, or a secretary, or a musician, or a man of any other occupation, if you depended upon him to enlighten you.

There seems to have been a mutual respect between the pair. It is possible the author saw something of his curmudgeonly but well-meaning father in this man who was later used as the template for the rather fractious, opinionated old Captain Nares in his book *The Wrecker*. This cordiality between Stevenson and Otis was very important, for, in the cramped environs of a yacht, there was little room for friction between captain and owner and Stevenson was essentially the owner of the *Casco* for the duration of the cruise. The ladies liked him far less, and he did little to ingratiate himself to Margaret when, on being asked by her if he had read any of Stevenson's novels he replied that he had read *Treasure Island* and this made him disinclined to read any more. Margaret was mortified but her son, who heard the exchange, came up and congratulated him on his frankness. It is possible that Otis' bluntness contrasted well with the many sycophants Stevenson must have encountered as a successful novelist.

When assessing Otis, you must also understand how annoying it is for a skipper who constantly finds guests interfering and getting in the way and there are a number of references to his irritation with the ladies. Fanny is admonished for talking with the helmsman and distracting him, the ladies are constantly nagged about leaving the portlights open, which let in water if the yacht heeled over excessively. Perhaps Margaret notes the most revealing exchange thus: 'Fanny said to the captain one day, "What would you do if Mrs. Stevenson were to fall overboard?" And the captain, who loves a joke, solemnly replied, 'Put it in the log!'

Otis also had other worries; he was concerned at how shorthanded he was in the heavy conditions. Indeed, had he fallen overboard, the remainder would have been in quite severe straits, as there were no other competent navigators aboard. Thankfully, he held on tight and on the fifth day out the *Casco* was treated to the stirring sight of a British windjammer running full and bye before the breeze and racing along at 15 knots and more. The vessel overhauled them and then vanished sail after sail below the horizon, a beautiful interlude to the tedium of an ocean voyage.

By day nine, the *Casco* was still flying before the breeze, breasting the feathery swells with joyous abandon. As a matter of fact, she was right on the edge of a severe cyclonic storm and Otis must have been deeply preoccupied with what to do next. He knew from all the signs in the weather that he was either on the extreme eastward or westward edge of the storm and must turn away to avoid it. Make the wrong decision and he would plunge the *Casco* into the heart of this fearsome adversary. Otis rolled the dice and turned west, running before the breeze setting every stitch of canvas that he dared carry.

As luck would have it, he made the right decision and the *Casco* sailed serenely on. Approaching the Marquesas, however, the schooner received a true dusting down at the hands of these unpredictable waters when she was almost overwhelmed by a white squall, which caught the crew unawares, as Otis later recalled:

The squall, which was as black as a black cat, first passed the yacht to leeward; when well off the quarter, it suddenly turned and came down upon us, like the dropping of a cloak. All whips were let go, and the wheel was put hard down; but before the Casco *could be brought into the wind, she was struck and knocked down until the wind spilled out her sails, and the edge of the house was under water, with the sea pouring over the cockpit in a torrent. It looked dangerous for a while, and I can imagine that those below, except, perhaps, Stevenson, must have been in a pretty tremor.*

Stevenson put it in even more picturesque, if somewhat incomprehensible, terms when he wrote: 'We cam' so near gaun heels ower hurdies, that I really dinnae ken why we didnae athegither.'

Make of that what you will. The big plus side of the trip so far was that it was doing Stevenson's health the absolute power of good and never has the term 'a new lease of life' seemed more fitting than in his case. He was clearly the most comfortable and robust traveller aboard the *Casco* and was also thoroughly enjoying himself. His final reward was the first sight of land at 5am on 28 July 1888. He described the moment beautifully:

The first experience can never be repeated. The first love, the first sunrise, the first South Sea Island, are memories apart and touched a virginity of sense. On the 28th of July 1888 the moon was an hour down by four in the morning. In the east a radiating centre of brightness told of the day; and beneath, on the skyline, the morning bank was already building, black as ink ... the customary thrill of landfall heightened by the strangeness of the shores that we were then approaching. Slowly they took shape in the attenuating darkness. Ua-huna, piling up to a truncated summit, appeared the first upon the starboard bow; almost abeam arose our destination, Nuka-hiva, whelmed in cloud; and betwixt and to the southward, the first rays of the sun displayed the needles of Ua-pu. These pricked about the line of the horizon; like the pinnacles of some ornate and monstrous church, they stood there, in the sparkling brightness of the morning, the fit signboard of a world of wonders.

The land heaved up in peaks and rising vales; it fell in cliffs and buttresses; its colour ran through fifty modulations in a scale of pearl and rose and olive; and it was crowned above by opalescent clouds. The suffusion of vague hues deceived the eye; the shadows of clouds were confounded with the articulations of the mountains; and the isle and its unsubstantial canopy rose and shimmered before us like a single mass. There was no beacon, no smoke of towns to be expected, no plying pilot. Somewhere, in that pale phantasmagoria of cliff and cloud, our haven lay concealed ...

Thence we bore away along shore. On our port beam we might hear the explosions of the surf; a few birds flew fishing under the prow; there was no other sound or mark of life, whether of man or beast, in all that quarter of the island. Winged by her own impetus and the dying breeze, the Casco skimmed under cliffs, opened out a cove, showed us a beach and some green trees, and flitted by again, bowing to the swell. The trees, from our distance, might have been hazel; the beach might have been in Europe; the mountain forms behind modelled in little from the Alps, and the forest which clustered on their ramparts a growth no more considerable than our Scottish heath. Again the cliff yawned, but now with a deeper entry; and the Casco, hauling her wind, began to slide into the bay of Anaho. The cocoa-palm, that giraffe of vegetables, so graceful, so ungainly, to the European eye so foreign, was to be seen crowding on the beach, and climbing and fringing the steep sides of mountains. Rude and bare hills embraced the inlet upon either hand; it was enclosed to the landward by a bulk of shattered mountains. In every crevice of that barrier the forest harboured, roosting and nestling there like birds about a ruin; and far above, it greened and roughened the razor edges of the summit...

It was longer ere we spied the native village, standing (in the universal fashion) close upon a curve of beach, close under a grove of palms; the sea in front growling and whitening on a concave arc of reef. For the cocoa-tree and the island man are both lovers and neighbours of the surf. 'The coral waxes, the palm grows, but man departs,' says the sad Tahitian proverb; but they are all three, so long as they endure, co-haunters of the beach. The mark of anchorage was a blow-hole in the rocks, near the south-easterly corner of the bay. Punctually to our use, the blow-hole spouted; the schooner turned upon her heel; the anchor plunged. It was a small sound, a great event; my soul went down with

these moorings whence no windlass may extract nor any diver fish it up;
and I, and some part of my ship's company, were from that hour the
bondslaves of the isles of Vivien.

This was Nuku Hiva, in the heart of the Marquesas Islands, a beautiful island first visited by Captain Cook in 1774. Nuku Hiva is fourteen miles long and ten miles wide. It is dominated by a ridge of mountains; great verdant pinnacles of rock which plunge down to the waters' edge. Most agree that the anchorage of Anaho – once so favoured by whaling ships as a watering place – is one of the most beautiful anchorages in the South Seas. This was where Herman Melville had embarked upon the adventures related in *Ty-Pee*. Stevenson's long romance with this intricate maze of islands began here; he capered around this paradise barefoot, and was delighted with his early encounters with the local population, noting in a letter to a friend in London that:

From this somewhat (ahem) out of the way place, I write to say how
d'ye do. It is all a swindle: I chose these isles as having the most beastly
population, and they are far better, and far more civilised than we. I
know one old chief Ko-o-amua, a great cannibal in his day, who ate his
enemies even as he walked home from killing 'em, and he is a perfect
gentleman and exceedingly amiable and simple-minded: no fool, though.
The climate is delightful; and the harbour where we lie one of the
loveliest spots imaginable. Yesterday evening we had near a score natives
on board; lovely parties. We have a native god; very rare now. Very rare
and equally absurd to view.

The next two weeks were spent exploring the island and paying the inevitable visit to Melville's Ty-Pee and Happar valleys. The few colonials were fascinated by the famous author and one later described him, 'He used to go about barefoot, with his trousers and singlet-sleeves turned up, and never wore a hat'; and, 'most every one thought he was a little crazy.'

In turn, Stevenson was largely repelled by the colonial whites and equally fascinated by the native population; delighted by almost everything about them apart from the sight of cannibal feasting places. These were a bit too much for his sensitive nature and he noted that, 'To consider it too closely is to understand, not to excuse, these fervours of self righteous old ship captains who would man their guns and open fire in passing, on a cannibal island.'

While all of this exploring was going on, Captain Otis was wrestling with the *Casco*, which seemed far more at ease upon the rolling seas than the sheltered harbour and kept threatening to drag her anchor into the steep cliffs and jagged pinnacles of lava that surrounded the anchorage. After several days, she did indeed drag and it was only swift action that prevented her becoming a total loss. It was doubtless a relief to her captain when the anchor was hove up and departure was made. The relief was, however, short lived. The *Casco* was bound for the nearby island of Hiva Oa and endured a miserable passage, as Stevenson noted:

It was what is called a good passage, and a feather in the Casco's cap; but among the most miserable forty hours that any one of us had ever passed. We were swung and tossed together all that time like shot in a stage thunder-box. The mate was thrown down and had his head cut open; the captain was sick on deck; the cook sick in the galley. Of all our party only two sat down to dinner. I was one. I own that I felt wretchedly; and I can only say of the other, who professed to feel quite well, that she fled at an early moment from the table. It was in these circumstances that we skirted the windward shore of that indescribable island of Ua-pu; viewing with dizzy eyes the coves, the capes, the breakers, the climbing forests, and the inaccessible stone needles that surmount the mountains. The place persists, in a dark corner of our memories, like a piece of the scenery of nightmares.

Eventually they made the shelter of Hiva Oa, but there was little relief to be found here, for the anchorage was exposed and exceedingly rough. Nevertheless, the Stevenson party headed ashore and into the interior, visiting the Atuona Valley where, a few years later, the artist Paul Gauguin was to live out the remainder of his days in a kind of languid daze until his very paintbrush seemed to ooze with the sensuality of the place. Stevenson thought it the 'loveliest and by far the most ominous spot I have ever visited.' It was at this point that the aforementioned yacht *Nyanza* arrived on the scene with Cumming Dewar in command. Dewar, a Scotsman, was actually known to the Stevensons, which makes this chance meeting all the more extraordinary. A yacht cruise through the South Seas was, in 1888, almost, but evidently not quite, a unique experience.

Nevertheless, the destination that they pointed the bows of the *Casco* toward next, few had dared to venture before: These were the Tuamotus, also known as the Paumotus or Dangerous Islands and one of the most tricky and treacherous stretches of water you could wish to encounter. The Tuamotus is made up of a huge labyrinth of low atolls and islands barely visible until you are almost upon them. The islands seem to interfere with the regularity of the trade winds, which are often fickle and squally in this area, while strong currents tend to race between the islands. These factors conspire to make navigation extremely difficult, particularly for a sailing yacht like the *Casco*, which had no auxiliary power to get her out of trouble. In a calm, it was eminently possible for a sailing vessel to simply be swept on to one of these reefs and completely destroyed. Just to make matters that little bit worse, the charts of the time were far from complete and often placed islands where there were none or in a slightly different position. 'It was not without misgiving that my captain risked the Casco in such waters,' Stevenson noted.

The first part of this trip was an unmitigated success; the friendly trade winds were at their best and the *Casco* was wafted blissfully before them, Margaret Stevenson noting: 'This truly is pleasure sailing and the ocean has been truly Pacific.' Stevenson recalled this idyllic sail in more poetic terms in *The Wrecker* when he wrote:

I love to recall the glad monotony of a Pacific voyage, when the trades are not stinted, and the ship, day after day, goes free. The mountain scenery of trade-wind clouds, watched (and in my case painted) under every vicissitude of light – blotting stars, withering in the moon's glory, barring

the scarlet eve, lying across the dawn collapsed into the unfeatured
morning bank, or at noon raising their snowy summits between the blue
roof of heaven and the blue floor of sea; the small, busy, and deliberate
world of the schooner.

Yet the crew would have still looked ahead with dread, and their misgivings soon turned into a full-blown nightmare for Captain Otis. On the fifth day out, poor visibility meant that he was unable to get a decent 'fix' of his position with a sextant and was forced to rely on dead reckoning. This essentially means calculating your speed over the ground to work out your position and is fine if you know what the current is doing, but hopeless if you do not. Captain Otis did not and, as darkness closed in, he had to admit he was totally lost. True, he was in the vicinity of the islands of Raraka and Kuahei, but between them was a vast uncertain mass of reefs and shallows, any of which could rip the bottom out of the beautiful schooner. All around came the low boom of surf pounding on jagged reef while the glow of white water perceived by the lookout meant that there were breakers and death in the vicinity.

The modern yachtsman with his radar, GPS and engine to help him can only imagine the misery of Captain Otis as he peered in to the dark, velvety night, disorientated and helpless. The schooner was in a desperate situation, for the Tuamotus archipelago is essentially a trap and the little vessel had sailed right into the middle of it. Captain Otis recalled the situation later:

It was a night filled with perils for all, but it turned out to be our lucky
night. Only occasionally the look-out could see ahead to advantage; and
when the surf could not be seen they had to depend on the sharpness of
their ears for the vessel's safety. One of the crew was kept until midnight
with ear to the main-mast, as the water conveys the sound of a threatening
surf farther and more clearly than does the air. During the rain-squalls
the darkness was intense; and it seemed to the anxious crew that they
were picking up the surf dead ahead about every ten minutes. Later on it
was learned that the confusion had been caused by the variable currents

running through a channel, formed by the two islands, which lay nearly at right angles to each other, and about six miles apart. Happily, when daylight came we found the yacht lying quite in the centre of this channel and out of all danger.

It is likely that the Stevenson party was only partly aware of the extreme danger that they were in, although Robert certainly had a better conception than the others. It is telling, however, that as darkness drew in and this nightmare closed around Captain Otis, the famous author was enjoying a blissful reverie as he later recalled:

The night fell lovely in the extreme. After the moon went down, the heaven was a thing to wonder at for stars. And as I lay in the cockpit and looked upon the steersman I was haunted by Emerson's verses:
　　'And the lone seaman all the night
　　Sails astonished among stars.'

The contrast in emotions between edgy captain and dreamy owner could not have been more marked. Nevertheless, Captain Otis, through extreme skill and a good deal of luck, had got away with it and the cruise continued along its merry way. The next day, the *Casco* pointed her knife-like bow through the jagged coral heads of Fakarava, a low atoll with an inner lagoon of glassy water many miles wide. The *Casco*'s travails were still not at an end, however for entering was not a particularly simple manoeuvre. An atoll contains a huge volume of water ringed in by the low coral that makes up the body of the island. Thus the tide can run with extreme ferocity through the narrow entrances into these atolls and vessels can find themselves literally sucked in if the tide is on the flood. Fortunately, this hazard was successfully negotiated and the schooner dropped her anchor in a stunning stretch of azure water almost entirely surrounded by coral reef, and fringed on all sides by palm trees and water as smooth as a sheet of glass. As the anchor tumbled from the cat head and kissed the virgin white sand many fathoms below, all on board breathed a collective sigh of relief.

The *Casco* was now completely off the beaten track, and there was much here that Stevenson learned to love, not least the Tuamotans themselves, who he found far more open and uncomplicated than the Marquesans. Stevenson opted to spend a couple of weeks ashore and rented a small shack. From here, he was able to fully appreciate the strangeness of life on an atoll, as he later recalled:

> *So long as I stayed upon that isle these thoughts were constant. I lay down to sleep, and woke again with an unblunted sense of my surroundings. I was never weary of calling up the image of that narrow causeway, on which I had my dwelling, lying coiled like a serpent, tail to mouth, in the outrageous ocean, and I was never weary of passing – a mere quarter-deck parade – from the one side to the other, from the shady, habitable shores of the lagoon to the blinding desert and uproarious breakers of the opposite beach.*

He was also intoxicated by the peace of the place and it is a great shame that the sojourn in this lonely little slice of paradise was cut short, for after a two-week stay, it was clear that the writer was becoming dangerously ill. He had contracted a cold in Hiva Oa and had never fully shaken it off. Weeks later, his breathing suddenly became laboured. In a panic, Fanny insisted that they leave at once to seek medical aid in Papeete, Tahiti, but this was patently not possible as it was dark and there was very little breeze. To raise the anchor would have meant certain destruction for the *Casco* and an unpleasant dunking for her crew. No doubt Captain Otis dealt with Mrs Stevenson with all of his usual tact and finesse. Whether she sulked following this encounter is not clear but the upshot was that the *Casco* did not sail until early the following morning, when the schooner once again threaded the atoll's narrow entrance and in a little over 48 hours was back in the relatively civilised port of Papeete. Which, as Margaret Stevenson noted, was: 'A sort of halfway house between savage life and civilisation, with the drawbacks of both and the advantages of neither.'

Nevertheless, it did have a hospital and the patient was immediately taken ashore. By this time he was at death's door and many did not expect him to set foot on the *Casco* again: An interview with Captain Otis gives an indication of the gravity of the situation and also an insight into Stevenson himself and his ambivalent relationship with death:

> *That evening, he sent for me. When I arrived at the hotel he sat propped in the bed; he appeared to be quite weak, but he greeted me cordially, and I remember that he was smoking a cigarette as usual. He was, in fact, the only one present who did not seem anxious and distressed – but then, his nerve never deserted him; and he was facing death as he had faced life and sickness, with a smile and a jest.*
>
> *He told me in his ordinary tone, and without a flicker of excitement, that he had sent for me, fearing that he might take a turn for the worse; if he did, he said, the doctor had told him he probably would not live until morning. Then he added with a smile, 'You see, the doctor does not give me much time; so I have divided what there is left into three equal portions, one for each, only reserving the last for Mrs. Stevenson.' He then proceeded to inform me, as calmly as though he had had a century to spend, how I was to dispose of the yacht and settle the business, if disaster fell – which happily it did not. After that he bade me adieu as quietly as if no danger threatened his life and hopes. The man did not seem to realize that he acted the hero in the little things of his life, as well as where he stood face to face with life's greatest evil – Death.*

After this brush with mortality, the patient convalesced rapidly, spending a month in a small cottage within the town. He grew to dislike Papeete as much as everyone else in the *Casco* party. It was noisy, squalid and run by the colonial French in such a high-handed manner that it was impossible not to be infuriated. It is worth noting that the beginning of his rather brutal story *The Ebb Tide*, which features a trio of down-and-out beachcombers plumbing new depths, is set in Papeete. Thus with the author well on the way to recovery, it was decided that a change of scene was called for, and the decision was taken to run the *Casco* around to the windward side of the island, where the village of Tavaroa offered good shelter and stunning scenery. The trip proved to be something of an epic, for there was a deeply unpleasant cross-sea running, which, coupled with a fresh gale, made the voyage extremely dangerous for all aboard. At times the gale threatened to overwhelm the *Casco* and it was with some relief that the entrance to Tavaroa was espied. This was another narrow gap in a long reef and, lying on the windward side of the island, huge swells were rolling on to the reef and hurling themselves with unnerving fury at its base. To aim straight for this must have been a severe test of nerve, and I leave the narration of the entry to Captain Otis:

> *The entrance to the harbour is through a narrow break in the reef, marked by beacons placed on the hill behind, while beating up to the passage heavy seas with variable winds were encountered; this made it quite uncomfortable and somewhat risky, as the plunge was to be made through a line of heavy surf. While there was actually little danger to be anticipated from the sailor's point of view, yet here, as elsewhere, wherever there was a possibility of an accident, the skipper had the boats properly cleared. When the trying moment came and the* Casco's *bows pierced the seething belt of spray and fume, she apparently stood on end for a hesitating moment before she leaped, like a thing alive, through and over what seemed certain destruction; and, before the breath could be in drawn, she fell again into the smooth basin inside, hardly having wet her decks in the passage. After a run of half a mile, the yacht was moored in a beautiful land-locked harbour, nearly a mile wide, that was wooded to its shore. When the anchorage was reached, suppressed excitement was still visible among those on board; even Stevenson, who seldom made comment, felt constrained to ask in careless manner, and with the ghost of a smile on his lips, 'if Captain Otis did not think such yachting gymnastics were rather risky sport for invalid authors to indulge in.'*

You will note that the skipper had the ship's boats cleared away and ready to launch, which gives some idea of the gravity of the situation. At this point, Fanny Stevenson did little to help the situation by commenting: 'Isn't that nice? We shall soon be ashore!' You can almost hear the grinding of Captain

Otis' teeth as he had to humour such fatuousness in the face of very real danger. Stevenson himself, usually so tolerant, was disgusted at his wife's witlessness, noting: 'Thus does the female mind unconsciously skirt along the verge of eternity.'

The yacht, crew and passengers were safe, but it was soon deemed that Tavaroa, being rather damp and mosquito ridden, was not conducive to Stevenson's health and it was therefore determined that the Stevenson party should decamp overland to nearby Tautira, a far more suitable spot, which they soon came to love. By now he felt he had completely lost touch with life back home, as he noted in a letter: 'Whether I have a penny left in the wide world, I know not, nor shall know, till I get to Honolulu, where I anticipate a devil of an awakening. It will be from a mighty pleasant dream at least: Tautira being mere Heaven.'

The Stevensons stayed in the house of one of the chiefs, Ori-Ori, and awaited the arrival of the *Casco*. The schooner had enjoyed a lively time of it on the trip round, having been forced to run almost into the breaking surf in order to pass back through the reef. Had Captain Otis got this wrong, the *Casco* would have stalled out and almost certainly been rolled right over and destroyed by the powerful breaking waves. Once again the smart vessel did not let them down, but it was after this severe thrashing that Otis perceived that the masts were out of line and, once anchored off Tautira, he sent hands aloft to investigate. The news was bad; for it transpired that the masts were far gone with dry rot and it was a miracle that they had withstood the recent heavy battering. There was nothing for it but to head back to Papeete, but, given the Stevensons' dislike for the place, the decision was taken to leave them in Tautira.

Captain Otis was furious and blamed the previous master for misleading him about the condition of the vessel. Stevenson, however, was altogether more philosophical and wrote to a friend back home, 'Our mainmast is dry-rotten, and we are all to the devil; I shall lie in a debtor's jail. Never mind, Tautira is first chop.'

Papeete proved a tricky hunting ground for new masts, for it soon became clear that both fore and main were far gone and would need to be replaced. Infuriating delays and dilatory working hours meant that it would be many weeks before the brave vessel was able to put to sea again. If the *Casco* was ailing, the same could be said of her owner. Stevenson had taken another turn for the worse and spent his days hallucinating with fever. It was at this point that he was visited by the Tahitian princess, Moe, daughter-in-law to the King of Tahiti, who hurried from Papeete to attend to the island's sickly visitor and plied him with restoring lime juice, coconut and other healthy treats. Soon he was on the mend, and always maintained that this member of the Tahitian royal house had saved his life.

It was fortunate that the Stevensons got on well with their host, Ori, for otherwise they would have long outstayed their welcome as they waited for the elusive *Casco* to make her return. In the meantime, the party made themselves comfortable and were very content, Margaret Stevenson describing the experience as 'camping with none of the drawbacks'. Meanwhile, Robert worked on *The Master of Ballantrae*, one of his finest novels. Fanned by the warm, soothing trade winds and hypnotised by the glistening palms and verdant emerald slopes of Tahiti, Stevenson's imagination travelled back to the frosty airs and purple glens of the Highlands of his youth and recalled them with pin-sharp accuracy in a novel viewed by many as his masterpiece. Stevenson's great friend and fellow novelist Henry James once commented that the South Seas did Stevenson's writing the power of good when recalling Scotland, but precious little for work he produced which covered his immediate locality.

The former point may well be true even if the latter seems grossly unfair, for the literature that Stevenson produced in the South Seas was, in many ways, his most innovative and progressive work. He set about portraying the islands as he saw them, warts and all. There was none of the romanticism of his earlier novels. He worked instead on a form of brutalism that looked at the relationship between the rapacious whites and hard-used natives with an unblinking eye. Stories such as *The Ebb Tide* and *The Beach of Falesa*, portrayed the colonists in a most unflattering light and were badly received by a Victorian readership obsessed with the glory of empire. A prime example of this can be seen in his short story, *The Beach of Falesa*, which related a practice used by white traders in the South Seas at the time of 'marrying' a native girl with a contract that read thus: 'This is to certify that Uma, daughter of Fa'avao is illegally married to John Wiltshire for one night, and Mr John Wiltshire is at liberty to send her to hell the next morning.'

This practice of getting one's way with local girls, made virtuous by the preaching of the missionaries, was common at the time. In *The Beach of Falesa*, the aforementioned Mr Wiltshire falls in love with his fraudulent bride and then reflects that, '... she was no even mate for a poor trader like myself.' The clear inference of a native girl being viewed as the superior to the white trader was repugnant to the Victorians, many of whom still believed that whites were inherently superior to people of any other colour. Stevenson was accused from some quarters of doting on the natives and presenting a rather skewed vision of evil, avaricious whites and virtuous, put-upon natives. This is also unfair, for his portrayal of the South Sea Islanders was balanced. He later summed up Samoans in simple but effective terms: 'Like other folk; false enough, lazy enough, not heroes, not saints, ordinary people damnably misused.'

As Stevenson wrote, the rest of the party awaited the return of the *Casco*, to all intents and purposes marooned in this beautiful spot. After a month, their supplies were out and, given that most of their money was aboard the schooner, they were in something of a fix. It was at this point that Ori stepped in, as Margaret related:

> *After much talk, Ori made a solemn oration to Louis, which was translated to him by the chief, and was to this effect: You are my brother, and all that I have is yours. I know that your food is done, but I can give you fish and fei as much as you like. This place suits you, and it makes us happy to have you, – stay here till the* Casco *comes, be happy, et ne pleurez plus!*

Such an offer could not be declined, and the Stevensons remained until the *Casco* finally returned on December 22. In fact, they did not manage to fully make their departure until Christmas Day, for their farewell was a long, protracted affair with much feasting. Stevenson regained the deck of the *Casco* in fine fettle; he had even taken to sea bathing towards the end of the stay in Tautira and was well prepared for the next stage of the trip, which would take them to Honolulu, Hawaii. The Stevensons had now been five months cruising the islands and, at least according to Captain Otis, were ready to return to civilisation, as he recalled:

> *It took all of five weeks before I was able to return to Tautira and pick up Stevenson; but when I got there at last, I found him in fine health, and as brown as a berry, yet I am certain he had grown tired of Tahiti, and certainly he hailed the* Casco *like a welcome friend.*

On Christmas Day, the *Casco*'s anchor clanked aboard and, the vessel once more headed out to sea. A 13-gun salute resounded from the captain's Winchester rifle, and from shore, the crack of a distant gun echoed in friendly reply. Once more the voyagers were on their way on what was to prove the final lap of their voyage aboard the *Casco*. As it happened, it was also to be the most trying leg of them all; for the 3,760km (2,336 mile) trip to Hawaii was dogged from the very start by ill fortune. As Louis noted in a letter to a friend back home while on passage:

> *At last our contemptible ship was ready; to sea we went, bound for Honolulu and the letter-bag, on Christmas Day; and from then to now have experienced every sort of minor misfortune, squalls, calms, contrary winds and seas, pertinacious rains, declining stores, till we came almost to regard ourselves as in the case of Vanderdecken.*

In all, there were 17 days of calm before the trade winds were finally picked up, 17 days of glassy water and heat that seared the deck until the pitch bubbled in the seams. Up above, the lifeless sails flogged and clashed against the mast in a most infuriating manner until most of the party was exasperated. Captain Otis later recalled that many of the crew were 'down in the dumps' the only exception being Stevenson, whose persistent good humour only seemed to irritate the rest of the party all the more. In their defence, the end of the cruise was in sight, for the intention was to make Honolulu a long, possibly indefinite, stop. With the coming of the end a trip, one's patience is often tried.

On 20 January, the trades were picked up and the gallant *Casco* once more kicked up her heels and flew, skimming across the waters, trembling under the strain of her canvas like a thing alive. Once more there was purpose and hope after those listless weeks of calm. The relief of all was palpable, but it was also short lived. It was around this time the cook discovered that the vessel was dangerously low on supplies. Captain Otis grumpily blamed the extravagant Christmas and New Year feasts the guests had enjoyed, combined with the unforeseen delay of the calms. Whatever the reason, all sail was piled on in order to make Honolulu in record time. All the while, the wind freshened, and sail was shortened. Soon the *Casco* was running before a gale of wind, which showed every sign of worsening.

Captain Otis found himself in a quandary: he desperately needed to make land as soon as possible, but as conditions grew ever more severe, a decision needed to be made. There was a real risk that one of the heavy seas that chased the *Casco* would overwhelm her, washing away her helmsman and flooding the cockpit. With the helmsman gone, the vessel would 'broach', slewing beam on to the seas and most likely be overwhelmed and rolled over by the next heavy sea. In such circumstances, the prudent sailor would opt to heave to, shorten down to one tiny sail and lay beam on to the sea, riding out the storm. All, however, were impatient to get on, and the shortage of supplies was now so dire that Otis, after careful consultation with Stevenson, opted to run on before the storm come what may. From this point, there would be no turning back, for once the storm worsened, heaving to would be impossible. Stevenson later recreated this moment in *The Wrecker*:

'Captain,' I returned, with my heart in my mouth, 'risk is better than certain failure.'

'Life is all risk, Mr. Dodd,' he remarked. 'But there's one thing: it's now or never; in half an hour, Archdeacon Gabriel couldn't lay her to, if he came down stairs on purpose.'

'All right,' said I. 'Let's run.'

'Run goes,' said he; and with that he fell to breakfast, and passed half an hour in stowing away pie and devoutly wishing himself back in San Francisco.

Thus the *Casco* roared on before the mountainous seas, and some idea of the dizzying ride can be gathered from this brief account by Stevenson himself:

One stirring day was that in which we sighted Hawaii. It blew fair, but very strong; we carried jib, foresail, and mainsail, all single-reefed, and she carried her lee rail under water and flew. The swell, the heaviest I have ever been out in – I tried in vain to estimate the height, AT LEAST fifteen feet – came tearing after us about a point and a half off the wind. We had the best hand – old Louis – at the wheel; and, really, he did nobly, and had noble luck, for it never caught us once. At times it seemed we must have it; Louis would look over his shoulder with the queerest look and dive down his neck into his shoulders; and then it missed us somehow, and only sprays came over our quarter, turning the little outside lane of deck into a mill race as deep as to the cockpit coamings. I never remember anything more delightful and exciting. Pretty soon after we were lying absolutely becalmed under the lee of Hawaii, of which we had been warned; and the captain never confessed he had done it on purpose, but when accused, he smiled. Really, I suppose he did quite right, for we stood committed to a dangerous race, and to bring her to the wind would have been rather a heart-sickening manoeuvre.

An indication of how bad things were during this part of the passage can be witnessed by the fact that Captain Otis later stated that these were, 'the worst seas I had ever seen'. God knows what the rest of the Stevenson party made of it, but doubtless they did not share their leader's exhilaration. Certainly Fanny was ill for the entirety of the storm and must have longed to once more step foot on dry land. Indeed, after the trip, she declared that she would, 'never go to sea again' which was a brave statement for someone who was stranded in Hawaii.

Once in the lee of Hawaii, they were essentially home and dry, although there were several hours spent infuriatingly becalmed before they finally dropped the hook off Oahu. The trip was over, for Stevenson took the decision to pay off the *Casco* and shortly after, she made her way back to San Francisco, and the awaiting Dr Merritt. Stevenson, writing to his cousin Bob, noted that: 'My extremely foolhardy venture is practically over. How foolhardy it was I don't think I realised.'

He continued by stating that the *Casco* was over-rigged and unsuitable for the trip. In this, he could not have been more wrong. The vessel had looked after the Stevensons better than they could have ever hoped and, as Otis late recalled, 'It was her extreme handiness that got us out of many a tight corner.' As for the friendship with Captain Otis, this had been severely strained by the tough trip up to Hawaii, but Stevenson later wrote that, 'I really liked the man'. They never met again. In essence, the yarn is over. We leave the *Casco* sailing the darkening seas on her way back to San Francisco, and bid adieu to the famous author in good health and, 'oppressed by civilisation' as he put it, in Honolulu.

Yet this is a tale where both author and yacht deserve a postscript, and we will begin with the *Casco*, for her adventures had only just begun. She returned to San Francisco, but all was not well with her owner, Dr Merritt, who died shortly after her return. Her days as a yacht with snowy white decks and plush interior were over, for in 1892 a syndicate purchased her for use in seal-hunting and trans-Pacific trading to the Far East. Her decks would have been stained with the grease of blubber and her opulent accommodation must have been at least partly ripped out to increase the size of her hold. Yet her reputation as a flyer remained and there is a claim that she made the crossing from Yokohama, Japan, to the US in 20 days, one of the fastest trans-Pacific runs on record for a sailing yacht of this era.

Her great speed was to get her into trouble, though, for in 1898 she was purchased by new owners and operated as an opium smuggler, running the drug in to Canada and the US from China. According to later accounts by some of her crewmembers, in this same year she was involved in an extremely grisly incident off the Canadian coast. At the time she was nearing the completion of one of her smuggling voyages and was loaded with opium and around 30 illegal immigrants. As she made her way along the coast, a revenue cutter was perceived making its way under power and gaining on the schooner in the fickle breeze. Panic ensued, and the decision was taken to jettison the cargo in order to escape the inevitable severe punishment for drug and people trafficking. In the case of the opium, this was a simple case of throwing the cargo overboard, but, shockingly, the decision was taken to bring the hapless immigrants up on deck, one by one, kill them and dump them into the sea weighed down with sacks of coal. As the revenue cutter slowly gained, this grisly massacre went on, hidden from the view of the authorities in the lee of the *Casco's* sails. By the time the cutter ranged alongside, the *Casco* was free from incriminating evidence and the authorities had little choice but to let the deeply suspicious vessel go.

The whole shocking occurrence is more gruesome than anything the depraved pirates of *Treasure Island* managed, although it does chime somewhat with a conundrum faced by Robert Herrick, anti-hero of Stevenson's South Sea story *The Ebb Tide,* who is faced with a similar dilemma of facing the long arm of the law or butchering his host.

After this unpleasant incident, the doomed vessel continued her wandering, changing ownership on many occasions and working in the West Coast trade and later in the fur trade. Several owners threatened to convert her back to a yacht, but none ever got round to it. In 1919, she was chartered by a desperate bunch of adventurers seeking gold far up the coast of Alaska. It was on this voyage that her luck ran out, for she ran aground off Anchorage and was later declared a total loss. Thus passed the beautiful *Casco.*

As for Stevenson, his adventures were far from over either and, after a sojourn in Hawaii, he decided that he was ready to slum it a bit after the luxury of the *Casco* and shipped aboard the trading schooner *Equator,* bound for the Gilbert Islands under the command of Captain Dennis Reid, a Scots-Irishman with whom the writer got on famously. He was quite a contrast to the rather dry, flinty Otis and the passage to the Gilberts passed pleasantly. Sadly, its details belong to another chapter altogether.

Stevenson was never much of a sailor in terms of handling ropes and giving out orders, but he was a true voyager and a man who saw the infinite freedom and beauty of the ocean. He also saw it as his ultimate resting place, and this is perhaps why he faced its perils with the *sang froid* that Captain Otis had so greatly admired. Certainly he had lived with death on his shoulder for so long that it held no fear for him. He wrote of his relationship with the sea in these terms, 'I cannot say why I like the sea; no man is more cynically and constantly alive to its perils; I regard it as the highest form of gambling, yet I love the sea as much as I hate gambling.'

So he pressed on once more, out onto its rolling hills and foaming billows, deeper into the unknown. He never left the Pacific again and only briefly left the South Seas for a trip to Sydney. He settled with his wife and ever-intrepid mother in Apia, Samoa, where he built a magnificent house and saw out the rest of his days, known to the locals as *Tusitala*, or the teller of tales.

He died in 1892 at the age of 42. Ultimately it was not his lungs that gave out, for he appears to have suffered a brain haemorrhage. It is perhaps fitting that the final book published before his death was *The Ebb Tide,* a nasty little tale of greed, drunkenness, murder and repentance. What made this story such an appropriate epitaph to the great author was how unlike much of his earlier work it was, how innovative in dialogue he had become. In addition to this his portrayal of one of the book's central characters, Attwater, is a masterstroke. This smooth, Cambridge-educated religious lunatic, replete with black cat on his shoulder and Winchester rifle at his hip, is both utterly repellent and fascinating, anticipating later maniacs such as Conrad's Kurtz in *Heart of Darkness,* while also opening the door to an exploration of the twisted cruelty often at the heart of imperialism. The South Sea adventures provided Stevenson with a new chapter and a forum within which he could innovate and develop as a writer, and it is a shame that his untimely death deprived us of further stories from this obscure corner of the globe.

There is no doubt, at his death, the words he wrote back in the Marquesas when the *Casco*'s anchor first kissed the sand of Aneho, Nuku Hiva still rang true: 'I, and some part of my ship's company, were from that hour the bondslaves of the isles'. For Stevenson, the South Seas put paid to his own famous quote: 'To travel hopefully is a better thing than to arrive'. There is no doubt that the South Seas were the first true home he had ever known. His epitaph, placed on his headstone where he lies to this day, high on a hilltop above his home in Apia, could not ring more true. Taken from his poem, *Requiem*, it reads as follows:

> *Under the wide and starry sky,*
> *Dig the grave and let me lie*
> *Glad did I live and gladly die,*
> *And I laid me down with a will*
> *This be the verse you 'grave for me;*
> *Here he lies where he longed to be;*
> *Home is the sailor, home from the sea,*
> *And the hunter, home from the hill.*